Veritatis Splendor and the
Renewal of Moral Theology

Veritatis Splendor

and the Renewal of Moral Theology

Edited by
J.A. DiNoia, O.P.
and Romanus Cessario, O.P.

SCEPTER PUBLISHERS

OUR SUNDAY VISITOR, INC.

MIDWEST THEOLOGICAL FORUM

Veritatis splendor *and the Renewal of Moral Theology* is published by

SCEPTER PUBLISHERS
P.O. Box 1270
Princeton, New Jersey 08542
e-mail: general@scepterpub.org

OUR SUNDAY VISITOR, INC.
200 Noll Plaza
Huntington, IN 46750

MIDWEST THEOLOGICAL FORUM
712 South Loomis St.
Chicago, Illinois 60607
Tel. 312-421-8135 Fax 312-421-8129
e-mail: mail@mwtf.org

ISBN 0-87973-739-5

Printed in the United States of America.

CONTENTS

LIST OF CONTRIBUTORS

Romanus Cessario, O.P., is professor of systematic theology at St. John Seminary in Boston and serves as Dean of the Theological Faculty for the Pastoral Provision.

J.A. DiNoia, O.P., is Executive Director of the Committee on Doctrine, National Conference of Catholic Bishops, and Professor of Theology at the Dominican House of Studies, Washington, D.C.

Avery Dulles, S.J., is the Laurence J. McGinley Professor of Theology at Fordham University.

Russell Hittinger holds the Warren Chair of Catholic Studies in the Department of Philosophy and Religion at the University of Tulsa.

Pio Cardinal Laghi is prefect of the Sacred Congregation for Catholic Education.

Alasdair MacIntyre is Arts and Sciences Professor of Philosophy at Duke University.

William E. May is the Michael J. McGivney Professor of Moral Theology at the John Paul II Institute for Studies on Marriage and Family.

Livio Melina is Ordinary Professor at Pontificio Instituto Giovanni Paulo II per gli studi su Matrimonio e Famiglia in Rome.

Servais (Th.) Pinckaers, O.P., is emeritus Professor of Moral Theology at the University of Fribourg, Switzerland, and serves as a member of the International Theological Commission.

Martin Rhonheimer does pastoral work in Zurich, Switzerland, and teaches moral philosophy at the Pontifical University of the Holy Cross in Rome.

INTRODUCTION

In the apostolic letter *Spiritus Domini*, issued on August 1, 1987, the second centenary of the death of St. Alphonsus Maria de Liguori, Pope John Paul II announced his intention "to write an encyclical with the aim of treating more fully and more deeply the issues regarding the very foundations of moral theology." The fulfillment of that promise was the encyclical letter *Veritatis splendor* (The Splendor of Truth) issued on the feast of the Transfiguration, August 6, 1993.

Since its appearance, *Veritatis splendor* has attracted the interest of theologians and laity alike. Scholarly journals and popular publications both have acknowledged the significance of the encyclical as a statement of the pope's moral vision; even among Protestant communities there has been an interest in investigating this articulation of abiding moral truth. *The Thomist* has been pleased to be able to contribute to the scholarly reception of this encyclical. Not only has the journal attracted articles on the subject, but these articles have shown a remarkable consistency in appreciating the encyclical as both a call to renewal in moral theology and a theological statement on the nature of the moral life. *Veritatis splendor* is much more than an exhortation to a populace that shows a tendency to wander away from moral absolutes and the guidance of the Church in matters of morality; it is a reconnection of morality and theology.

The fifth anniversary of the publication of the encyclical seems to be an appropriate time to emphasize its contribution to the Church's life. It is also significant that this appreciation would appear in the midst of the preparation for the new millennium. Pope John Paul II has called for a new evangelization for the new millennium. *Veritatis splendor* is part of that call, in that it situates the Church's understanding of the moral life in the pursuit of eternal life, the participation in the perfection of the imitation of Christ. The moral life cannot be understood, finally, apart from its connection with beatitude. The casuistic systems that dominated the moral theology of the Church for much of the past four hundred years encouraged Christians to think of morality largely in terms of laws, the following of which was a necessary part of the integrity of Christian life. That is, it presupposed that Christians lived in a secure and solid framework of doctrine, sacraments, devotions, etc., and presented the moral laws as limits for behavior that achieved their meaning in that framework. Today very few Christians regard their participation in the life of the Church primarily in juridical terms. Furthermore, the relation between the life of the Church and the life of the broader culture has undergone considerable change, especially in Western Europe and the United States.

Taking account of the present circumstances, the pope has called for a new kind of evangelization. The tone of this evangelization is personal, not juridical. We see in retrospect that it is a logical consequence of the Second Vatican Council, and has more recently been prefigured by the *Catechism of the Catholic Church* and *Veritatis splendor*. These texts have profoundly altered the teaching of morality as it had developed in the immediate post-conciliar period, and have dissuaded the ordinary Catholic from conceiving the good life either in terms of a moral (legalistic) minimalism or in terms of a spirituality significantly separated from the requirements of Christian morality. *Veritatis splendor* encourages us to think about the moral life in teleological terms, that is, in terms of the life centered on love.

The encyclical is, then, a substantive contribution to theological reflection on the Christian life. Yet it is overly optimistic to suppose that this is enough to grant it a serious hearing. Theological discourse today is often dominated by historicist interests. The question addressed by researchers is not "What is the truth of the matter?" but "What did a particular author think about the subject?" In part, this reflects an understandable timidity: the body of research is so vast that one is easily cowed into limiting oneself to one little corner of specialization. However, understandable though it may be, this kind of approach is fatal to true theology, for it prevents the theologian from developing the habit of systematically understanding the truths of the Faith.

The present volume is happily free of this restraint. Though many of the essays do take account of the history of moral theology, they do not end there; nor do they confine themselves to a dialectical exchange with previously published assessments of the encyclical. The ten internationally known scholars who have contributed to this volume are united in their effort to take the encyclical as a source for serious theological thinking.

It is appropriate to linger over the shift in perspective enacted by the encyclical, for it is in this way that we can see its permanent significance in the life of the Church. Part I of this collection, "Perspectives," contains three appreciations of this significance, by J. Augustine DiNoia, O.P., Servais Pinckaers, O.P., and Alasdair MacIntyre. The contributions vary in emphasis, but each supports one conclusion: *Veritatis splendor* has reintegrated morality with the Christian understanding of the way to eternal life, exemplified in Christ and revealed in the Gospel.

It has been noted many times that Pope John Paul II has a strong appreciation of the concerns of contemporary philosophical anthropology. It is no less true that he has displayed a keen awareness of the abiding truths that are indispensable to moral understanding. In Part II, "Issues," Russell Hittinger (natural law), Avery Dulles, S.J. (freedom), Livio Melina (desire for happiness), Martin Rhonheimer (intrinsically evil acts), and Romanus Cessario, O.P. (moral absolutes), take up topics of perennial significance and examine the teaching of *Veritatis splendor* on them. Each of these authors sees that the encyclical formulates these topics in terms of the gospel call to the fullness of Christian life.

Veritatis splendor has not been spoken in an academic vacuum: the second part of the encyclical addresses the errors of teleologistic ethical theories, specifically those of "consequentialism" and "proportionalism." Not surprisingly, one very visible public response to the encyclical has been the reaction of theologians commonly recognized as proportionalists—although, as is typical in documents of this kind, the encyclical does not name any particular proponent of any given theory. Part 3 of this book, "Reception," contains essays by William E. May and Martin Rhonheimer that advance the discussion of the issues raised, particularly the question of the accuracy of the encyclical's portrayal of these theories.

The Epilogue to this volume continues the theme that informs the whole collection: the impact of the encyclical's reformulation of morality in terms of a theology of the moral life. Pio Cardinal Laghi offers some reflections on the transformation of education demanded by the encyclical, both within the Church and by the Church in the world.

Veritatis splendor is addressed to the bishops of the Church; this is appropriate, for it is the bishops who are given the task of leading the Church in the way of Christ. There has been a tendency in some circles to regard the encyclical as a set of "musings," or a papal exhortation. However, the occasion of its appearance, its connection with the *Catechism*, the fact that it is addressed to the bishops, and, most of all, its substance, all point to a much different evaluation: *Veritatis splendor* is a magisterial document, intended to be a normative teaching of the Church. Many Catholics have already recognized this point; others have publicly objected to it. We are pleased in this volume to offer the first collection of essays that is both serious and sympathetic to the objectives of the magisterium in the encyclical.

Gregory F. LaNave
Managing Editor, *The Thomist*

I. Perspectives

Veritatis splendor: Moral Life as Transfigured Life

J. A. DiNoia, O.P.

Pope John Paul II put his signature to *Veritatis splendor* on August 6, 1993, the feast of the Transfiguration of our Lord. While the encyclical did not become public until October, considerable significance attaches to the date on which documents of this magnitude are actually signed. *Veritatis splendor* is arguably the most important encyclical of this pontificate, and will probably be judged to be one of the most significant of this century. I have a single aim in this paper: I want to argue that the date upon which this great encyclical was signed provides a key to unlocking its meaning, that transfiguration and communion are at its heart.

But I shall begin with a quotation, not from *Veritatis splendor*, but from *Pastores dabo vobis*: "There are spiritual and religious values present in today's culture, and man. . . cannot help but hunger and thirst for God. However, the Christian religion is often regarded as just one religion among many or reduced to nothing more than a social ethic at the service of man. As a result, its amazing novelty in human history is quite often not apparent. It is a 'mystery,' the event of the coming of the Son of God who becomes man and gives to those who welcome him 'the power to become the children of God' (Jn 1:12). It is the proclamation, nay the gift of a personal covenant of love and life between God and man."[1]

In these powerful words, Pope John Paul is trying to get us to see the stunning truth of the destiny to which human beings are called, a truth proclaimed by Christ and a destiny made possible for us by his passion, death, and resurrection. Human persons are called to nothing less than communion with the Father, Son, and Holy Spirit. To put it as forcefully as possible, Christianity affirms that the triune God could not bring about a more intimate union with created persons than that which has begun in Baptism and is to be consummated in the life to come. Ultimate communion involves nothing less than becoming part of the Trinitarian family.

Just as Christ is Son by nature—a member of the divine family of the Trinity in virtue of his being the only Son of the Father—so we human persons are to be sons and daughters by adoption. Our fellowship with Christ and with each other in him brings us into the divine Trinitarian family.

For a variety of reasons, we have lost a sense of the "amazing novelty" of this message. For one thing, we simply take it for granted. For another, our culture inclines us to see all religions as in some sense equally concerned with something vaguely called the Transcendent and more or less equally fit to lead people to experience and enjoy it.

One of the overriding objectives of *Veritatis splendor* is to affirm that the Christian moral life makes sense only within this understanding of our calling to "life on high in Christ Jesus" (Phil 3:14). If we are destined to enjoy ultimate communion with the Father, Son, and Holy Spirit—and with each other in them—then we must change. We must be transformed into people who can enjoy this high destiny.

As the encyclical strives to make clear, this transformation will be a conformation: the more we become like Christ, the more surely do we discover our true selves, the unique persons created by the triune God to share in the divine life and to enjoy the family life of the Trinity. A moral life is a life lived in Christ and through his grace. The ultimate aim of a morally upright life is not so much to "please God" by successfully keeping the Commandments as to render us fit for the eternal company of the triune God. We become good by seeking the Good.

The encyclical makes this clear in the long meditation on the encounter between Christ and the rich young man with which it begins. In response to the young man's question, "What good must I do to have eternal life?" Jesus says, "There is only One who is good. If you wish to enter into life, keep the commandments" (see Mt 19:16–22). Our Lord's teaching here indicates that only by seeking the Ultimate Good—God himself—can we become good. In other words, he connects keeping the Commandments with becoming good. The more we seek the Ultimate Good through the keeping of the Commandments, the more we become good and the more fit we become to enjoy the communion with the triune God that is our destiny. Only in Christ can we discover and become enabled to seek the Good through the keeping of the Commandments.

Thus, in the encyclical's first chapter, Pope John Paul II summons us to see the Christian moral vision as a matter of increasing transformation in and intimacy with Jesus Christ. Then, in the second chapter, the pope takes up some of the fundamental principles of the Christian moral life understood in this perspective. In taking up these topics, *Veritatis splendor* is unique among the documents of the magisterium. There has been a great deal of teaching on specific issues of Christian morality, like sexual and social ethics, for example, but this is the first occasion when there has been a sustained discussion of the most basic principles of the Christian moral life. In effect, the question in the encyclical is not simply how to act morally in this or that situation, but the more radical question, Why act morally at all? The resounding response offered by the encyclical is framed in terms of our destiny in Christ to enjoy communion with the triune God and with each in God.

It is true that in this chapter, the pope takes up in turn the topics of authentic freedom, conscience, sin, and the nature of the moral act. In part, his concern is to correct certain mistaken ideas about these matters put forward in recent years by some Catholic theologians and popularized among people in the Church. His concern here is not academic but pastoral: mistaken ideas about these issues can undermine a true Christian moral life. But more important than what the encyclical denies is what it affirms.

When talking about the big changes that Vatican II has caused in Catholic life, most of us tend to think immediately about changes in discipline and liturgy. In fact, one of the most dramatic shifts occurred in the area of moral theology. After a practically undisputed reign of nearly four hundred years, legalism (and the kind of casuistry associated with it), which had governed a lot of Catholic life and sacramental practice, slipped away without so much as an obituary notice.

The reasons for the powerful hold of legalism in moral theology since the Council of Trent are complex and could be the subject of a lengthy discussion all their own. The important thing to notice for our purposes today is that legalistic moral theology tended to put matters not in terms of good and evil but in terms of the permitted and the forbidden. In this style of moral theology, moral norms were viewed more as laws to be enforced and obeyed than as principles for a good life, lived in view of God's invitation to ultimate communion. In a legalistic perspective, happiness is a kind of extrinsic reward for a life lived in conformity to an arduous code of conduct. The framework is contractual rather than virtue-centered and personalist.

The fundamental importance of *Veritatis splendor* is that it embodies a complete rejection of this legalistic moral theology. It seeks to recover and reaffirm a more complete biblical, patristic, and authentic Thomistic vision of the whole of the Christian life and to locate the moral good within this vision. According to this vision, happiness is the flourishing of a life lived in seeking the good in order to realize and enjoy personal communion with the triune God and with other persons in God.

A simple example will help to dramatize the nature of this shift away from legalism. If you tell a child to stop eating cookies before dinner, and he asks you why, you have at least two possible answers to give. You could say, "I'm your mother, and I told you to stop. I make the rules in this house." Or, you could say, "You'll ruin your appetite." The first answer is an authoritarian one, a very simplified form of the kind of explanation associated with legalistic moral theology. The second answer appeals in a simple way to what is good and bad for you. The new encyclical exemplifies, at a highly sophisticated and theologically dense level, the second kind of answer.

In its rejection of legalism, the new encyclical is solidly in the tradition of Vatican Council II. That council called specifically for a renewal of moral theology that would restore to primacy the biblical categories of love, grace, discipleship and transformation in Christ.[2] The council thus inaugurated a period of tremendous creative ferment in which a variety of new avenues were explored. The new encyclical reviews twenty-five years of reflection and debate in moral theology and resoundingly affirms the best trends in the ongoing renewal of Catholic theology, and at the same time expresses a series of cautionary notes about certain trends in moral theology that seem to be going in the wrong direction. But the crucial point that must not be lost in the controversy that the encyclical has generated among some Catholic authors is the affirmation that morality makes sense only within the perspective of the call to ultimate communion.

The first Truth here is the truth of God himself, as embodied in the person and teaching of Jesus. If we want to live in the truth, we must be conformed to the Truth who is Christ himself. Our happiness is to be found in seeking and attaining the ultimate Good. Moral goodness in human beings is a participation in the divine goodness.

If we are to enjoy communion with the triune God, then we must become fit for it. Interpersonal communion with God, though, is "natural" only to uncreated persons. However, for created persons, who are also sinners, such communion is possible only through grace. It is through the grace of Christ, and, specifically, through the transformation that this grace makes possible, that we are rendered "fit" participants in the communion of the Father, Son, and Holy Spirit.

It is at this point that the central significance of the mystery of the Transfiguration emerges.

We are all familiar with the gospel accounts of the Transfiguration. Matthew, Mark and, Luke agree in the basic details: Peter, James and John, witnessed a remarkable transformation in the countenance of Christ. The ordinary, dusty Jesus who was their companion and master was transformed before their eyes in a dazzling display of glory. The disciples were at a loss even to describe what they saw. Jesus' clothes became whiter, as Mark's gospel quaintly puts it, than any bleach could make them. In fact, as would become clear to the disciples later, what they saw was not so much a "transfiguration" by which Jesus was changed into something he had not been beforehand, but rather a revelation in which his true nature was exposed to view. For a fleeting moment, the veil that concealed his glory from their sight was removed and they beheld the glory of God's only Son.

But we need to go deeper. We need to ask why Christ allowed the disciples to behold his glory. St. Leo the Great can be of assistance at this point. In a sermon on the mystery of the Transfiguration, Leo suggested that there were are least two reasons why Christ revealed his glory to these chosen witnesses.[3]

The first reason, Pope St. Leo suggests, was "to remove the scandal of the cross from the hearts of his disciples, and to prevent the humiliation of his voluntary suffering from disturbing the faith of those who had witnessed the surpassing glory that lay concealed." In other words, when the disciples saw Christ dead on the cross, they would not despair or lose heart. Those who had been to the top of Mount Tabor—according to tradition, the locus of the Transfiguration—would know that beneath the appearance of defeat and death lay the reality of victory and life. Appearances to the contrary notwithstanding, as we might put it, the cross constituted a victory over sin and death, a victory that would be confirmed and made manifest in the Resurrection on the third day.

But, Leo goes on, there was another reason why Christ let his disciples witness the Transfiguration. Christ wanted more than to sustain the faith of his disciples in the face of events that would sorely try it. In the Transfiguration he revealed not only his own hidden glory, but our future glory as well. In short, he wanted to show us what would become of us. "The whole body of Christ," Leo says, "was to understand the kind of transformation that it would receive as his gift. The members of that body were to look forward to a share in that glory which first blazed out in Christ their head." Naturally, from our point of view, we seem to be sinking into decrepitude rather than rising to glory! But, again, appearances to the contrary notwithstanding, "all of us, with unveiled faces, seeing the glory of the Lord as though reflected in a mirror, are being transformed from one degree of glory to another" (2 Cor 3:18).

It is Leo's second reason for the Transfiguration that sheds light directly on the meaning of the encyclical. Let the text of the encyclical speak for itself at this point: "The light of God's face shines in all its beauty on the countenance of Jesus Christ, 'the image of the invisible God' (Col 1:15), the 'reflection of God's glory' (Heb 1:3), 'full of grace and truth' (Jn 1:14). Christ is 'the way, and the truth, and the life' (Jn 4:16). Consequently, the decisive answer to every one of man's questions, his religious and moral questions in particular, is given in Jesus Christ, or rather is Jesus Christ himself. . . "(VS 2.2). Moral life—the struggle to become good by seeking the good—finds its ultimate pattern and principle in Jesus Christ. Why? Because in him, the perfect image of God is found, and it is in being conformed to him that the image of God in us is made perfect. The Transfiguration signals to us that our transformation must be a conformation. It is this conformation that gives us our entry into the Trinitarian family. As we pray in one of the Sunday prefaces: "Father, . . . [y]ou sent him as one like ourselves, though free from sin, that you might see and love in us what you see and love in Christ."[4]

What must be made clear here is that this conformation does not amount to a mere conformity. The conformation to Christ which is the principle of our transformation is not a mere cloning but the realization of our distinctive and unique personal identity. This must be so, for otherwise the communion to which this transformation is directed could not be consummated. The image of God in us consists precisely in the spiritual capacities of knowing and loving that make interpersonal communion possible. But authentic interpersonal communion presupposes the full realization, not the absorption or dissolution, of the individual persons who enter into it. Thus, if Christ is to be the principle of our transformation, it can only mean that in being conformed to him, we each discover and realize our unique identities as persons.

This is an astounding claim, and we should pause over it. Consider the following saying of the Lord (I shall quote the saying from Matthew, but in each of the Synoptic Gospels it is placed, significantly, just before the account of the Transfiguration): "If a man wants to be my disciple, let him deny himself and take up his cross and follow me. For whoever wants to save his life will lose it, and whoever loses his life for my sake will find it. For what will it profit a man if he gains the whole world but loses his life? Or what will he give in return for his life?" (Mt 16:24–26; cf. Mk 8:34–37; Lk 9:23–25). What Christ is asserting, in effect, is that each person will find his or her true self only by being conformed to Christ.

We need only to consider our ordinary experience to grasp how startling, even outrageous, Christ's assertion is. None of us, whether as teachers or parents or pastors—no matter how inflated our conceptions of ourselves or how confident our sense of our abilities—would ever dare say to any of our charges that they will find their true selves by imitating us. Naturally, we do sometimes feel that they would be a lot better off if they followed our example at certain points! But we cannot want any children or students of ours simply to be clones of us. On the contrary, we want them to discover themselves, to become independent and self-confident (even if not, these days, self-supporting!). None of us could say to another person: you will find your true self only if you imitate me.

Yet this is precisely what Christ asserts. In effect this means that an indefinite number of human persons will find their distinctive identities by being conformed to Christ. A moment's reflection shows us that only the Son of God could make such an assertion. Only the inexhaustibly rich *perfect* Image of God who is the Person of the Son could constitute the principle and pattern for the transformation and fulfillment of every human person who has ever lived.

The encyclical locates the moral life within this all-encompassing mystery of communion and transfiguration.

Since we are persons, and precisely as persons, we must freely embrace the personal communion that is offered to us by the triune God as our ultimate happiness and good. Christ's grace empowers us to do so, but it empowers us to do so freely. The meaning of authentic freedom—a central theme of *Veritatis splendor*—lies here. The encyclical is critical of modern notions of freedom for their exaltation of individualism and autonomy. Christian freedom is not a matter of untrammeled choice, but a participation in God's freedom. In effect authentic freedom is the God-given capacity to enter in a personal way in the realization of our true happiness. Precisely as persons invited into personal communion, we must freely embrace this invitation or, of course, fail to. In this way, persons are different from non-personal, or as we usually put it, the non- or sub- rational creatures with whom we share the cosmos. Chipmunks and cabbages cannot embrace their good, or for that matter fail to. Only persons are free to join their hearts and souls to the endeavor to realize their true good—which, as we have seen, is the authentically personal good of ultimate communion.

It follows that, since we are persons, and precisely as persons, our actions count for something. We do not become good, or fail to become good, willy-nilly. Nor do we become good, or fail to become good, once and for all—at least on this side of the grave. No, in each action, and in some actions more than in others, we choose the good, or fail to. And through each action, and through some more than others, we become good, or fail to. In the moral life—which is nothing other than the whole realm of our human actions—something is happening to us. We are growing into fitness, or failing to, for the consummation of our already initiated communion with the Father, Son, and Holy Spirit. Christ is the principle and pattern of a gradual transformation—to which we freely and in grace join our efforts—by which this fitness takes hold in us. And since through his passion, death, and resurrection he has already overcome the deadly effect of our failures, he makes it possible for us to rise above them through forgiveness and repentance.

In conclusion, a brief remark about the bearing of the encyclical on the theme of this year's workshop, "Faith and Challenges to the Family."

At the beginning of his message for the 1994 Day of Peace, Pope John Paul II stated: "God wished humanity to live in harmony and peace, and laid the foundations for this in the very nature of the human being, created 'in his image." The divine image develops not only in the individual but also in that unique community of persons formed by a man and a woman so united in love that they become 'one flesh' (Gn 2:24). . . . This specific community of persons has been entrusted by the Lord with the mission of giving life and of nurturing it by the formation of the family."[5] There are several references to the importance of morality for family life in the encyclical, but it does not contain a lengthy discussion of the issue. As the passage just quoted indicates, however, the themes that are central to the encyclical also afford a fundamental theological perspective on the family. The family is in a true sense an image of Trinitarian communion itself.[6] Indeed, family relationships have provided a persistent inspiration for Trinitarian theology throughout Christian history. Our destiny of "life on high in Christ" is in a real sense a participation in the Trinitarian "family" life. As we noted above, the language of family relationships plays a central role in Christian understanding of the life of grace: we become the adopted sons and daughters of the Father in the Spirit by becoming brothers and sisters of the only Son. Since the image of God in us is realized precisely in interpersonal communion, our transformation into Christ is always in part experienced within the context of our relationships with other persons in whom grace is similarly at work. In this way, the family is central to both our understanding and our experience of communion and transfiguration.

I have argued in this paper that the principal message of the encyclical lies in this: without the mysteries, morals do not make ultimate sense. In the Christian vision of things, we can understand the significance of human action only within the context of the prior divine action. It is only in the perspective of the divine invitation to ultimate communion and the concrete initiation of this communion in Christ that the full significance of morality can be experienced and understood.

Endnotes

1. John Paul II, *I Will Give You Shepherds: On the Formation of Priests in the Circumstances of the Present Day* (Washington, DC: United States Catholic Conference, 1992), paragraph 46, pp. 125–26.
2. Vatican Council II, *Optatam totius*, n. 16 states: "Special care should be given to the perfecting of moral theology. Its scientific presentation should draw more fully on the teaching of holy Scripture and should throw light on the exalted vocation of the faithful in Christ and their obligation to bring forth fruit in charity for the life of the world."
3. Leo the Great, Sermon 51, 3-4, 8; PL 54: 310-311, 313. See *Liturgy of the Hours*, volume 2, pp. 149-50.
4. Preface 7, Sundays in Ordinary Time, in *The Sacramentary* (New York: Catholic Book Publishing Company, 1974), p. 443.
5. John Paul II, "Message for the 1994 World Day of Peace," *L'Osservatore Romano*, 23/29 December 1993, p. 1.
6. The new *Catechism of the Catholic Church* makes this point explicitly when it states in paragraph 2205 that "[t]he Christian family is a communion of persons, the image and reflection of the communion of the Father and the Son in the Holy Spirit."

An Encyclical for the Future: *Veritatis splendor*

Servais (Th.) Pinckaers, O.P.
(translated by Sr. Mary Thomas Noble, O.P.)

The encyclical *Veritatis splendor*, following in the wake of the *Catechism of the Catholic Church*, has met with great success in bookstores. Reactions in the press, in reviews, among publishers, and from theologians, have been varied. Nowhere does it meet with indifference. Now that the first wave of commentaries and critical revisions has played itself out, it seems the time has come for deeper reflection.

On taking up the text, it is good to remind ourselves that our reading of this encyclical must be a real dialogue in which both reader and document have a part. A minimum of openness and good will is indispensable if we are to welcome and grasp any writer's thought, discover his message, and draw profit from it. The suggestion of the apostle St. James is also relevant: "Be quick to listen and slow to speak." In other words, we first have to read it through attentively, a little as if we were listening to a friend. We need to take time out, too, for reflection, to make sure we really hear what it is saying. Then we shall be able to make an informed judgment and perhaps later some pertinent comments. We cannot race through *Veritatis splendor* as we would a newspaper. It calls for thought, some experience of the subjects discussed, and a bit of theological formation. But it offers far more substantial fare than the daily news: solid nourishment, and doctrine to guide us in living.

My object is to help the reader to discover the true dimensions of the encyclical and to perceive both what is at stake in the questions it raises and the significance of the answers it proposes. Among other things, I should like to demonstrate that *Veritatis splendor* is far more innovative than first appears. It is not satisfied to defend traditional positions. It points out paths that will lead to a profound renewal in the way Catholic moral theology is taught. I might even say that it launches a kind of discreet revolution in the concept of Christian morality, down to its very foundations. It carries us far beyond the so-called progressive positions which it critiques, and invites us to revise many ideas which have been accepted unquestioningly or are too narrow.

Introduction: The Reason for the Encyclical; its Preparation

Before examining the encyclical chapter by chapter, I should like to mention several points which will be helpful for a balanced interpretation.

A. The Twofold Purpose of *Veritatis splendor*

Initially, we are faced with the question: *What was John Paul II's purpose in writing this encyclical?* It had been announced as far back as 1987 in the Apostolic Letter *Spiritus Domini*, which celebrated the second centenary of the death of the patron of moral theologians, St. Alphonsus Liguori. It doesn't take a genius to guess the reason for it: indubitably it was the crisis in morality which had been developing within the Church and society for the last quarter of a century. Even some priests had come to wonder if such a thing as Christian morality still existed. Many moralists had abandoned the teaching on natural law that had formerly been the foundation of morality. Parents bemoaned the fact that the Ten Commandments were no longer taught to children in catechism class, and were rarely mentioned in sermons to the laity. The moral theology which had formerly been taught, and which had been a significant part of Christian formation, seemed to have been considerably watered down, if indeed it was not viewed as altogether obsolete. Furthermore, almost everyone was attempting to construct a moral system according to his own conscience (read opinions) and personal convenience.

Nevertheless, the particular preoccupation that inspired the project of the encyclical was *the teaching of moral theology within the Church,* or more precisely: "the lack of harmony between the traditional response of the Church and certain theological positions, encountered even in seminaries and in faculties of theology, with regard to questions of the greatest importance for the Church and for the life of faith of Christians" (*VS* 4.3). Such are the positions or opinions critiqued in Chapter 2 of the encyclical. Clearly, this quotation gives us the determining goal of *Veritatis splendor.*

However a second purpose, and one of equal importance, complements the first rather polemical one. It is well to stress it, because it could easily go unnoticed. In conformity with the council's recommendation that moral theology should be enhanced through a presentation more richly nourished by Sacred Scripture (Decree *Optatam totius* on the formation of priests, n. 15), John Paul II has wished to *renew the weakened link between Catholic moral teaching and the Gospel.* An essential condition for any true renewal of the teaching of moral theology is the reestablishment of a profound and sustained contact with that primary source of inspiration for Christian life and theology that is the Word and Person of Christ. This is the aim of Chapter 1 of the encyclical. It gives an evangelical dimension to the entire document. These two goals, the one constructive in the gospel sense and the other more controversial, are complementary and balance each other like two columns giving proportion and strength to the architectural structure of the document. We cannot interpret any section of it without taking both aims into account.

B. Discussions that Preceded *Veritatis splendor*

It will also be helpful to take a look at the theological and ethical debates which were the forerunners of the encyclical.

Without a doubt, the stand taken by Pope Paul VI in 1968 on the means of artificial contraception, articulated in his encyclical *Humanae vitae,* played a historic role in the development of the morality crisis among theologians. This document aroused a wave of shock which in one case—the problem of contraception—went so far as to challenge traditional teaching on moral laws in general, and the manner of their application. Thus in opposition to post-Tridentine morality a new and widespread system of morality has gradually been worked out. It is this development, earmarked by the names "proportionalism" and "consequentialism," that *Vertatis splendor* challenges.

In this connection I might mention two publications brought
out before the encyclical which indicate the *state of the question*
before the latter was drawn up. These are reports of a Symposium held in Rome in 1981. Present were classical and "innovative" moralists, exegetes, and patrologists, come together to
discuss the theme of universal and unchangeable moral laws.
The reports were published for the German- and English-read-
ing sector by Father W. Kerber under the title *"Sittliche Normen.
Zum Problem ihrer allgemeinen und unwandelbaren Geltung"*
(Düsseldorf, Patmos, 1982) and for the other participants by
Father J. C. Pinto de Oliveira and me in *"Universalité et permanence des Lois morales."* (Fribourg, Editions universitaires, 1986).

In these exchanges the two principal objects of the encyclical can already be distinguished: the linking of morality with
the Gospel and the discussion of the "new" theories proposed
by some moralists as solutions to ethical problems. The plan of
the book, *"Universalité et permanence des Lois morales,"* follows
this order. The first part studies moral law in Sacred Scripture
and especially in the Sermon on the Mount, while the second
follows a historical plan, treating law and the forming of a
moral judgment according to the Fathers of the Church, particularly St. Augustine and St. Basil, and then according to St. Thomas Aquinas with his study of natural law. Next come post-
Tridentine theology, Newman's teaching on conscience, and finally the question of the authority of the magisterium in the
field of morality. The third part is devoted to current discussions on the universal application of ethical norms, the question of intrinsically evil actions, and the objectivity of the judgment of conscience, while the final part situates these studies
within the framework of the gospel Law. A later contribution
to the debates is found in my book, *What One May Never Do: The
Question of Intrinsically Evil Actions. History and Discussion*
(Fribourg, Editions universitaires, 1986).

C. A Look at the Teaching of Moral Theology before the Council

In order to take an accurate measure of *Veritatis splendor* from
the point of view of its background and the contributions it
makes, we need some point of comparison. This is actually presupposed: it is the organization of morality found in textbooks

used in seminaries after the Council of Trent. Their presentation of material, which became standard, shaped preaching and
catechesis. It is characteristic of what has come to be called *casuistry*. While in no way denying the solidity of this teaching,
the encyclical renews its perspectives and enriches its content,
so that morality may the better harmonize with the Gospel.
Thus it indicates, for Christians and moralists alike, the paths
to be followed in the effort for moral renewal, together with the
task of a "new evangelization," which is the concern of all the
baptized.

This point of comparison also enables us to situate the "innovative" morality, which the encyclical critiques. Despite its
new interpretations, this systematization is, in fact, an out-
growth and variant of casuistry, whose basic categories and
some of whose typical methods of judging it revives.

The fundamental plan followed by the textbooks in the presentation of moral theology—and it is easily recognizable as the
most prevalent concept of Catholic morality observable in recent centuries—can be summarized as follows.

Moral theology is divided into two main parts: fundamental and specific morality. The four treatises that make up *fundamental morality* are:

1. *Law*, chiefly natural law as expressed in the Decalogue. Law is seen
   as the source of moral obligation, setting limits to freedom.

2. *Conscience*, which in its capacity as witness to and interpreter of law, plays the role of an interior judge of actions;

3. *Human acts*, considered chiefly in relation to cases of conscience, whence the name of casuistry, which is given to this
   type of morality;

4. *Sins*, which form the matter of the sacrament of Penance, the
   principal object of post-Tridentine morality. These will be
   studied in detail.

Specific morality borrows its principal divisions from the Ten
Commandments and adds the commandments of the Church
and certain prescriptions of canon law. Here, morality is understood to be the domain of strict obligations that are imposed on
all, and the Decalogue to be the code of commands and prohibitions dictated by God. This limitation of morality to duties

and prohibitions has become generally accepted. Thus a French TV correspondent in Rome explains that the moral section of the *Catechism* is, so to speak, the Church's civil code, to be completed by the penal code.

Ascetical and mystical theology, preferably termed *spirituality* today, or spiritual theology, have been added to the moral system described above. Ascetical and mystical theology deal with the ways of perfection which, transcending the ordinary requirements of morality, are proposed in the form of counsels rather than precepts. They are the concern of an elite, generally identified as religious. Ascetical theology studies the search for perfection through the virtues, with the aid of ordinary grace, while mystical theology presupposes special graces, easily confused with extraordinary phenomena, and attributed to the gifts of the Holy Spirit.

Basically, these are the divisions and categories which have become standard in moral theology. While taking the will of God, the supreme Legislator, as its principal reference, this moral system tends to be mainly rational. It belongs to the same school as that of the modern moralists of obligation, who situate the source of morality in the imperatives of reason, like Kant, or in the prohibitions of society. These moral categories have been transposed in exegesis where, for example, a separation has been made between ethics, which formulates obligations in the imperative mode, and parenesis, viewed as a simple exhortation relating rather to spirituality. This explains the scant attention paid by exegetes and moralists to apostolic catechesis, which they view as parenesis. Such a systematization is thus suited to the mentality of a period. As serious critics have already done even before the council, we need to note the limitations of this method of organizing morality, particularly in view of its separation from Scripture and its neglect of the teaching on the virtues.[1]

D. Some Helpful Clarifications

It is helpful to observe the correspondence between the *Catechism of the Catholic Church* and *Veritatis splendor*. The two documents were drawn up at the same time. Yet it was appropriate, as the encyclical itself affirms, that the *Catechism* should appear first, because it is set in a broader perspective and has the more general purpose of providing an overall, well-ordered teaching on morality as related to the Creed, sacraments, and prayer. The encyclical is more limited in its object, since its focus is limited to certain basic questions and theories which are open to criticism in view of Catholic tradition. In carrying out its purpose, it looks to the *Catechism* as to "a sure and authentic reference text" (*VS* 5.3; *Fidei depositum*, 4).

The encyclical states that this is *the first time* the magisterium of the Church has pronounced with authority on *fundamental elements of moral teaching* and explained them in such detail (*VS* 115.1). Formerly, the Church had taken stands in particular areas, such as marriage and social justice. In the seventeenth century, at the time of the dispute over probabilism, which offers many analogies with the current crisis, Rome had been obliged to condemn a number of laxist or rigorist propositions. For example, in connection with problems of that period, the following propositions held by some moralists were condemned: "If a knight is challenged to a duel, he may accept the challenge for fear of being accused of cowardice" (DS 1102); or again, "It is lawful for a religious or a priest to kill a person who threatens to spread grave calumnies about himself or his Order, if there is no other way of defending himself" (DS 1117). We recognize here one of the propositions which Pascal had opposed, saying that in this case the Jansenists were already dead men (*7th Provincial*). But here is something which actually remains to this day: "It seems likely (and therefore tenable) that the fetus does not have a rational soul as long as it is in the womb of its mother and only acquires it at birth. Therefore it must be admitted that murder is not committed in any abortion" (DS 1185). The encyclical takes its stand on a different plane than these questions of cases of conscience, and addresses fundamental problems.

Again, it is helpful to know that translations of the encyclical were based on the Italian text, while the *Catechism* was first drawn up and published in French. We may then consider the Italian text as a reference for other translations of the encyclical, since translations are not always perfect.

E. The Plan of the Encyclical

We are now ready to take our document in hand, beginning with the *Table of Contents*.

Veritatis splendor is divided into three chapters, the first of which is entitled, "Christ and the Answer to the Question about Morality." This is not simply a preamble, a kind of introductory spiritual meditation. Rather, it is a constructive chapter presented in the form of an in-depth reflection on the incident of the rich young man. This is indicated in the quotation added to the title: "Teacher, what good must I do . . . ?" It is within the framework of this question that the entire encyclical is written and must be interpreted.

Chapter 2 discusses "The Church and the Discernment of Certain Tendencies in Present-Day Moral Theology." This section is critical in the main and addresses the determining purpose behind the encyclical.

The principal object of Chapter 3 is to spell out how the encyclical should be applied by those responsible for teaching in the Church: moral theologians and bishops, to whom this letter is directly addressed. It is entitled: "Moral Good for the Life of the Church and the World."

I. Moral Theology and the Gospel: Six Guidelines for the Renewal of Catholic Moral Theology

The first chapter of the encyclical is undoubtedly the easiest to grasp. Because of its gospel presentation of morality and its spiritual content, it has aroused the greatest interest among ordinary readers. It has also for the most part won the approval of theological commentators, but these, after a few words of praise, give it very little attention. They apparently view this first section as a spiritual meditation, meant to introduce the discussion of moral problems in Chapter 2. It is an introduction which in their view calls for no particular comment. Their interest lies elsewhere.

This simple observation is an indication of precisely the basic problem which the encyclical's introduction wishes to address: the gap between morality and the Gospel which exists in the minds of many moral theologians. For them, a reflection on the Gospel would seem to betoken spirituality rather than morality and to have no direct, inevitable effect upon moral problems. Therefore it could not, in their view, be anything more than a preamble.

I maintain that the first chapter of *Veritatis splendor* is every bit as important as the second, because it traces the broad lines of a renewal of Catholic moral theology through a return to its chief source—the Gospel—which means bridging the gap which has been created between morality and spirituality. In doing this, the encyclical carries forward the work of biblical research undertaken by the *Catechism of the Catholic Church*. Chapter 1 is basically constructive, and for this reason it merits profound study. At the same time it offers a major censure of the moral theories critiqued in Chapter 2, namely, that in systematically separating morality from revelation by means of their categories, they have definitively moved away from evangelical renewal.

As I see it, we can distinguish in Chapter 1 *six guidelines for the evangelical renewal of moral theology*. They stand out most clearly when we contrast them with the preconciliar moral theology whose characteristic traits and divisions we have described above.

A. The Relationship Between Moral Theology and Scripture

In line with the council's wishes regarding the teaching of theology, and notably moral theology, *Veritatis splendor* reestablishes profound and sustained ties between moral theology and Scripture, particularly the Gospels. Three examples of this follow.

1. *The Frequency of the Citations*

As in the *Catechism*, Scripture is quoted far more often than in the textbooks of moral theology, which date from a period when anti-Protestant reactions had set extreme limitations on the use of the Bible in the Catholic Church. The gospel texts serve as a source of doctrine and a basis for reflection. They are no longer merely props, used to "confirm" the arguments of reason. Even the encyclical's Table of Contents is studded with scriptural quotations. Here we gather the fruits of the biblical renewal encouraged by the council, which truly restored the Bible to the People of God. The Pope gives us an example of a reading of Scripture that is shot through with moral teaching.

Some have faulted *Veritatis splendor* for its manner of reading and exploiting Scripture. This is a basic problem for exegetes as well as theologians: how to draw theological teaching from Scripture, particularly in the field of moral theology; and how to extract Scripture's moral and spiritual riches without losing sight of them in discussions about history and hermeneutics—while at the same time maintaining due respect for the contributions of positive study. The encyclical does not have to deal with such problems. It traces out the path and shows every Christian that the Gospel contains a word addressed to him personally even as it was addressed to the rich young man, a word which goes deeper than any human word.

2. *At the Heart of the Gospel Stands the Person of Christ*

   This is a point of major importance, transcending our initial observation, which was still at the material level: morality drawn from the Gospel focuses on the very person of Christ. The Bible is a book like no other. Far from being simply a historical document, Scripture is the bearer of a Word which touches us personally and puts us in an intimate relationship with Christ in faith. And according to the encyclical, the moral teachings of the Gospel too converge in the person of Jesus. Christian morality cannot be reduced to a code of commands and prohibitions. It consists basically in "holding fast to the very person of Jesus . . . sharing in his free and loving obedience to the will of the Father." "Following Christ is thus the essential and primordial foundation of Christian morality" (*VS* 19.2). This is how one becomes a true disciple. The imitation of Christ, particularly in the practice of fraternal love, constitutes the moral rule of Christian life (*VS* 20).

3. *Jesus' Conversation with the Rich Young Man is the Starting Point of* Veritatis splendor

   It introduces a concept dear to John Paul II, posing the most fundamental moral question: "What good must I do to have eternal life?" (Mt 19:16). Jesus replies that God alone is good and tells his questioner to observe the Commandments. As the young man is still not satisfied, Jesus exploits his desire for the good to show him the way of perfection, which means giving up his possessions, distributing them to the poor, and following him. Meditation on this passage carries us far beyond the realm of pious considerations. It poses the most basic of moral questions and continues with an in-depth reflection on the dominant themes of Christian morality, shaping them into closer conformity with the Gospel. The story of the rich young man thus becomes the setting for the entire encyclical. This method has the merit of presenting morality to us concretely, in a dialogue with Jesus. It moves us to question ourselves personally in our turn, in a similar conversation with the Lord. In this way the encyclical provides us with a model for reflection on moral questions in the light of the Gospel.

B. The Moral Question, "Teacher, what good must I do?" and the Question of Happiness

Another important change is indicated by the formulation of the moral question, which is different from the rich young man's, "What good must I do to have eternal life?" The encyclical sees in his words a question in the moral order that arises in the heart of every person who, consciously or not, approaches Jesus. It is about the full meaning of life, rather than about rules to be followed. It expresses a yearning for absolute good, which reveals to man the "call which comes from God who is the origin and goal of man's life." It directs the Church's mission to every man's encounter with Christ (*VS* 7).

This phrasing of the moral question opens up to us a much broader horizon than that of casuistry. Morality is not now limited to the problem of what is permitted or forbidden in cases of conscience. From the start it is situated within a perspective as vast as human life, thanks to this basically positive question, "What is good in life?" It is a clear invitation *to place at the very beginning of moral teaching the question of happiness and of the purpose of life*, as did the Fathers of the Church and St. Thomas. The *Catechism of the Catholic Church* has clearly shown the way at the opening of its section on morality, by linking man's creation in the image of God to his vocation to happiness, which finds its expression in the gospel Beatitudes (*CCC* 1716–29).

This modification of the moral question has an important result. It used to be possible to address the problem of what was permitted and forbidden by formulating purely rational laws, and to remain within the parameters of a purely human morality. However, one cannot give a fully satisfactory answer to the question of "what is good," and the desire for happiness, without bringing in God. In fact, God is the only one who can an-

swer the question about what is good, since he is Goodness itself, according to Jesus' word, "No one is good but God alone."
Thus the encyclical restores its religious dimension to morality
by relating it to the love of God, who is "the source of man's
happiness and . . . the final end of human activity" (*VS* 8–9).
The consideration of beatitude and of our final end once more
lays the foundation needed for complete harmony with Christ's
moral teaching and for the elaboration of an authentically Christian morality, based on charity.

C. The Reinterpretation of the Decalogue with Love as the Starting Point

Basing morality on the question of goodness leads to a reinterpretation of the Decalogue with significant consequences. According to the standard presentation in textbooks and cat-
echisms, the Decalogue had appeared as a summary of obligations, commands and prohibitions imposed on man by God under pain of sin, with the threat of punishment. Considered to
be the expression of the natural law inscribed in man's heart by
the Creator, as we read in St. Paul (Rom 2:15), it was nonetheless experienced as an external, restrictive law, a kind of legal
or natural authority set up in opposition to our freedom.

The encyclical maintains the interconnection between the
Decalogue and natural law, seeing the latter as the work of God
the Creator acting within man's heart as "a light of the intelligence infused in us by God," to use St. Thomas's definition,
which is corrective of legalistic voluntarism. However, it puts
the law back into the scriptural setting of God's covenant with
his people. *The Decalogue is a gift of God*, which has "brought
into existence the people of the Covenant" and made of them
"a holy nation." It is *linked with the promises of God* concerning
the promised land which was shown to Moses and which is a
symbol of eternal Life. God's Commandments "show man the
path of life and they lead to it" (*VS* 12.2). The Decalogue is not
simply a barrier that may not be crossed; it takes on a positive
role in pointing man to the kingdom of God.

Thus conceived, the Decalogue elicits from man something
far greater than material and servile obedience. *It calls for "a response of love"* in keeping with the fundamental command-

ment of Deuteronomy: "Hear, O Israel: The Lord our God is one Lord; and you shall love the Lord your God with all your heart, and with all your soul, and with all your might (6:4–5)" (*VS* 10). In keeping with the structure of the Decalogue, this response takes on the twofold form of love of God and neighbor.

It will be helpful to pause for a moment over this response of love which is asked of us. In reality, *Veritatis splendor* changes the foundation supporting morality and brings out its quintessence: *Is it love or is it obedience to obligations?* In the traditional textbooks, the general foundation lay in obligations and the predominant virtue became, in actual fact, legal obedience. The section on charity was revealing in this connection, since, practically speaking, it was limited to an explanation of man's obligations to, and sins against, God and neighbor. The study of charity itself, viewed as an upward thrust of the heart toward God, pertained to spirituality rather than to moral theology. Here we are faced with the question, Is it possible to love out of a sense of duty? If morality is the domain of obligation, then it can have little connection with the question of love.

The encyclical reverses this outlook, which has been too heavily influenced by the legalism of a historical period. It quite openly returns to Scripture and specifically to the gospel interpretation of the Decalogue, beginning with the commandment of love. It quotes St. Augustine, who explains this decisive question of priorities with acumen. "Does love bring about the keeping of the Commandments, or does the keeping of the Commandments bring about love? . . . But who can doubt that love comes first? For the one who does not love has no reason for keeping the Commandments" (*VS* 22.3). The encyclical invites us, therefore, to correct our idea of morality so as to assure the definitive primacy of charity, thanks to a rereading of the Ten Commandments. The *Catechism of the Catholic Church* does the same thing.

1. *Love's Twofold Response to the Decalogue*

Taking its inspiration from the teaching of St. Thomas, and in particular from his preaching on the two commandments of love and the Ten Commandments of the Law, *Veritatis splendor* shows how the Decalogue gives a twofold form to the response of love, which it enjoins on us. In the first place it teaches us about loving God "with our whole heart," exemplifying this in *the Commandments of the first tablet*. Here, in adoration, we recognize God as "the one and absolute Lord," and follow through with obedience and the exercise of justice and mercy. This is "the very core, the heart of the Law," from which its particular precepts flow (*VS* 11.1); or to put it differently, it marks the "centrality of the Decalogue" (*VS* 13.2).

Then comes love of neighbor, regulated by *the precepts of the second tablet*, which are summed up in the Commandment, "You shall love your neighbor as yourself." Here the encyclical introduces the personalist themes so often developed in John Paul II's catechesis: respect for the particular dignity of the human person, to be shown by safeguarding his spiritual and material goods in relationship to God, his neighbor, and the material world. Placed at the service of charity, these commandments indicate the duties and guarantee the fundamental rights of the human person (*VS* 13.2).

Taking up once more the pedagogical perspective, which was all too rare in post-Tridentine morality, the encyclical explains how necessary the role of the Decalogue is during the first stage of the development of the moral personality on its journey toward spiritual freedom. As St. Augustine affirms, avoidance of the serious sins forbidden by the Commandments forms in us "an initial freedom. . . but this is only the beginning of freedom, not perfect freedom" (*In Ioannis evangelium tractatus*, 41, 10: CCL 36, 363; cf. *VS* 13.4).

The encyclical concludes its reflection on the Decalogue by making an important point about *the relationship between the two commandments of love*: "They are profoundly connected and mutually related." We cannot separate them (*VS* 14.2). We cannot separate love of neighbor from love of God. Love of God is first and it alone gives the complete answer to the moral question about what is good from the viewpoint of eternal life. This point has its application in the theories, critiqued by the encyclical, that attempt to limit morality to human relationships on the so-called horizontal plane. Obviously it is impossible to conceive of love of God apart from love of neighbor without contradicting the formal teaching of St. John and the Synoptics.

In such a scenario we would be talking about an entirely vertical morality. In former periods the tendency to do this could be observed in a contemplative life marked by a certain asceticism in regard to human relationships. Let us note that the same tendency can also emerge in "horizontalist" teachings, in the form of an ideology that loses sight of the concrete individual flesh and blood neighbor who is the object of gospel love.

D. The Reintegration of the Sermon of the Lord and the New Law in Moral Theology

We have come to a central point. On several occasions (nn. 12, 15–16, 24, 25), the encyclical appeals to the Sermon on the Mount and the teaching of the New Law. In discussing Jesus' second answer to the rich young man, in which he reveals to him the way of perfection, it shows them at the summit of Christian morality.

1. *The New Law in St. Thomas and in Moral Theology Textbooks*

At this point we need to take a glance at the history of theology, in order to appreciate the innovation and gauge its importance. After a first elaboration in the Franciscan Summa of Alexander of Hales, the teaching on the New Law received from St. Thomas Aquinas its definitive theological formulation (*STh* I–II, qq. 106–8). This is an expression of the powerful spiritual movement of the thirteenth century, exemplified by St. Francis of Assisi and St. Dominic. Its originality lies in the fact that it defines the gospel Law as an interior law. The source of this teaching is the prophetic text of Jeremiah about the new Covenant, the law inscribed in hearts and minds (31:31), which the Letter to the Hebrews cites and applies to Christ (8: 6–13). St. Paul does the same thing when he speaks of the law of the Spirit (Rom 3 and 8), as also St. Augustine, in his commentary on the Sermon of the Lord, and his work, "The Spirit and the Letter," which is a meditation on these beautiful texts. To sum up, the entire scriptural and patristic tradition is gathered together and emphasized in the work of the Angelic Doctor. According to St. Thomas the New, or Gospel, Law is fundamentally, at its powerful core, *an interior law*. It is *the very grace of*

*the Holy Spirit, received through faith in Christ who justifies and op-
erating through charity which sanctifies*. This is its inmost essence.
But the New Law also possesses secondary and more material
elements, necessary in order that the grace of the Spirit may act
in us. These are *the text of Scripture*, epitomized in the Sermon
on the Mount—which thereby becomes the New Law's specific
text as the Decalogue was for the Old Law—and *the sacraments*
insofar as they are the means adopted to communicate the grace
of Christ to us (*STh* I–II, q. 106, a. 1, and q. 108, a. 1). Thus defined, the New Law fulfills the Decalogue and brings it to perfection (q. 107). It regulates man's interior acts at the level of
the "heart," where faith and charity operate with the other virtues, while the Decalogue bears directly on external actions (q.
108, a. 3).

This teaching, which attributes a primary role to the action
of the Holy Spirit and the theological virtues in the Christian
life, and which takes so exact an account of the evangelical dimension of morality, had unfortunately been neglected by
moralists since the rise, in the fourteenth century, of nominal-
ism, which restricted morality to the domain of obligation. Thus
the New Law and the Sermon on the Mount are never mentioned in modern textbooks or in the moral section of cat-
echisms appearing after the Council of Trent. If they are alluded
to, they are never assigned an important role in the scheme of
moral teaching. This is evident in the rift which has been created between the Gospel and the teaching of moral theology.
The result has been a real impoverishment of tradition.

2. *The New Law in the* Catechism of the Catholic Church

We had to wait until the middle of this century for the first
signs of a rediscovery of the New Law by exegetes and theologians. The *Catechism* takes full advantage of this renewal (nn.
1965–86). In its discussion of moral laws, after considering natural law and the Mosaic Law it takes up *"the New or gospel Law,"*
which it places *at the head of all moral legislation* in direct relation to grace (nn. 1965–74). The New Law is presented as "the
perfection here below of the divine law, natural and revealed,"
a reference to St. Thomas's definition, which we gave above.
The *Catechism* then comments briefly on the Sermon on the
Mount, which explains this Law as it corresponds to the new

commandment of love found in St. John (13:34), and shows us how this law causes us to act out of love, not fear. The New Law is a law of grace, conferring the strength we need; it is a law of freedom, giving rise to spontaneous action, which advances us from the condition of servants to that of friends of Christ and liberates us from the old observances. Such is the freedom of love, set in motion and manifested by the evangelical counsels.

Finally, we note that the *Catechism* (n. 1971), which is clearer on this point than the encyclical (*VS* 26), adds to its commentary on the Sermon on the Mount *"the moral catechesis of the apostolic teachings,"* or paraclesis. (I believe this term is to be preferred to paranesis, because of its frequent, almost technical, use in the presentation of moral teaching.) This paraclesis is found in the great Epistles containing the moral teaching of the apostles: Romans 12–15; 1 Corinthians 12–13; Galatians 5; Ephesians 4–5; Philippians 2:1–17 and 3:1–4, 9; Colossians 3–4; 1 Thessalonians 4–5; James; 1 Peter; 1 John. Clearly, therefore, the Sermon of the Lord is not an isolated text, but rather the privileged apogee of the moral teaching of the New Testament and of all Scripture.

3. *The Future of the New Law*

The introduction of the New Law into fundamental moral theology is an innovation which I believe is prophetic. It is still far from being generally accepted. Yet it is an absolute condition for the evangelical renewal of moral theology and an essential contribution to the undertaking of "re-evangelization" promoted by John Paul II. In this regard *Veritatis splendor* is ahead of current ideas in the field of moral theology, which are still determined by casuistic categories. Even the various editions of the *Catechism* demonstrate the difficulty encountered in introducing the New Law into the generally accepted moral categories. The thematic index of the French edition, which has been adopted by the Italian edition, does not include the Sermon on the Mount, although several Numbers of the *Catechism* deal with it and it is cited in a number of instances. The German edition compiled its own index; but it too fails to mention the "Bergpredigt." The English edition which has just come out has not corrected the omission. Yet if we consult the biblical index we find 139 quotations from Matthew 5–7. The Sermon of the Lord, which is the representative text of the New Law, does not yet seem to have a place among the familiar concepts of moral theology. Our mental categories lag behind.

4. *The Sermon and the New Law in* Veritatis splendor

The difficulty I have just pointed out is understandable. The Sermon on the Mount cannot be fitted into a moral system that is conceived to be the domain of obligations and prohibitions. It introduces quite a different type of morality, in which love takes precedence over legal obligation. The encyclical itself notes this: we are no longer dealing with commandments "understood as a minimum not to be exceeded, but rather as a path on which we pursue a moral and spiritual journey toward perfection, at the heart ['soul,' in the Italian text] of which is love" (*VS* 15.2). In other words, we are moving from a static morality, primarily bent on determining what we should not do, to a dynamic morality in which the impulse of love urges us on to continual progress.

This is very much the thrust of the encyclical. The interpretation of the Sermon on the Mount which it proposes is based on growth in charity. The Beatitudes at the beginning of the Sermon can in no way be opposed to the commands which follow them, the encyclical remarks. Quite the contrary: through their promises they orientate the commandments to the perfection of charity. If we study them in depth, they present "a sort of *self-portrait of Christ*" and invite us to follow him and to live in communion with him (*VS* 16.3). Actually, it is possible to discern the spiritual physiognomy of Christ throughout the Sermon. He offers himself as a model and companion on our journey along the paths of the Kingdom which its precepts indicate.

In its second part, the Sermon deals with the principal Commandments of the Decalogue. It interiorizes and radicalizes love of neighbor, and proposes as our model the perfection of the Heavenly Father in his merciful love. It shows us in Jesus the living fulfillment of the Law, the Master who would have us communicate in his love and who gives us the power to bear witness to it in our actions and choices (*VS* 15).

For this reason, the Sermon on the Mount could be called the *magna carta of evangelical morality*. We can consider it as the fundamental constitution of the Christian people. It is also the first rule of religious orders and of all who consecrate themselves to the evangelical life. Should it not serve as the foundation of canon law?

Further on, in connection with the relationship between law and freedom (*VS* 45), *Veritatis splendor* explicitly presents *the Thomistic teaching on the New Law,* namely, that it is an interior law written in the hearts of the faithful, a law of perfection and freedom. A passage is cited from St. Thomas' commentary on the Letter to the Romans, which shows the close link between this Law and the Holy Spirit and which paves the way, through the grace of the Spirit, for the definition which the *Summa theologiae* was to give: the New Law is the Spirit himself dwelling in the soul to enlighten and incline it to act rightly, or indeed the effect of the Spirit, that is, faith, operating through charity. The New Law is likewise evoked in connection with the need for grace (*VS* 24). I shall return to this point later.

5. *Return to the Patristic Tradition*

In its presentation of Catholic morality, the encyclical is profoundly intent on renewal, for it returns by way of St. Thomas to the patristic tradition growing out of the New Testament. It is essential to understand that this tradition is not something material and static like the transmission of a text or a piece of legislation. According to the very definition of the New Law, we are dealing with a living tradition, and with the communication of the source of life and permanent renewal, which is the grace of the Holy Spirit. The encyclical invites us therefore to return to the interior source of all spiritual renewals which have ever been produced in the life of the Church, through recourse to the Gospel. Guided and rendered authentic by the Sermon of the Lord and the apostolic catechesis, our effort for renewal should also be nourished by the sacraments in a liturgy animated by the spirit of prayer.

St. Thomas' definition of the New Law can be of enormous help to us in disposing the various elements of the Christian life in their proper order. The formulation of this teaching, the fruit of one of the great spiritual renewals of history, has acquired a universal value and may be considered as the theological expression of gospel living for all times. In the structure of the

Summa theologiae the treatise on the New Law is the keystone supporting all of moral theology in its relation to the life of the Trinity, *through* the Holy Spirit who communicates the Father's love to us (*Prima pars*), and *to* the person of Christ, through faith and the reception of sacramental grace (*Tertia pars*). It is very fitting, therefore, that the encyclical should have turned to this teaching. Yet St. Thomas is no more than an interpreter of the Gospel. He leads us to the Spirit, our Sanctifier, and to Christ our Savior, "the way of truth by which we may come, through the resurrection, to the blessedness of eternal life" (prologue of *Tertia pars*).

E. The Link between Observance of the Commandments and the Search for Perfection

Let us return with the encyclical to our meditation on the story of the rich young man. Jesus, aware of his eager desire for the good, which will not allow him to settle for mere observance of the Commandments, reveals to the rich young man his call to complete goodness, the perfection of love. He would have him transcend, in a sense, the Old Law regulated by the Decalogue, and pass on to the New Law.

1. *The Problem of a Double Standard of Morality*

Here we come to an important problem of interpretation, which the encyclical resolves with perception and vigor. The story of the rich young man has often served as an illustration of *the separation between morality and the search for perfection*, and a basis for it. When Jesus in his first response quotes the chief Commandments of the Decalogue, he is reminding the rich young man of the precepts which are imposed on everyone and which constitute morality. His second response, phrased conditionally, "If you wish to be perfect. . . ," indicates something special, a higher kind of life reserved for those who, like the apostles, have freely committed themselves to the search for perfection. This story has therefore served as an evangelical basis for the setting up of two states of life, or two degrees, within the Church: one for the generality of the faithful, for whom the observance of the Decalogue in the form of a series of obligations is sufficient; and another for those whom the evangelical counsels have summoned to a higher perfection, and who are generally identified as religious. This is what led Protestant writers to speak of a double moral standard in the Catholic Church, one for ordinary Christians and the other for monks.

This division corresponds to the teaching of the textbooks on moral theology mentioned above. On the one hand there is morality properly so called, with obligations based on the Decalogue and incumbent upon everyone. On the other hand we find asceticism and mysticism, which treat of ways of perfection reserved for the elite. The first moral system is reduced to a minimum of observances and a concern to avoid mortal sin; the second entails a search for perfection aided by asceticism and additional observances. One of the disadvantages of this view of things has been to cut ordinary Christians off from the vocation to perfection and the desire for sanctity. They could safely assume that for the generality of the faithful it was enough to conform to the minimum which was strictly required.

2. *The Response of the* Catechism *and the Encyclical*

The *Catechism* takes a definite stand in opposition to these divisions and corrects the perspective. It recalls the teaching of *Lumen gentium* on *the universal call to holiness*: "All Christians in any state or walk of life are called to the fullness of Christian life and to the perfection of charity." This it confirms with a quotation from the Sermon on the Mount: "Be perfect, as your heavenly Father is perfect" (Mt 5:48; cf. CCC 2013). It makes it clear that the life of every Christian possesses a mystical dimension: "Spiritual progress tends toward ever more intimate union with Christ. This union is called 'mystical' because it participates in the mystery of Christ through the sacraments—'the holy mysteries'—and, in him, in the mystery of the Holy Trinity. God calls us all to this intimate union with him." It is well, however, to distinguish this life of union with Christ, which constitutes the essence of the Christian life, from "the special graces or extraordinary signs of this mystical life [which] are granted only to some for the sake of manifesting this gratuitous gift given to all" (CCC 2014). We should not therefore identify mysticism, as has often been done, with the extraordinary phenomena which may accompany an intense participation in the "mystery" of Christ, such as the stigmatization of St. Francis of Assisi. The mystical life unfolds in the day-to-day events of the

Christian life, through the profound working of the theological virtues and the gifts of the Holy Spirit.

This is a confirmation of the renewal of spirituality initiated by Msgr. Saudreau in France at the end of the last century and continued by Fr. Arintero in Spain, by Fr. Garrigou-Lagrange in Rome, and by many others. They all maintained that the spiritual life, even in its mystical dimension, is accessible to every Christian through the reception of the sacraments, the liturgy, and the practice of prayer under the impulse of the Holy Spirit. It now remains to reintegrate spirituality, thus renewed, into the mainstream of the teaching of moral theology.

Along the same lines, *Veritatis splendor* presents *a renewed interpretation of the story of the rich young man.* According to the encyclical, there is no separation, still less a break, between the two successive responses of Jesus. Rather, there is *a profound continuity based on the charity* already evidenced in the young man's inclination toward "the good," in such wise that the two responses express two stages, and not two independent states, in the progress of the one charity toward its perfection.

Appealing to St. Augustine, who sees moral growth toward the perfection of love as coinciding with freedom's growth toward maturity, aided by the Law of God (*VS* 17), the encyclical differentiates between two attitudes: the observance of the Law seen as a burden and a restriction if not denial of freedom, as would be the case where obedience is rendered purely out of a sense of obligation; and on the other hand an observance inspired by love, which senses "the interior impulse" of the divine law and spontaneously seeks to live out all its exigencies in their fullness, going far beyond the Beatitudes' required minimum (*VS* 18). The root of the problem of our relationship to God's law is this: either we observe the Decalogue with love, and it becomes a teacher leading us beyond itself toward the New Law, or we obey it under the constraint of obligation and experience it as a burden which we seek to lighten.

Taking as its foundation and starting point the presence of inchoate charity at the origin of every Christian life, *Veritatis splendor* can affirm that "the vocation to perfect love is not restricted to a small group of individuals," but is addressed to everyone, since charity, like all life, tends spontaneously to grow toward "that perfection whose measure is God alone" (*VS* 18.2). According to the teaching of Jesus, this perfection will take on a twofold form: the radical exercise of love of neighbor expressed in giving one's possessions to the poor, and love of God proven in the following of Jesus. Clearly, the concrete modalities of the response to such a call will vary considerably, according to vocations and personalities. From the viewpoint of the Gospel, the essence of the response lies at the level of the heart. The question is, whom do we love, whom do we prefer and choose to follow? The conditional phrase, "If you wish to be perfect. . ." does not signify a counsel which we are free to follow or reject indifferently. In calling the rich young man to follow him, Jesus, by his exhortation, wishes to awaken love in his heart and to entice him beyond his chrysalis of observance of the Commandments.

3. *The Following and Imitation of Christ*

Veritatis splendor thus leads us to recapture the gospel theme of the Christian life understood as a following and imitation of Christ. This will enable us to restore to moral theology its personal and spiritual dimension.

We should note that the encyclical is at pains to associate the two expressions, "following" and "imitation" of Christ, in contrast to Luther, who set them in opposition, moving away from the theme of imitation, which is so important in Catholic spirituality, and which he faulted for giving too much emphasis to human effort and merit. The expression "followers of Christ," used to indicate the disciples, is found chiefly in the Synoptics, who describe Christ's life with his disciples as they followed him about in his wanderings through Galilee and Judea. The theme of imitation appears in the two Letters to the Thessalonians (1 Thess 1:6; 2 Thess 3:7; see also Phil 2:5; and 1 Pt 2:21), which are addressed to Christians who, after the death and ascension of Jesus, were following him no longer physically but spiritually. The two expressions are therefore complementary. *Imitation is an interior following*, at the level of heart and morality, under the impulse of the Spirit; it means *being conformed to Christ*. St. Augustine puts it very clearly in a homily on St. John: "'If anyone would serve me, let him follow me'. What does 'let him follow me' mean, if not 'let him imitate me'? For 'Christ,' says the apostle Peter, 'suffered for us, leaving us an example that we might follow in his footsteps' . . . What is the result of this, what is the reward, the advantage? That 'where I am, there also my servant will be.' May he be freely loved, and may this be the reward for work done in his service: to be with him" (*Homily* 51.11).

The encyclical orientates the following and imitation of Christ to the fraternal love shown by Christ in the account of the washing of the feet, the prelude to the Passion, and indicates its measure in the new commandment: "Love one another as I have loved you" (Jn 15:12). Thus, seen from the viewpoint of charity, "Jesus' way of acting and his words, his deeds, and his precepts constitute the moral rule of Christian life" (*VS* 20.1).

F. The Need for Grace

The beauty and nobility of the moral teaching in the New Law, which Christ proposed first to the rich young man and then to all the disciples, gives rise to a crucial question. *Is it possible to put such lofty teaching into practice?* The question had already been raised regarding the Decalogue, as it is raised in regard to every demanding moral system. But it becomes more pressing in the case of gospel morality, above all when it is to be applied universally, as the encyclical proposes.

Here we encounter the major difficulty with which modern exegesis and theology have grappled in their interpretation of the Sermon on the Mount. Doesn't the Lord's Sermon demand the impossible in presenting an ideal too high for ordinary people to attain? The difficulty becomes insurmountable when we think of morality as consisting entirely of obligations. From this perspective the precepts in the Sermon, which reach down into our most intimate depths, seem to increase the burden of our obligations beyond endurance.

This problem posed by the Sermon has elicited various responses. Some Catholics have distinguished between morality properly so called, which is meant for all and limited to the Decalogue, and the spirituality which the Lord's Sermon proposed, not to the crowd but only to those chosen disciples who drew near to Jesus to hear him—according to one interpretation of Matthew 5:1. This spirituality would be meant for an elite called to a perfection defined by the evangelical counsels. On the other hand, Luther challenged the distinction between precepts and counsels and ascribed to the Sermon the same role as that of the Law of Moses. As with the latter, the first aim or function of the Sermon, according to him, was to convince us of our sinfulness and make us turn to pure faith. Christ alone had lived out the teaching of the Sermon, said Luther, and he clothes us, by means of faith, with the justice which this discourse sets before us. Others have spoken of the Sermon on the Mount as an ideal moral system, unattainable yet still useful in encouraging moral progress. Again, it has been interpreted as an exceptional morality appropriate for those Christians who believed that the Parousia was imminent, but hardly one to be extended to the Church of all times.[2]

Veritatis splendor presupposes this problem regarding evangelical morality and also takes into account the very concrete difficulties which Christians can encounter in the practice of the Church's moral teaching.

The answer comes to us from St. Paul and the Fathers of the Church. *Man cannot imitate Christ's love by his own power, but only by virtue of a gift of God.* This, precisely, is the grace of the Spirit of Love, who defines the New Law. In relation to this needed help, the law has a teacher's function. It makes us aware of our sin and powerlessness and incites us to pray and to welcome the Spirit (*VS* 23). The encyclical repeats a formula of St. Augustine which is remarkable for its clear expression of the interaction between law and grace: "The law was given so that we might ask for grace; grace was given so that we might fulfill the law" [and not: "the obligations of the law," as the French translation has it]. This question is brought up again in Chapter 3 of the encyclical at the end of the section on moral problems. Whatever may be the temptations and difficulties, the Lord always enables us to observe his commandments through the gift of his grace in cooperation with our human freedom (*VS* 102–3). The very consciousness of our weakness prepares our hearts to receive God's mercy and awakens in us the desire for his help, which we express in prayer.

With this as a background, we need to perceive the Sermon on the Mount not as a code of supplementary obligations but as an expression of the manner in which the Holy Spirit acts. It is an exhortation to perform the works he wishes to produce in us by means of faith and love. Supported by the Our Father, which is placed at the center of the Sermon, we keep our eyes fixed on the promises of the Beatitudes.

1. *The Treatise on Grace in Moral Theology*

Those who are familiar with theological systems will quickly notice the changes that have been introduced. *The treatise on grace must be restored to its place in fundamental moral theology,* alongside law. This change is a direct consequence of the insertion of the New Law in the section which treats of laws. According to *Veritatis splendor,* we can no longer teach moral theology without referring to grace, giving it a major role and showing how it intervenes in the life of every Christian. This is true not only of all the concrete actions of a person but also of his prayer, where faith, hope, and charity are expressed and where the loftiest action of the Spirit is experienced—for he is the teacher of prayer as well as the inspirer of our actions.

Clearly, the rich young man's question about what is good in view of eternal life has changed the moral question and broadened it. Only God, who alone is good, can give the complete answer. In the light of Scripture, we have revised the interpretation of the Decalogue by considering it as a gift of God calling for a response of love. Viewed under the impulse of love, which it guides and protects in its first stages, the Decalogue prepares us to rediscover the way of perfection traced in the Sermon of the Lord and elucidated by the New Law. Thus a continuity can be reestablished between the various stages of progress in love and a profound unity at the heart of the Christian people, in keeping with the appeal addressed to all to follow Christ and to walk in the ways of holiness. Finally, the teaching of the Lord and the very awareness of our weakness show us our need for grace in order to respond to such a vocation. This grace has happily gone before us. All we need do is welcome it in faith with the free spontaneity of love.

Central to this renewal of perspectives on morality is the teaching of the New Law, which expresses theologically the heart of the Gospel. Because of the connection between the New Law and natural law, we are able to reconstruct a moral system which will be at once authentically Christian and fully human. It remains for us to develop the potentialities contained in the gospel teaching. In my opinion, the most fruitful way to do this is to recapture a morality that is based on the virtues and the gifts of the Holy Spirit, according to the model supplied by St. Thomas Aquinas, always with the condition that we give full value to the evangelical elements that his teaching presents. The encyclical has, in its first section, restored to morality its Christian foundation. It is up to moral theologians to build on it. There is still much work to be done.

II. The Church and the Discernment of Certain Tendencies in Current Moral Theology

Chapter 2 is considered the most difficult chapter in the encyclical. It should not be faulted for that, however. It was necessary to discuss the theories of certain moral theologians who make waves and often express themselves in very technical terms. We should be thankful that these theories have been brought forward and answered in a simple manner that focuses on essentials and avoids the excessively abstract terminology so dear to specialists. We should note too that the encyclical summarizes the theories it critiques without naming authors, and thus avoids personal polemics. It gives nuanced answers, discerning both the admissible and the unacceptable in a calm and reasoned way. The subjects under consideration are treated with seriousness and composure. Doubtless the discussion is open to further clarifications and more technical details, but that is the business of theologians. The encyclical has given us the essential points. The reactions of those who feel they have been targeted confirms the fact that it has brought to light the real problems that underlie a tangle of opinions and the subtleties of reasoning.

The central question in the debate is about the range of moral law and its application. We can formulate it in this way: are moral laws, stemming from natural law and formulated principally by the Decalogue, universal and unchangeable, and do they remain permanent through all the changes of history? Or more precisely, are there certain moral laws which always apply, without exception, because they have to do with intrinsically evil actions—things one may never do—such as the murder of an innocent man or abortion? Or should we rather say that moral laws and their application change with changing periods of history, places, cultures, circumstances, and personal situations? Obviously the solidarity of the entire body of morality is at stake, particularly in regard to natural law, which has served as a fundamental base for classic moralists. If the foundation is shaken, the whole building is at risk of collapsing. And how is it to be restored? The need for an answer to this question is urgent if we are to ensure a firm defense of human rights and dignity at a time when ethical problems are uppermost in our minds and their gravity is most apparent.

Veritatis splendor classifies the problems according to the four principal elements of morality current today:

1. Freedom and law.
2. Conscience and truth.
3. Fundamental choice and concrete performance.
4. The human act and criteria for judging its moral quality.

A. Freedom and Truth. Autonomy Received from God.

Without a doubt the pivotal point of *Veritatis splendor* lies in the coordination it establishes between human freedom and truth. The connection is already apparent in the chosen title, "The Splendor of Truth." The word "truth" is placed first in the Latin so that it will stand out in bold relief. Let me note that we are not speaking of abstract truth here. Truth is related to the desire for the good, which is at the root of human freedom. Hence the meaning of truth and the meaning of the good together form the fundamental moral question: what is true good, and therefore true happiness? What is it that is truly good, in terms of the rich young man's question? Far from diminishing freedom, the exigencies of truth in regard to the good are necessary for its implementation, and above all for the formation and growth of love. Our freedom is therefore freedom for truth, for the good, for love, for happiness. It is in touch with reality (*VS* 34).

With this in mind, we turn to a passage in the *Catechism*: "Freedom is the power, rooted in reason and will, to act or not to act, to do this or that, and so to perform deliberate actions on one's own responsibility. By free will one shapes one's own life. Human freedom is a force for growth and maturity in truth and goodness; it attains its perfection when directed toward God, our beatitude" (*CCC* 1731). "The more one does what is good, the freer one becomes. There is no true freedom except in the service of what is good and just. The choice to disobey and do evil is an abuse of freedom and leads to 'the slavery of sin' " (*CCC* 1733). So we are not talking about a freedom which has been reduced to the power to choose between contraries, between good and evil—which has been called freedom of indifference. Rather, the freedom we mean tends spontaneously toward whatever possesses truth and goodness—and this we call freedom for excellence, because it consists in the power to perform deeds which are true and good. Thus we can say that freedom is "at once inalienable self-possession and openness to all that exists, in passing beyond self to knowledge and love of the other" (*VS* 86).

1. *John Paul II's Experience*

To understand John Paul's concern and determination on this point, I believe it is helpful to recall his experience under the Communist regime, where he lived under the threat of a veritable system of lying. The only way a person could defend himself against it was to adopt, with the dissident Russians, the watchword "never to lie," never to be caught up in the system. In this situation it was clear that loyalty to the truth was the necessary condition for freedom. The smallest concession to lying would lead to slavery. Therefore acceptance of truth was clearly a source of interior freedom and the only defense of human dignity.

In connection with this, it is enlightening to reread Galanskov's "Human Manifesto," proclaimed in a square in Moscow and quoted by V. Boukovsky in his book, *And the Wind Blows Round and Round*:

I shall go out
  into the square
  and there,
  for all the city to hear,
  I shall fling out
                    a cry
                              of despair.
  It is I.
    I appeal to truth—to justice
    To revolt!
    I am he who will no longer serve.
    I smash your black fetters
    Tissue of lies.
    I have no need of your bread
    Mixed with our tears
    I fall to earth and I vanish
    In a half-delirium
    A half-sleep . . .
    And I feel
                    the human within me
                              stifled.

The problem has not disappeared with the fall of communism in the Eastern countries. It is present in the West in more subtle forms. In the very name of freedom people have lost interest in truth and have reduced it to mere personal opinion, feeling, or advantage. Since they are no longer sustained by a strong and challenging idea of truth, their freedom has grown weak and proves powerless against the drives of passion or selfishness and the external pressures of their social or intellectual environment, the mass media, and political power. In Western countries as in the East, the rift between freedom and truth leads to enslavement. Only a vigorous love of truth can empower us to defend our freedom and give us courage enough to face up to life's problems and trials.

2. *The Debate on Freedom, Conscience, and Law*

In discussing the connection between truth and freedom, the encyclical strikes at the root of the present moral problem. It has the merit of revealing the two fundamental questions underlying the current debate: what is the nature of freedom and how does it relate to the moral law?

Veritatis splendor takes a stand against an ideology which would make freedom a kind of absolute and its own justification, and which would cede to it the power to determine what is good or evil. Where this is done, freedom becomes the principal criterion of moral judgment: whatever favors freedom is morally good; whatever diminishes or opposes it is evil.

This concept in turn leads to the claim of autonomy for individual freedom, in the strict sense of the word. In such a system freedom, aided by reason, becomes a law unto itself, with a resulting purely rational and human morality. This is an application of the Kantian problematic, which opposes autonomy to heteronomy. (As "nomos" means law or rule and autonomous means self-rule or self-made law, and as we speak of an automobile as a vehicle which has its own motor, so heteronomy refers to rule by another, "heteros," and to laws coming from another.) Similarly we speak of "theonomy" when the rule or laws are received from God ("theos") (*VS* 36). The question of the autonomy of morality has been discussed at length by moralists; the discussion is still going on.[3] The claim to complete autonomy has as its corollary the rejection of all law imposed on man from without or from above, particularly divine authority. It goes hand in hand with secularization.

In the same line of thought we find a "creative" concept of the moral conscience. While taking into account the indications of general laws or norms, "the individual conscience . . . would in fact make the final decision about what is good and what is evil" (*VS* 56.1). It would thus enjoy decisive autonomy in concrete moral judgment, at the risk of confusing conscience with personal, subjective opinion.

Here we see man focusing on freedom and considering it, in one way or another, as the source of moral values. Because of his freedom and reason the human subject, the personal conscience, would be the ultimate judge of what is good and evil. Moral law would thus become relative to subjective judgment. Of course it would be given a certain general value, but exceptions could always be made according to circumstances, and its application would ultimately depend upon the judgment of the individual. This sublimation of freedom is very widespread in our liberal societies.

So we are witnessing a kind of revolution in Catholic moral theology. The casuistry of recent centuries had placed morality in the framework of a debate between freedom and law, conceived as two opposite poles, with law having a restrictive effect and imposing itself upon freedom with the force of obligation. Freedom and law confront each other like two landowners, disputing the territory of human acts. Generally speaking, moralists would say: "Law governs one kind of action, freedom another." For example, law takes over Sundays, when manual work is forbidden, while freedom takes over the rest of the week, when we are free to work. Formerly, moralists were the traditional representatives of moral law and it was their duty to show conscience how to apply the law in a given case or "case of conscience." Today we observe a strong tendency to reverse the roles. Moralists now see themselves as defenders of freedom and personal conscience. As for moral law, it has become the servant of freedom, providing it with general indications, which may be followed according to personal judgment. These new theories are actually outgrowths of the concept of freedom of indifference, which underlies casuistry. Freedom of indifference attributes to the will alone the power to choose between contraries, between good and evil, to choose for or against the law. It thus sets up a tension in relation to law, which it sees as a purely restrictive, external will. The claim to this kind of freedom is at the origin of modern individualism. The encyclical rightly notes, moreover, that this heightened freedom is being widely contested by the human sciences, which are busy demonstrating the conditionings it is undergoing.

3. *The Convergence of Freedom, Law, and Conscience*

Veritatis splendor proposes a different concept of man and freedom, inspired by Scripture and Christian tradition. Man was created in the image of God in his spiritual nature. Hence he is capable of knowing and loving God and is given mastery over his actions, or freedom, which is patterned on the freedom of God. This freedom, quickened by the desire for truth and goodness, enables man, both in his own regard and in regard to those who depend upon him, to share actively in God's legislative power, his government, and his providence. The origin of moral law is in God—from this viewpoint we call it the divine or eternal law—but this law is inscribed in a unique way in the human heart and mind, and in man it is called natural law. It is placed within man, and makes him a collaborator with God in the regulation of his actions and his own life (*VS* 42–43).

Man thus enjoys a real moral autonomy, understood as a participation in the sovereign autonomy of God. The encyclical, while recognizing this autonomy as did the council, prefers to speak of a "participated theonomy" in order to show clearly that moral law has its original source in God (*VS* 41.2). Furthermore, we can say—and Christian experience confirms this—that the more closely a man conforms through obedience to the light of God shining in the depths of his soul, the freer he becomes interiorly. He is autonomous in regard to all external pressures and capable of responding personally to the call of truth, goodness, and love. This is his natural vocation, according to Psalm 4, quoted by the encyclical and also by St. Thomas in connection with natural law: "There are many who say: Who will make us see good? The light of your face, Lord, is signed upon us" (4:5). Upon us, that is, within us, in the depths of our hearts where you have inscribed your law.

Let us note that natural law is represented here as an inner light. It is a work of God's wisdom which speaks to the human mind and heart. This accords with the relationship between freedom and truth which the encyclical establishes. A contrary concept views law as the sheer determination of the legislator's will, imposed from without upon a freedom it wishes to restrict. This sets up a relationship of force, which no reason can resolve.

As for conscience, which receives from God "that primordial insight about good and evil," it is like an indestructible spiritual spark (*scintilla animae*) which shines in the heart of every man. The Scholastics called it synderesis. It is also said to be the voice of God. Thanks to this higher light, conscience becomes for man an inner imperative and a call to do what is good in concrete situations. This is the origin of moral obligation, also called the obligation of conscience. Hence conscience is "the proximate norm" of concrete actions insofar as it is the witness and instrument of that interior light which finds its expression in natural law, "the universal and objective norm of morality" (*VS* 59–60).

Doubtless conscience can be deceived in its judgment, since human reason, faced with complex situations, is fallible. But it always retains that inner, primordial light which spurs it on to seek the truth unwearyingly and ever to advance in doing good. (*VS* 60–64).

Thus man's freedom, conscience, and the law of God, far from being opposed, "meet and are called to intersect," in spite of tensions which may arise (*VS* 41.1). Freedom needs to be taught and supported by the law of God. It depends on the inner light of conscience to show it what is truly good and to foster its growth in truth.

4. *Conscience according to John Henry Newman*

The encyclical follows the lines of great Christian tradition, as recalled by Newman in his "Letter to the Duke of Norfolk," quoted in part by the *Catechism* (*CCC* 1778):

> Conscience is but an ensemble of natural principles more primordial than nature itself. It is a law of the mind; yet [Christians] would not grant that it is nothing more; I mean that it was not a dictate, nor conveyed the notion of responsibility, of duty, of a threat and a promise . . . . [Conscience] is a messenger of him who, both in nature and in grace, speaks to us behind a veil, and teaches and rules us by his representatives. Conscience is the aboriginal Vicar of Christ. It is the prophet who reveals the truth to us, the king who imposes his orders upon us, the priest who anathematizes us and who blesses us. If the eternal priesthood of the Church were to disappear, the chief priest would survive this ruin, incarnate in conscience.

In contrast with this Christian concept of conscience, Newman describes for us the new meaning of the word "conscience" being adopted by many people:

> But what does the man in the street think about conscience? . . . When our fellow citizens claim the rights of conscience they no longer consider the rights of the Creator nor what creatures owe him in their thoughts and actions; they think of the right to speak, write and act according to their own opinion or mood, without the least concern for God or the world. They do not dream of obey-

ing the moral law. They claim the right for every English-
man to act as he pleases; the right to believe what he likes
and to ask no one's advice; the right to regard any priest
or pastor, speaker or writer as outdated, who takes the
liberty to react against this way of rushing without let or
hindrance to perdition. If conscience has its rights, it is
because duties are implied. But in our day, in the minds
of a great number of people, the rights and freedom of
conscience serve only to dispense conscience. They would
like to ignore the Lawgiver and Judge, and be free of all
interior obligation . . . . In former times, conscience was
a strict counselor. Nowadays it has yielded its place to a
sham unheard of in eighteen centuries, which would
never have taken people in if they had known of it: the
right to do as you please.

Surely this text sounds a prophetic note.

Cardinal Newman indicates the criteria by which we can
discern the difference between a true conscience and what we
might call a conscience formed by opinion. The authentic conscience places us before God who stands "behind the veil" of
his mystery. It subjects us to his Word, precepts, judgment,
appeals, and rule. It is forever challenging us—and this is a sure
sign that it is at work—because it wants us to advance toward
God by that path which the Gospel calls narrow. If we follow
its voice, the true conscience will win for us inner peace and
joy even in the midst of trial and spiritual combat intensified
to the point of persecution. Such a conscience will really make
us autonomous, capable of judging for ourselves, "in secret,
where the Father sees us," and of serenely resisting all pressures of public opinion or force contrary to truth and goodness.
Conscience is like an inner citadel. It strengthens us, because
together with the moral law it communicates to us the light and
grace of God.

A conscience formed by opinion is pure illusion. It is a conscience fallen captive to our opinion and to our determination to
defend and justify our own feelings and their worth. It refuses to
submit to the judgment of another or the command of any authority whatsoever. This so-called conscience attempts to set itself up
as the judge of good and evil and to shape law, the moral world,
religion, and even God himself, according to its whim. It would

rob God of his right to condemn and punish. But despite its apparent power, the conscience formed by opinion remains weak in its individualism. It is unable to resist the pressures of its intellectual environment, the media, and the crowds to whom it instinctively looks for support and protection from the inner Voice. It allows itself to be drawn into agitated discussions about freedom, conscience, and peace, which end in divided opinions, turmoil of hearts, inner emptiness, and dissatisfaction.

So the formation of conscience of which the encyclical speaks is clearly indispensable (*VS* 64). It begins with the discernment of what a true conscience is and with the joyous humility of one who has discovered the Light. It grows by attending the school of the Word of God, with the help of the Church's teaching. It needs to be strengthened by experience, through the exercise of virtue, in the light of faith, under the impulse of hope and charity; and it operates in prudential discernment. Through docility to the Word of God, which it inculcates in us, conscience frees us from our isolation and integrates us in the communion of the Church. Thus it fulfills its role as "Vicar of Christ."

B. The Temptation of Rationality and Technology: The "Proportionalist" System

In order to see clearly what is at stake in the debate in which *Veritatis splendor* is engaged, we need to understand the theories it is challenging. It is not enough to know their salient features and certain aspects which are open to criticism. We also need to see how they coordinate ideas and categories to form a complete system of moral thought which is firmly constructed and has its own specific characteristics and logical consequences. The encyclical provides us with the principal elements of this systematization, but I believe it will be helpful to regroup them so that their significance and consequences may be the more clearly assessed. What, then, are "proportionalism" and "consequentialism," so often referred to in the encyclical? How have the authors who subscribe to them systematized them, and how have they put them into operation in moral theology?

It is not easy for the uninitiated to form a precise idea of "the proportionalist system," of which "consequentialism" is a variant. The authors who, with the help of theoretical reflection, have worked it out in the wake of the encyclical *Humanae vitae* often use very technical language in which Kantian categories shore up and intensify scholastic abstraction in such a way that theologians of other disciplines such as dogma or exegesis have difficulty following them. Moreover, none of these authors have written a book offering a presentation of the system in its totality. They have only published articles or collections of essays that give us partial insights, depending on the writers' views and preoccupations. Then too, their defensive attitude sometimes leads them to nuance their positions and explanations to such an extent that it is difficult to be sure what their chief tenets actually are.

However, once we become familiar with the literature on the subject we can more easily distinguish the main categories used by these authors, their interconnection, and their internal logic. Actually, the "proportionalist" system is heir to the casuistry of recent centuries and proposes a revision of it constructed with the aid of elements borrowed from St. Thomas—such as the predominance accorded to finality—together with categories or problematics of Kantian inspiration. What we are presently witnessing is an updated version of the crisis of "probabilism," which shook the Church in the seventeenth century. We certainly have to credit the authors, like their predecessors, with the laudable desire to adapt Christian moral teaching to the ideas of our age and its technological mentality, in order to address the ethical problems posed at the personal level and within the parameters of our society. The question is, whether the moral system which they propose provides an adequate response, or whether on the other hand it does not systematically ignore the essential dimensions of human and Christian action, which leads to regrettable consequences at the level of the foundations of morality and the treatment of cases. This is precisely what *Veritatis splendor* faults them for.

I shall now sketch "proportionalism" in broad outline, basing my analysis on the data provided in the encyclical and taking into account at the same time current literature on the subject.

Basically, we could say that the construction of the new system has been aided and abetted by two separations or disassociations at work in the teaching of Christian morality: first, the rift created between the transcendental and categorical levels, and second, the breach between the pre-moral and moral levels.

1. *Transcendental and Categorical Levels*

A first cutoff is the distinction, at the heart of Christian morality, between the transcendental and categorical levels. Borrowed from Karl Rahner, this distinction has been used in moral theology to address the question of Christian morality.[4] At the transcendental level we find personal attitudes, general intentions, and behavioral patterns which engage the entire person and all of life in its commitment to God, Christ, and neighbor. "This refers to virtuous ways of acting, such as faith, love, openness to redemption, the vision of life as a sacrament, the imitation of Christ, etc." In simpler terms the encyclical calls it the order of salvation (*VS* 37). At this level the contribution of revelation is incontestable, and numerous scriptural texts bear it out. From this point of view we can certainly affirm the existence of a Christian moral system.

The categorical level includes concrete actions which can be grouped according to various commandments and virtues such as justice, fidelity, chastity, etc. At this level scriptural texts do not give us specific, clear, and precise norms that can be applied at all times. Here Christian morality is identified with a purely human morality, justifiable by reason; Christian data obtained at the transcendental level simply provides a favorable and supportive background.

It is easy to see the consequences of this distinction, which many authors have adopted without too much nuancing. Actually, all the concrete moral problems under discussion today, together with the norms being directly applied to them, are found at the categorical level, and should therefore, according to this theory, be solved by purely rational criteria and arguments. Thus the domain of morality, along with cases of conscience and the norms they include, would be confined to the categorical level. This would be the proper field of ethics.

We should note that this distinction between the two levels is a prolongation of the now classical distinction between morality, where rational arguments predominate, and spirituality. But the distinction has become solidified among "proportionalists" and is now equivalent to an actual separation, because of morality's claim to autonomy—made in the name of reason—and because morality has been limited to the level of human relations within the framework of a secularized society. The end result is a morality which will yield only to the magisterium of reason and will claim independence of the magisterium of the Church founded on revelation. The problem is that this rational magisterium, which would set itself up in the name of science, has caused many moralists to abandon the teaching on natural law which had hitherto been a firm foundation for them. They have not grasped the fact that no positive human science, being in principle and methods a science of facts and not of right action, can be normative and teach moral law, still less the entire scope of natural law. These sciences are of a different order. Hence the moral edifice, if placed under the umbrella of scientific reason, will rest on very fragile and uncertain foundations. The right of the Church's magisterium to intervene in the field of morality in the name of natural law will likewise be disclaimed.

We are witnessing an initial narrowing of the field of morality as it cuts itself off from its specifically Christian sources, moving away from them in the direction of a purely rational and secular morality. Clearly, proportionalists treat morality in a sense diametrically opposed to the goal set forth in the first chapter of *Veritatis splendor,* which is, as we have seen, to reestablish the bond between morality and the Gospel, a bond so weakened by casuistry. The fact that the evangelical contribution is considered to be a favorable context for morality does not prevent it from remaining marginal, since it is taken for granted that it cannot provide proper norms and criteria at the categorical level. Here we have reached the heart of the debate over Christian morality.

2. *The Pre-moral and Moral Levels*

Morality being situated henceforth on a rational, human plane, the "new moralists," as they have sometimes been called, wish to determine more precisely the role of the concrete moral judgment. They again distinguish two levels within the realm of morality: first the pre-moral level, also called physical or ontic, and second the specifically moral level.[5]

Let us note that this distinction, too, is the prolongation of a concept elaborated by moralists in recent centuries. They have approached the human act from the point of view of its physical being in relation to its object and circumstances, prior to the intervention of the will in relation to law.[6] But here again the distinction has been stressed and the data and its organization modified.

A distinction is made, then, between the pre-moral level—where we have the relationship of the action to all the circumstances in view of the end pursued—and the properly so-called moral level, where the will intervenes, determining whether or not to perform the action previously judged at the pre-moral level as good or evil.

So we are dealing with yet another separation. The judgment, which forms the basis for moral qualification, will work exclusively at the pre-moral level, where the action is related to its circumstances, consequences, and end. The will's intervention will only come later, acting on the judgment previously formed. Its role will be limited to an option: to will or not to will what has been judged good or evil. The essential note of morality lies in the good or bad intention.

In their concern to distinguish levels, proportionalists have adopted a special terminology. At the pre-moral level they speak of an action as appropriate or correct (in German, *richtig*; in English, *right*), while at the moral level they will call it good (in German, *gut*; in English, *good*).

3. *Judgment of Actions Based on Results or Consequences*

We have come to the heart of the new system. If the fundamental judgment of actions is situated at the pre-moral level, how, and according to what criteria, will it be formed?

Here is what we might call the system's root concept. It is borrowed from the classic theory of double effect used in casuistry to resolve certain difficult cases. An action, a surgical operation, for example, or the administration of medication, may have a good effect on the mother of a family, such as the cure of a grave illness, together with an evil effect such as an eventual abortion.

The root idea of the system was to apply the principle of double effect to all moral actions, thus giving this principle a general impact in moral teaching, but revising it in such a way as to order the effects to the end sought. In the classic teaching, the good effect had to precede the bad effect in the temporal, material, or causal order so as to avoid contradicting a principle taken from St. Paul: "it is not licit to do evil that good may come of it" (cf. Rom 3:8). One could not do something evil in order to achieve some good, or in other words, one might not use an evil effect as the means for obtaining a good effect (cf. *VS* 79). In line with the new concept, priority among effects will be established according to the requirements of a proportionate reason for acting, and more precisely with the help of a comparison of the good and evil effects in view of the end sought. If the good effects outweigh the evil effects, they are given priority by the will and the action becomes lawful, correct, and good.[7]

A procedure for forming a judgment is thus set up in such a way that it can be generalized. Considered at the pre-moral level, all of our actions have both good and evil effects or consequences. Medication can have harmful side effects. The construction of an industrial complex brings prosperity but causes pollution. An atomic factory poses ecological danger. The choice of a priestly vocation obliges a man to renounce marriage. Hence, since all of our choices are directed to partial goods, they are bound to have some negative consequences, at least insofar as they may deprive us of alternate possible goods.

The judgment of actions will therefore consist in weighing their good and evil consequences in relation to the end sought; thus a proportionate reason for acting will be provided. This is what the Germans call a *Güterawägung,* or balance, an assessment of goods which aims at a maximum of good effects and a minimum of evil ones (*VS* 74). Hence the two terms used for the new system: we speak of consequentialism when our chief consideration is the consequences of an action, and of proportionalism when actions are judged by the presence of a proportionate reason for acting, even if they run counter to some law. In this case as well the judgment is based on a calculation of consequences.

These authors insist, moreover, on the necessity of taking into account *all the consequences* of an action, whether proximate or remote, and *all the circumstances* entailed at personal, social, cultural, and historical levels. This totality should be, in principle, weighed in its proportionality in order to arrive at a correct, appropriate judgment, to which the will communicates a moral character. These moralists do not therefore make the classic distinction between the essential elements of an action, which are for St. Thomas the object and the end, and the secondary elements, which are precisely the circumstances.

In order to parry objections, some authors try to lift the assessment of circumstances and consequences to a universal plane. Thus judgment of the proportionality of an action to its end should not stop at a consideration of the advantages and disadvantages to accrue in the near or not too distant future, but should take a broader view and weigh all possible untoward effects "from all angles over the long haul" (*auf die Dauer und im ganzen*).[8] This transposition to the universal changes nothing in the system however, nor in the problems it poses when we come down to the concrete and look at norms and actions, because the entire system remains dominated by a finality which is by its very nature technical.

If it is true that the term "circumstance" includes, for these moralists, everything that goes to make up an action, then we have a right to marvel that they can be so heedless of the inner, profound, and spiritual circumstances that are present in every concrete action. Such would be, for example, the active dispositions of the subject, his virtues, and most especially that unique "circumstance," his relationship to God. All these have been set aside as pertaining to the moral or transcendental level. The only things to be considered therefore, are external circumstances and certain psychological data of the pre-moral order, insofar as they can be measured.

4. *The Tendency to Utilitarianism*

Ideas have their logic and their built-in tendencies. Current proportionalism is inclined to judge everything from a finalist, or teleological, viewpoint, so called because it relates the means to the end. Because of this *it inevitably moves toward utilitarianism*, since usefulness is defined precisely as the adequate relationship of means to end. We should not be surprised therefore that proportionalism has been faulted for lapsing into utilitarianism, and that the accusation persists in spite of the responses made, some fine tuning, and subtleties. Writers have, for example, distinguished several kinds of utilitarianism: utilitarianism of action and utilitarianism of norms, strict utilitarianism, and mitigated utilitarianism. This has led to the terms: strict or mitigated proportionalism or consequentialism.

Utilitarianism of norms, elaborated in response to objections made to the fact that the consideration of utility should enter into the judgment of individual acts, admits as criteria of action certain norms having universal significance, which must however have been justified beforehand at the utilitarian level. An example of this would be the fact that long experience has shown that such or such behavior is always harmful. We wonder, however, if this recourse to experience provides a solid enough foundation for our contemporary world, characterized as it is by a break with the past, change, and love of novelty. Whatever may be the arguments for a utility forged in order to maintain the existence of universal moral laws, it seems in fact that the predominance of the useful in this type of system leads inevitably to a certain relativizing of moral reality, as well as to the admission of some exceptions to all law.[9]

C. Toward a Moral Technique

This new system of judging actions at the pre-moral level turns morality into a kind of technique. Its rational methods are much like those used in industry for evaluating projects by calculating profit and loss in relation to efficiency and utility. *We are dealing with the reduction of morality to a kind of technique* in which the moralist plays the role of director. This is confirmed by the choice of examples which proportionalist writers use, borrowed as a rule from medical, industrial, economic, or social techniques. Actions, for example, are often described as "productive" or "counterproductive." This reduction of morality to a technique fits in well with the technological, scientific, and pragmatic mindset of our Western society. To some extent this explains its success and utility, but we should also be alert to its inherent dangers and weaknesses, stemming from the diminishment of morality which proportionalism entails.

The first defect of this system is that *it cannot be integrated or used* in judging specifically moral qualities such as *virtues.* These have no place in calculations of utility or efficiency, since they must be sought for their own sake and demand the eventual sacrifice of all material or pre-moral *interests*. Such, for example, are love of truth and justice, love in itself, extending in its generosity to forgiveness; uprightness and honesty; or again, friendship. Insofar as they are perfections of persons, these qualities belong to a different order and cannot enter into the field of comparison proposed by proportionalists anymore than they could be computerized, since they are unpredictable. They are about a morality of excellence and cannot be reduced to a morality of utility.

With all the more reason *the theological virtues* are beyond calculation, to say nothing of the gifts of the Holy Spirit, which have, in any case, been automatically excluded from the system, since they belong to another sphere. Thus the gospel teaching is, in fact and in principle, excluded from the moral judgment. Any attempt to combine the two would be little more than a palliative.

D. The Encyclical's Fine-Tuning

Veritatis splendor *first emphasizes the danger of this system* vis-à-vis the major problem under discussion, namely, *the universality and permanence of moral laws*, particularly negative ones. *The negative commandments* forbid actions which are evil in themselves and which can never become good regardless of the circumstances, such as adultery and murder. They have binding force *semper et pro (ad) semper*—always and without exception. On the other hand *the positive precepts* are about acts of virtue to be performed, whose perfection requires due ordering of all the circumstances. An example of this can be seen in the gospel precept of fraternal correction. Positive precepts oblige *semper sed non pro semper*—always, but according to circumstances (*STh* II–II, q. 33, a. 2). Actually, in insisting that moral laws and their application depend upon the consideration of all the circumstances in their multiplicity and variations, and in particular upon the calculation of good and evil consequences in view of the end, proportionalists render it theoretically and practicably impossible to hold out for norms that are universally applicable without any exception. Hence they introduce into all moral norms an element of flexibility and relativity which weakens them and compromises the very foundations of the moral edifice, particularly the teaching on natural law, which is summed up in the precepts of the Decalogue.

The object of the encyclical is precisely to reestablish the solidity of this basic foundation of Christian teaching. Its critical section deals with the twofold split created in the sphere of moral action by proportionalism.

First, Veritatis splendor *challenges the separation made between the order of salvation and concrete actions* and their rational norms; between the transcendental and categorical levels; between the fundamental option and particular actions; and finally, between the Gospel and morality (*VS* 65ff.).

As we have seen, the encyclical shows how the desire for the good, which is natural to man, is directed to God and finds its complete fulfillment only in the teaching and person of Christ. It is impossible, therefore, to construct an ethical system which is exclusively human, avoids the question of God, and sets aside the Word of God. The question of true goodness and happiness is basically a religious question.

Above all, the encyclical reestablishes *a close link between the Decalogue*—the interpreter of natural law in the setting of the Covenant—*and the New Law* instituted by Jesus. He instituted this Law by means of charity, which is engrafted like a living branch upon our natural sense of goodness and love. Charity defends and teaches us through the Ten Commandments and grows in us through the gift of the grace of the Spirit. *Charity, therefore, cannot remain outside the field of morality and individual actions.* On the contrary, the entire thrust of Christian education and doctrine is to have charity penetrate our lives, our heart's intentions, and our concrete actions, in such a way that the love of Christ becomes the prime motivation and ruling criterion of our conduct. This in no way hinders us from acting reasonably as human persons—far from it. We can see an illustration of this in St. Paul's responses to the conscience cases submitted to him in First Corinthians. In addition to the rational criteria which a philosopher might have advanced, such as this reflection on fornication: "Every other sin which a man commits is outside the body; but the immoral man sins against his own body," St. Paul proposes decisive criteria drawn from our relationship to

Christ: "Do you not know that your bodies are members of Christ? . . . that your body is a temple of the Holy Spirit? . . . and that you are not your own?" (1 Cor 6:15–19). Charity thus becomes the chief criterion, as in the case of meat offered to idols, where we are shown how we should behave toward weaker brethren (1 Cor 8–10).

In Chapter 3 *Veritatis splendor* inveighs against *"the serious and destructive dichotomy which separates faith from morality,"* resulting in a separation between freedom and truth (*VS* 88). Faith is a decision which engages our entire being. It is a communion of love and life with Christ. It therefore has a moral content which strengthens and perfects the observance of the divine commandments and bears witness to the inviolable holiness of the Law of God. It can lead the believer even to the point of martyrdom (*VS* 89ff).

Pursuing the same line of thought, *we cannot separate general intentions and fundamental options from individual actions.* For example, we cannot say that love of God and neighbor is our basic orientation in life and our fundamental option, and at the same time commit contrary guilty actions such as adultery or injustice. Our most personal intentions are confirmed or corrupted by what we do, whenever we act with full knowledge and consent. To speak realistically, the concrete action engages the person in his totality. We cannot therefore confine mortal sin to the level of a fundamental option—a radical refusal of God—and distinguish it from individual choices and actions which are contrary to the moral law in serious matters (*VS* 69).

In contrast to the divisive theories which it critiques, *the thrust of the encyclical is strongly unitive.* We see this notably in its refusal to admit opposition between human freedom and nature, often understood in a biological sense (*VS* 46). Man has received from God a nature at once spiritual and corporeal, forming in the individuality of the human person a wholeness which includes and gathers up as in a sheaf all the inclinations which form the basis for natural law. The encyclical refers us to the five natural inclinations indicated by St. Thomas: inclinations to the good, to self-preservation, to the generation and education of children to truth, and to social life. To these *Veritatis splendor* adds a sixth, the contemplation of beauty (*VS* 51). The chief precepts of the natural law, together with all fundamental human rights and obligations, flow from these inclinations.

We note that some inclinations are obviously spiritual, for example the desire for goodness, truth, and justice, and that others, such as the sexual inclination, include a determining biological dimension. Yet the encyclical insists strongly, with good reason and in conformity with St. Thomas' thought, on the profound unity of soul and body in the human person, especially insofar as he is a moral subject. All the natural inclinations converge, in fact, to form a concrete moral action. Furthermore, we cannot "dissociate the moral act from the bodily dimensions of its exercise" (VS 48–50). This applies particularly in the case of sexual activity and related problems, where we cannot really separate the biological and moral spheres. Natural law has therefore a universal value, extending even to individual acts in which the body is engaged.

These considerations rule out a separation between moral and pre-moral levels. *But what about judging actions in light of their consequences?*

It is certainly good to take into account the foreseeable results and consequences of actions in order to assess their moral value. Classic moralists considered effects, but viewed them as "circumstances," that is, secondary elements, and did not attach excessive importance to them. I might add that attention to consequences has acquired greater importance in our day because of the increasing repercussions of our actions. The growing use of technology enables us to foresee results more clearly at social and even planetary levels. Nevertheless, this is not the primary element to be considered in the formation of a moral judgment. *"The morality of the human act depends primarily and fundamentally on the 'object' rationally chosen by the deliberate will"* of the person who acts, *"and whether that object is capable or not of being ordered to God"* seen as man's final end (VS 78.1–2). Let us note that the object, in moral theology, can doubtless be a thing, such as stolen money, but it can also just as well signify a person, as when we speak of an object of love, anger, or hatred: our brother. God himself is the object of our faith and love. The object, then, in moral theology, is not something purely material. It is tied up with our relationship to God and neighbor.

Consequently, an action whose object is evil, such as homicide, genocide, abortion, euthanasia, torture, or prostitution— here I am quoting the list given in the constitution *Gaudium et*

spes—cannot be rendered good by circumstances or by anticipated useful results or by a subjective intention, however good,
such as the turning over of the resulting financial gains to some
work of mercy (*VS* 80.1).

Actions which are intrinsically evil because of their object
and serious matter are incompatible with love of God and
neighbor, and correspond to negative precepts such as: You
shall not kill, you shall not commit adultery, you shall not steal
another's goods, etc. The consideration of circumstances and
effects alone could never enable us to establish such universal
and stable laws, for we can always imagine unforeseen circumstances in which a given law would not hold, and the calculation of consequences can be extended ad infinitum. Casuists
have never lacked imagination in this field.

In placing the object of the action once more at the center of
the moral judgment, *the encyclical restores its objectivity and realism.*
This point is essential. With St. Thomas in mind, we have to say,
further, that the consideration of the end is equally essential in
relation to the interior act, the voluntary intention; but with the
additional remark that this finality is itself objective, for we cannot will and love anyone or anything in any way whatsoever, indiscriminately. The supreme moral question is precisely this: to determine what is objectively our final end, where our complete happiness lies, and what the object which wholly satisfies all our
yearnings. This needs to be discussed at the very beginning of
moral theology, as the *Catechism* has done in its third part, because
the orientation and truth of human life depend upon it. Moral life
and actions are thus given a teleological dimension (from the
Greek *telos*, which means "end"), a value that proportionalism has
wished to restore. But it has understood it in too subjective a sense,
and has reduced it to a relationship between means and end established by technology within a context of sheer efficiency and
utility (*VS* 71ff). The kind of finality elaborated by a St. Thomas,
for example, pertains directly to the moral order, not simply to the
technological. It stems from the moral experience of a man who
orientates himself to his end by his actions, with wholehearted
commitment and especially with love. The means he takes, the
paths that lead him toward this goal, are, emphatically, the virtues.

Clearly, *Veritatis splendor* goes beyond the narrow perspectives within which the proportionalist concept of morality would confine us, and does away with its divisions. There is no pre-moral level of action in real life. This is a figment of the mind, an artificial separation which may hold some abstract interest for us—though even that is doubtful—but which we cannot transpose into the real world. A human or voluntary action is in itself moral because of its object, in relation to the one who performs it, to the neighbor whom it affects, and to God who has placed within us the attraction to the good, which will lead us to himself, our final end. Morality thus structured is open to receive the teachings of the Gospel and to live them, especially those about the gift of charity.

E. To Look to Christ

At the end of its critique, *Veritatis splendor* again turns to the positive outlook of the first chapter and invites us, when confronted with ethical questions, to raise our eyes with the Church to the Lord Jesus, for "the crucified Christ reveals the authentic meaning of freedom; he lives it fully in the total gift of himself and calls his disciples to share in his freedom" (*VS* 85). He sets our freedom free by his pardon and grace; he is its teacher by his instruction in the gospel Law and his example (*VS* 86). He shows us how "obedience to universal and unchanging moral norms can respect the uniqueness and individuality of the person and not represent a threat to his freedom and dignity" (*VS* 85). The encyclical teaches us that "the frank and open acceptance of truth is the condition for authentic freedom: 'You will know the truth and the truth will set you free' (Jn 8:32)." (*VS* 87.1) *"Jesus, then, is the living, personal summation of perfect freedom in total obedience to the will of God"* (*VS* 87.4). This obedience should of course be understood not as legalistic and voluntaristic, but as the obedience of love, carried out in the spirit of that charity which the encyclical has placed anew at the foundation of the Decalogue, and which finds its most wondrous expression in the obedience of Christ hymned in Philippians: "He, though he was in the form of God . . ., being found in human form, humbled himself and became obedient unto death, even death on a cross. therefore God has highly exalted him." (2:6–11).

After its appeal to Christ, the encyclical evokes the witness of *the martyrs and saints,* Susanna in the Old Testament, John the Baptist at the dawn of the New, the deacon Stephen, the apostle James, and countless others throughout the long history of the Church up to our own times. "Martyrdom [and Christian holiness] accepted as an affirmation of the inviolability of the moral order, bears splendid witness both to the holiness of God's Law and the inviolability of the personal dignity of man, created in God's image and likeness" (*VS* 92.1). This witness, which reawakens a moral sense and saves man from "*the confusion between good and evil*" (*VS* 93.1), surely has meaning for every man. It shows that "there are truths and moral values for which one must be prepared to give up one's life" (*VS* 94). Such a witness is a service to all mankind, at both individual and social levels, for the recognition of valid norms of intrinsically evil actions, always and for everyone, constitutes "the unshakable foundation and solid guarantee of a just and peaceful human coexistence, and hence of genuine democracy" (*VS* 96).

Thus *Veritatis splendor* gives *a firm response to the question of the foundation of ethical norms,* human rights, and the principles of justice in our society. This stands in marked contrast to the most carefully worked out modern theories of the procedural type which, following formal law, often give only a misleading response, designed for intellectuals.

III. The Mission of Moral Theologians and Bishops

A. Faith and Morality

Chapter 3 of *Veritatis splendor,* bringing its message to a conclusion, begins with a summary of the doctrine which has been explained, emphasizing the bond between Christian faith and morality. *Faith* does not consist merely in assent to a body of propositions. It includes knowledge and experience of the mystery of Christ. It is a truth to be lived; it *possesses a moral content* (*VS* 88). In fulfilling this practical role, faith finds its models in the very person of Jesus and in those outstanding witnesses of his, the martyrs and saints. The questions discussed in the second chapter are thus tied in, by means of faith, to the doctrine set forth in the first. We can note that in Chapter 1 the language is more normative and persuasive, in keeping with the usual formulation of problems by moralists, with whom the encyclical is concerned.

The insistence upon the connection between faith and morality is an important corrective for Catholic moral theology. Textbooks of recent centuries had already been faulted for separating these too much from each other. Faith, they had proposed, was about dogmatic theology, while morality was the domain of obligations. From this perspective, moralists who claimed the autonomy of their science believed they need only be concerned with faith where it involved obligations and sins. Furthermore, they considered that the teaching on virtues, presented under the aegis of faith in the documents of revelation, pertained rather to the field of spiritual exhortation than to morality properly so called. It became difficult from that time on to demonstrate clearly the moral significance of faith.

The new codification of moral theology proposed by the proportionalists only aggravated the problem by introducing categories that rendered the separation systematic. It emphasized the distance of an ethics elaborated as a rational technique from a teaching which is happily irreducible to such procedures.

The question therefore assumes major importance for moral theology. It is actually decisive for the future of theological work, for it involves the very existence of Christian morality and directly conditions the role of the Church's magisterium in the teaching of morality.

B. The Service of Moral Theologians

Faced with these problems, the task of moral theologians is a vast one. It cannot be limited to discussing particular ethical problems, but calls for constructive reflection which will give the teaching and practice of morality their evangelical, and at the same time profoundly human, dimension, in line with the orientations indicated by the encyclical.

Veritatis splendor has clearly defined the "service of moral theologians" in the context of the "vocation of the theologian in the Church," in accord with the instruction *Donum veritatis* of the Congregation for the Doctrine of the Faith (*VS* 109). The work of moral theologians is a service to the Church. Their task is to transmit and explain Christian doctrine to the faithful under the guidance of the magisterium, which bears the primary responsibility. In their research, they must indeed utilize the contributions of the human sciences, but it is indispensable that they preserve *a clear awareness of the specificity of morality*. Morality cannot be reduced to a body of knowledge worked out simply in the context of the so-called behavioral sciences (*VS* 111). These last are not actually normative. They are based on the empirical observation of facts, and do not suffice for the establishment of moral laws or the determination of what should be done. Hence they cannot distinguish between good and evil, especially if the spiritual and supernatural dimension of Christian action is taken into account.

The encyclical also warns moralists and other theologians against *a claim to the right to dissent*, which risks forming an aggressive and polemical mentality within the Church, directly opposed to "ecclesial communion and to a correct understanding of the hierarchical constitution of the People of God" (*VS* 113.2). This attitude is likewise opposed to the constructive work of charity which, according to St. Paul (1 Cor 12), orders all charisms and ministries for the good of the body of the faithful who make up the Body of Christ.

C. Moral Theologians and Agape

We theologians have a real need to meditate from time to time on the Apostle's description of charity in Chapter 13 of First Corinthians. Each characteristic can be applied to us, as to every Christian: "*Charity is patient* [among other things, it takes time to do careful theological work, to persevere in spite of contradictions and criticism, knowing how to wait for God's hour. *It is not envious* [even of those who win public favor].

Charity is not boastful [it doesn't assume a doctoral tone, or give itself airs]; *it is not arrogant* [as St. Paul has just said, knowledge puffs up, but charity builds up. Should not humility before the Word of God be the theologian's first virtue, as it is for the spiritual life?]

Charity is not rude [which would risk upsetting the faithful and would do no good; it tries rather to accommodate itself to each person]; *it seeks not its own interest* [for reasons of utility or personal ambition. Forgetful of self, it is happy to serve]. *It is not irritable* [When attacked or calumniated; it remains gentle and avoids aggressiveness like the plague]; *it is not resentful* [like those who love to talk about what they think is wrong with the Church, and who stir up discontent]; *it does not rejoice in what is wrong* [It loves and practices justice, even toward enemies, and does not favor injustice even if this would be advantageous to its own cause or opinion; it opposes party spirit]; *but rejoices in the truth* [which the theologian should love with all his heart and ever seek, according to the Augustinian definition of happiness: 'joy in the truth', the joy which truth brings].

Charity bears all things [like the Lord, it is always ready to understand and forgive, even in the case of personal attacks]; *believes all things*, [because of its faith in the grace of Christ and because it has confidence in others], *it hopes all things* [because of the promises of the Holy Spirit who acts in each person]; *it endures all things* [trials, sins, and weaknesses, including one's own, with the inner strength which faith and prayer give]." Such are the fruits of the Holy Spirit (cf. Gal 5:22).

D. The Collaboration of Moral Theologians with the Magisterium

To my mind the idea of the moral theologian simply as an intermediary between the Church and the faithful, like a servant whose chief virtue was a more or less blind obedience to the prescribed teaching, was a mistake. On the other hand, no opportunity has been lost to exalt the rebellious or dissident theologian as if he were the freest and most intelligent of all beings. Both of these simplistic views come from a voluntaristic mentality, which is still very prevalent and which causes us to envisage the relationships between the ecclesial magisterium, theologians, and the faithful, as trials of strength, where Church authorities hold the power and theologians the scientific knowledge. At times it has reached such a pitch that theologians have set up their own magisterium, with varying degrees of discretion.

In reality, whether we are bishops or theologians, priests or faithful, *we are all subject in faith to the Word of God*, who has called us personally and who moves us interiorly. The Word brings us a unique light which directs and leads us far beyond our own opinions, revealing to us *the mystery and the love of Christ and communion in his Church*. This faith which we hold in common consists in a loving and joyous obedience to a teaching which comes to us outwardly through the preaching of the Church and inwardly through the light of the Holy Spirit, the One of whom Jesus said, "When the Counselor comes, whom I shall send to you from the Father, even the Spirit of truth, who proceeds from the Father, he will bear witness to me . . .; he will guide you into all the truth" (Jn 15:26; 16:13). Such is the Spirit of Christ, who distributes charges and functions in the Church and teaches us to fulfill them with an intelligent, enlightened, and devoted love, as a service to the Lord and an aid to our brothers, in view of the common good. The same Spirit teaches us that particular form of patience whereby we accept to work imperfectly, enduring our own limitations and those of others, including the sins of churchmen and the defects of theologians.

In the light of faith and under the impulse of a devoted charity, relationships between the magisterium and theologians should therefore be established which take the form of *a contribution to the common task of building up the People of God*, in a collaboration that is strong enough to surmount any differences which may surface and introduce a note of antagonism between intellectuals and churchmen in the very measure of their good intentions.

E. The Theologian's Task

From the viewpoint of faith *the theologian's role in the Church seems important*. In communion with the successors of the Apostles, the theologian has received the charism of the "utterance of wisdom," the "utterance of knowledge" (1 Cor 12:8), so that he can share in the office of teaching. St. Paul exhorts him to acquit himself of this gift "in liberality," without counting the cost, and to practice this form of spiritual mercy "with cheerfulness" (Rom 12:8). His first task is to gather up the heritage of gospel teaching and the fruits it has produced in the rich tradition of the Church; to feed on these and live by them so as to know them experientially; and then to transmit them to the Christian faithful, explaining them to the best of his ability. Such a task calls for the complete dedication of a mind at once contemplative, active, and avid for the truth, and a will to which divine realities have become connatural, so that the theologian may discern the ways of God and apply moral law wisely in concrete life situations.

F. Fidelity to the Magisterium

Fidelity to the magisterium of the Church is a primordial condition for the excellence and fruitfulness of theological work. From the magisterium the theologian, like every Christian, receives the gospel heritage, which he is charged to transmit. The magisterium contains the seed of the Holy Spirit which renders all work in the Church fruitful and which has produced all spiritual and intellectual movements of renewal within the Church throughout her history. Without this fundamental harmony underlying ecclesial collaboration, the theologian's work, however scholarly, remains a human, individual work, easily engendering confrontation and division.

The question of "dissent" with the magisterium is often presented in too subjective and superficial a way, as if it were a matter of varying viewpoints and arose from the right to freedom of opinion in the face of authority. Hence it seems that among theologians there are only two attitudes to choose from: either a servile obedience to the magisterium at the expense of freedom of thought and research, or the claim to a freedom of opinion, which is manifested particularly by criticism of the magisterium and ends in superficiality.

This view of things is too narrow and misses the essential point. It does not take into account *the content of opinions, nor the exigencies of the truth* which breathes life into theology and gives it its power. Theology can only weaken and go around in circles if it yields to changing opinions and intellectual trends. The magisterium helps theologians to stand firmly on the rock of the Gospel so that they can build a structure capable of resisting contemporary crises, the pressures of the culture, and the devastating effects of time. In this sense it contributes to the freedom of theological thought. We can even observe that in general ecclesiastical authorities leave more latitude to theologians than do the "progressives," who often accept criticism with a very bad grace and in their own fashion excommunicate the opinions they dub "conservative."

In order to clarify the relationship of the theologian to the magisterium, it is helpful to make a distinction in regard to the heritage to be transmitted. There are in the first place *the essential and constitutive elements of the Christian faith* expressed in the Creed, and these correspond to the magisterium's doctrinal role. Then there are the basic precepts of morality, formulated in the Decalogue and perfected in the Lord's Sermon, which correspond to its practical function. Such is "the truth which has been entrusted" to us, which we have to "guard with the aid of the Holy Spirit who dwells within us" (2 Tm 1:14). Next comes the theological edifice built upon these foundations from the earliest Christian generations. Its object is to deepen the understanding of revelation and to further its presentation and defense before all peoples, whether Christian or pagan, so that the gospel message may be spread through varying languages and cultures and bear fruit in every nation.

We can speak on the one hand of the domain of the Gospel, which provides the foundations and the pristine source of the life of faith. On the other hand we can consider the domain of theology, which researches the knowledge gained through faith and shares in its light, on condition that it does not see itself as something separate from the Gospel. It derives precisely from the Gospel, in fact, and becomes sterile when it prescinds from the living faith.

In the realm of theology *the variety of schools*, spiritualities, and even liturgies, *manifests the great freedom given by the Holy Spirit* to believers who seek to understand the mystery of Christ. It can be compared to the varieties of fruit produced by nature. In moral teaching, we may note systems and presentations of material which differ considerably but which are based on a fundamental continuity. Examples of this are St. Augustine, St. Thomas, the Franciscan school, and the post-Tridentine manuals of moral theology. This is why *Veritatis splendor*, like the *Catechism*, can invite us today to reexamine our concept of morality, the better to relate it to the Gospel and the Fathers of the Church. Here we have a theological enterprise that will keep us perennially engaged.

At this level, *the magisterium of the Church has always wished,* in principle, *to respect the freedom of theologians* and to allow for the legitimacy of divergent opinions. Nevertheless, things are not so simple in the concrete, for ideas have their own logic and implications. Certain theological theories can, at least in their possible consequences, threaten important tenets of Christian morality. Quite profound divergences can thus surface, which call for common vigilance, frank dialogue between the representatives of the magisterium and theologians, and true love for the Church of God.

G. Respect for the Theologian

The relationship between the magisterium and theologians is in a sense unique. Actually, those who exercise magisterial functions have themselves received their theological formation from theologians. They have absorbed their orientations and mindsets, and the influence often lasts a lifetime. Furthermore, the documents of the magisterium always involve, in their preparation and composition, a good deal of theological reflection, in which the help of theologians is indispensable. Thus collaboration between the magisterium and theologians is necessary for the exercise of their respective ministries. It demands on the part of the magisterium what we might call *respect for the dignity of the theologian in the Church and esteem for his work,* as well as the encouragement of a freedom built on the foundation of faith. The theologian, for his part, should be *grateful to the Church,* which has transmitted to him the Gospel of Christ, and *to the magisterium,* which assures its defense in a difficult world. He should likewise have the courage to collaborate with the magisterium today lucidly and frankly, and also to defend it, when the occasion arises, from misunderstandings and all those problems which can surface in human relations, within the Church as elsewhere.

H. Moral Theologians Put to Work

To return to *Veritatis splendor*, some pollsters have thought that the encyclical has "frozen" the terrain of morality in the Church by taking away from moral theologians their freedom of speech and research and condemning them to repetitive teaching. The accusation is unfounded. Faced with the crisis which threatened to devastate Christian morality by shaking its very foundations, *the encyclical wished to reestablish firmly the groundwork* without which one cannot build constructively in theology: natural law and the Decalogue. It has returned its evangelical dimension to this foundation by restoring the Sermon of the Lord and apostolic catechesis to moral theology. Thus the encyclical has *put the theologian to work at the task of renewing Christian moral teaching* in fidelity to Scripture and living tradition. It appeals to his creative and constructive freedom and warns him against the temptation of a freedom which is limited to criticism and is spiritually sterile.

We find ourselves once again in the situation described by St. Paul: "According to the commission of God given to me, like a skilled master builder I laid a foundation, and another man is building upon it. Let each man take care how he builds upon it" (1 Cor 3:10). According to the Apostle, it is possible to build with gold, silver, wood, hay, or stubble. The point is to raise the building on solid foundations.

I. A Morality of Commandments and a Morality of Virtues

The work entrusted to moral theologians is considerable. The encyclical does not go into details but leaves great latitude. To return to St. Paul's comparison, it is a work of construction which affects the entire body of moral theology. In particular, we need to choose between *a morality of Commandments* in the tradition of recent centuries and *a morality based on the virtues and the gifts of the Holy Spirit* in the tradition of the Fathers of the Church and St. Thomas. We can also link the Commandments more closely to the virtues so as to give them a certain dynamism as the *Catechism* has tried to do, for a virtue-based morality must include the Commandments and take them into account. Needed, too, is a clarification and explanation of *the role of conscience*, which has become, in our day, a most appropriate setting for moral theology. And we must show how conscience, being the inner witness to truth and goodness, contributes to the prudential choices which lead to action. In this research, we cannot bypass *confrontation with current theories* which attempt to base ethics on justice, and law on dialogue and consensus.

It is likewise necessary to *rediscover the original and true meaning of the words* we use in moral theology, so that they will match the realities and experiences they signify. Many terms have grown outdated, impoverished, and distorted. The word "virtue," for example, which used to designate admirable human qualities of mind, heart, and action, today means little more than a habit of obeying the law, which in practice is difficult. The "virtue" which was once a joy has now become a bore. This is a sign that we are locked into a certain system of morality which prevents us from understanding and appreciating what virtue really is. Yet even if we hesitate to talk about virtue, we still haven't lost the experience of it, for we spontaneously praise the man who shows courage or that control of his feelings and appetites which we call temperance. We acclaim the one who can give us discernment, and wise counsel, and who can make prudent decisions, and we appreciate a sense of justice and honesty, uprightness and generosity. Happily, virtue is not dead for us; but our language has not kept up with virtue. We no longer find words capable of conveying the riches of the moral experience. It is our task to reestablish a balance between profound experiences and the vocabulary of moral theology.

Speaking of this effort for the renewal of language and structure in moral theology, I should like to mention a very hopeful sign: *the rediscovery of the teaching on virtue* in the tradition of Aristotle and St. Thomas. This has been developing in the United States in the field of philosophy ever since the appearance of the recent publications of Alasdair MacIntyre. It is a response to the failure of modern philosophies in their often contradictory attempts to base ethics and its norms on pure reason and to imitate the patterns of the natural sciences.[10]

J. The Question of Happiness

Finally, there is the question of happiness. This interests everyone. Yet rare are the moral theologians who dare to treat it as
a fundamental question, for fear of being taxed with
eudaemonism in the wake of the Kantian critiques. For several
centuries now, moralists of the obligation-and-imperative
school have avoided the question of happiness on the ground
that it introduces too much of a note of self-interest. In their
view, happiness can be envisaged only in terms of material
well-being, a sort of utilitarianism. The result has been a rift between the good—identified with sheer duty—and happiness;
and this has caused a veritable break between morality and the
desire for happiness. The breach has been extended to love itself, which cannot be separated from the desire for happiness.
Thus morality has taken on an austere, sad quality, and has
been diminished by rationality and juridical legality. Anything
to do with the heart or feelings has become suspect.[11] The
proportionalist system fits well in this scheme of things because
of the technology it has introduced and the finality of the useful which guides it.

We must have the courage to bring this question of happiness into the open once more: true happiness, which accompanies the delight of the senses and is the end of human life. We
need to rediscover the happiness the Gospel tells us about,
which is found in the spiritual experience kindled within us by
the Word of God, in accord with the teaching of the Beatitudes.
It is formed in us through the trial of faith, like the joy which
is born of Truth and faithful Love. Herein lies the permanent
source of the renewal of moral theology which the encyclical
Veritatis splendor proposes.

K. Everyone's Task

The work of the renewal of Christian morality does not pertain
exclusively to the Magisterium and to theologians. *It concerns
all the faithful.* Each one should make his contribution, precisely
because this renewal springs from the eager humility of faith
in the Word of God which is common to us all, and from loving obedience, the source of our experience and understanding

of spiritual things. As theologians, we should always keep in mind the prayer of Jesus: "I thank thee, Father, Lord of heaven and earth, that thou has hidden these things from the wise and understanding and revealed them to babes; yea, Father, for such was thy gracious will" (Mt 11:25–26). This in no way excludes theologians nor scholars nor bishops; but it reminds us that these are things we cannot understand unless we first become little ones through faith.

L. Looking to the Virgin Mary

The encyclical concludes with an invitation to look to the Virgin Mary. Why? Mary defined herself, in a sense, when she called herself "the handmaid of the Lord," and she invites us to praise God with her because "He has looked upon the lowliness of his handmaid." And in his mercy the Lord has done "great things" for her, which he wishes to reproduce in the Church "unto the praise of his glory." Which brings us full circle to the title of the encyclical: "The Splendor of Truth."

Endnotes

1. See, for example, Thomas Deman, "Probabilisme" in *Dictionnaire de théologie Catholique*, vol. 13, 1936, col. 417–619; Jacques Leclerc, *L'enseignement de la théologie morale* (Paris, 1950); G. Gilleman, *Le primat de la charité en théologie morale* (Louvain, 1954); S. Pinckaers, *Le Renouveau de la morale* (Tournai, 1964).
2. See H.-D. Wendland, *Ethique du Nouveau Testament* (Geneva, 1972), 27ff.
3. See J. C. Pinto de Oliveira, and collaborators, *Autonomie: Dimensions éthiques de la liberté* (Fribourg, 1978).
4. See J. Fuchs, *Existe-t-il e morale chrétienne?* (Gembroux, 1973), 12.
5. See L. Janssens, "Ontic Evil and Moral Evil," *Louvain Studies* 4 (1972): 115–56.
6. See S. Pinckaers, *Ce qu'on ne peut jamais faire* (Fribourg, 1986), 48ff.
7. See P. Knauer, "La détermination du bien et du mal pour le principe du double effet," *Nouvelle Revue théologique* 87 (1965): 356–76.
8. P. Knauer, "Fundamentalethik: teleologische als deontologische Normenbegründung," *Theologie und Philosophie* 55 (1980): 321–60.
9. For more details see Pinckaers, *Ce qu'on ne peut jamais faire*, 67ff.
10. A. C. MacIntyre, *After Virtue* (Notre Dame, 1981); *Whose Justice? Which Rationality?* (Notre Dame, 1988); *Three Rival Versions of Moral Inquiry* (London, 1990).
11. See S. Pinckaers, *La morale catholique* (Paris, 1991), 71ff.

How Can We Learn What *Veritatis splendor* Has to Teach?*

Alasdair MacIntyre

Veritatis splendor can be read in two very different ways. It can be read, and of course it should be read, as a papal encyclical, a piece of authoritative Christian teaching. As such, it is addressed to the Catholic bishops and its subject matter is not only Christian moral teaching in general, but more particularly the present condition of the academic discipline of moral theology.

I of course am neither a bishop nor a theologian, so it might seem that all that I can be asked to do in reading *Veritatis splendor* is to listen quietly to what is being said in a conversation between others. Yet the complexity of the experience of reading *Veritatis splendor* makes it impossible for me to restrict myself to this role of a more or less innocent bystander. For *Veritatis splendor* is not only a work of authoritative Christian teaching about moral judgment and the moral life, it is also a striking contribution by the Polish phenomenological and Thomistic philosopher Karol Wojtyla to ongoing philosophical enquiry, one in which an incisive account is advanced of the relationship between biblical and other Christian teaching, the various moralities of the various cultures of humankind, and the argumentative conclusions of moral philosophers. (I am well aware that generally several anonymous writers contribute to the drafting of encyclicals, and doubtless they did so on this occasion. But any reader of Karol Wojtyla's major philosophical writings, from his doctoral dissertation onward, will recognize, both in the style of arguments and in the nuances with which particular arguments are developed, a single namable authorial presence in this text.)

* I am indebted for very helpful comments on earlier drafts of this paper to my colleagues Alfred J. Freddoso, Ralph M. McInerny, and W. David Solomon, as well as to the participants in a discussion sponsored by the John Paul II Institute for Studies on Marriage and Family, *Communio, The Thomist,* and the American Maritain Society.

The central theses of this encyclical thereby challenge a range of rival philosophical accounts of that relationship: Kantian, utilitarian, and Kierkegaardian, to name only the most important. But how can any one text perform both of these very different tasks? Insofar as *Veritatis splendor* genuinely contributes to argumentative moral philosophy, must it not be precluded from presenting itself as authoritative teaching? And insofar as it is authoritative Christian teaching, how can it possibly be a contribution to the contentious debates of moral philosophy? Part of what is impressive about *Veritatis splendor* is that in the course of answering a number of other questions, it also answers these questions about itself.

Even so, any philosophical discussion of this encyclical which finds its argumentative conclusions compelling will be committed to an acknowledgment that philosophy itself, what it is and what it can legitimately hope to achieve, has to be understood in the light afforded by the Christian Gospel. *Veritatis splendor* never lets us forget this, so that even if I begin from the philosophy in the encyclical, I do so already knowing that it is going to direct me beyond philosophy. Nonetheless this is where I do have to begin, and this for two reasons. First of all, this encyclical has an important argumentative structure, and arguments are always matter for philosophy. Secondly, quite apart from any concern with *Veritatis splendor* itself, what is inescapable for moral philosophers who are also Catholics, such as I, is a strongly felt need for some definitive answer to the question of how their own peculiar philosophical conclusions about the nature of moral judgment and the moral life are related both to the dominant moral theories and practices of their own culture and to the biblical and Christian teaching by which they have been instructed. Each of these three presses upon us its own type of claim to our attention and allegiance, and these sometimes conflicting claims define the situation in which and formed by which each of us encounters the theses and arguments of *Veritatis splendor*. What then is my particular situation in these three respects, as Thomistic Aristotelian, as North American immigrant, and as Catholic?

Thomists do of course quarrel a good deal among themselves. But there are two distinctive sets of conclusions which many of us take to be of crucial importance in the practical life. What are they? A first set concerns those rules which we take practical reason to apprehend as precepts of the natural law. Those rules enjoin and prohibit certain types of action as such. It is only insofar as our actions conform to what those precepts require, and do so just because those precepts require it, that we can become the kind of people who are able to achieve that final good toward which we are directed by our nature. So the human good can be achieved only through a form of life in which the positive and negative precepts of the natural law are the norms governing our relationships.

Thomists support this first set of conclusions by a variety of arguments drawn from Aristotle, Aquinas, and others. These arguments can be reinforced by a second set of considerations which concern not so much the theories, but rather the practices of their anti-Thomistic philosophical critics, whether these are Humeans, Kantians, utilitarians, existentialists, relativists, or what you will. For it is a Thomistic contention that such anti-Thomistic philosophers inadvertently give evidence by and in their activities of the truth of just that Thomist view of the practical life which as theorists they suppose themselves able to refute. What is it about those activities, which warrants this conclusion? Such philosophers generally and characteristically pursue the truth about moral and philosophical matters in a way and with a dedication that acknowledges the achievement of that truth as one aspect at least of what seems to be being treated as a final and unconditional end. They do so moreover generally and characteristically under constraints imposed by rules which prescribe unqualified respect for those with whom they enter into debate, precisely as enjoined by the primary precepts of the natural law. So we find that relationships within philosophical debate about morality are themselves governed to a surprising extent among a variety of non-Thomists and anti-Thomists by a practical recognition of exceptionless norms whose point and purpose is the achievement of the final end of that activity, thus exemplifying something that Thomists take to be characteristic of well-ordered human activity in general. For it is indeed a Thomist thesis that all practical reasoners, often unwittingly and often very imperfectly, exhibit in significant ways the truth of the Thomist account of practical reasoning by how they act, even when, as in this case, they are engaged in the enterprise of constructing anti-Thomistic philosophical theories.

That this is so would of course be strenuously denied by such anti-Thomistic moral philosophers, moral philosophers who not only are in a large majority among our academic colleagues, but who enjoy one great advantage over us in contemporary debate. For they, unlike us, generally represent in their theories the standpoints of the dominant moral culture of everyday life in modern North America. Even in their fundamental disagreements with each other—Kantians against utilitarians, both against Humeans, all three against Nietzscheans—they articulate at the level of theory standpoints and disagreements which inform a good deal of everyday practice in our culture. This is after all a culture in which there is an unusual degree of awareness that moral thought and practice have varied from one culture to another and that disagreement between and within cultures has often been intractable. So that a Thomistic Aristotelian, unlike most of his or her philosophical colleagues, must in certain respects find himself or herself at odds with this dominant North American culture, involved in recurrent argument and contention at the levels both of philosophical debate and of everyday practice. We are participants in a conversation with many disputing voices.

Yet as Catholics we have to listen first to what a very different set of voices have to say to us, those inspired and authoritative voices which declare the Word of God concerning those same moral matters about which our own culture speaks to us so vociferously and about which we have arrived at our own philosophical conclusions. Part of what we have to learn, or rather to relearn, from *Veritatis splendor* is that, at least so far as the fundamental and central precepts of the moral law are concerned, the truths about those precepts declared to us by God through Moses and the prophets, in the revelation by Jesus Christ of the New Law, and in the teaching of the Catholic Church, culminating in this very encyclical, are no other than the truths to which we have already assented as rational persons, or rather to which we would have assented if we had not been frustrated in so doing by our own cultural, intellectual, and moral errors and deformations. Yet the encyclical also teaches us that what we encounter in Jesus Christ is immeasurably more than this. We also have to learn of our forgiveness and our redemption and of the transformation made possible in our acknowledgment of law when we come to understand it in the light afforded by Jesus Christ. Nonetheless the law declared to us by God in revelation is the same law as that which we recognize in the moral requirements imposed by our own human practical understanding and reasoning, when they are in good order. So that when we become able to hear and to respond to what Jesus Christ has to say to us, we do not have to leave behind or discard anything that we had genuinely learned concerning the moral law through reasoning. Grace often corrects, as well as completes, what we have so far taken to be conclusions of reason, but when grace does so correct us, it is always because we have in some way failed as reasoners. And therefore *Veritatis splendor*, just because it is true to this biblical teaching, will be grotesquely misunderstood if it is understood as an act of coercive imposition by an external authority, rather than an invitation to become more thoughtful and more perceptive. It does indeed speak in the name of an authority external to us, God, but that to which it invites us—that to which he invites us—is in part an act of moral and rational self-recognition. And *Veritatis splendor* as a work of philosophy does itself exhibit just that moral and rational awareness to which as an encyclical it invites its readers.

What, then, are those truths to which we are invited to attend? In *Veritatis splendor* we are presented not only with a reassertion of central truths, but also with a characterization of a number of types of contemporary error—philosophical, theological, and moral. It would be a great mistake to treat this focus upon errors as merely an irritable expression of the censoriousness of authority. It is rather that unless and until we have understood these particular errors, and why they are errors, we shall have failed to grasp important features of the relevant set of truths. So we cannot begin by attending exclusively to the statements of the truths and only afterwards go on as a secondary matter to that of the errors, for the exposition of the truths will remain radically incomplete until the four types of error have been characterized. What, then, are these truths which we shall sufficiently understand only by considering some mistakes about them into which we and our contemporaries are peculiarly liable to fall? *Veritatis splendor* begins with biblical and Christ-centered meditation and exegesis, as all Christian theology must begin. But because my commentary is that of a philosopher, I take the liberty of beginning elsewhere—in fact at a middle point in the encyclical's argument. I begin with the encyclical's creative and constructive restatement of what I have already noticed as the Thomistic account of natural law, an account that, as the encyclical stresses, the Church has included "in her own teaching on morality" (*VS* 44.1). And here in consequence there is a tension and a danger peculiarly for Thomists. We, like all other Catholics, have to receive this teaching with attentive obedience, and we must not be misled into thinking that our own philosophical conclusions, as philosophical conclusions, can make our attentive obedience unnecessary. Indeed, we, more than anyone else, may be tempted into treating *Veritatis splendor* as a restatement of what was already sufficiently known, so deceiving ourselves about our own need to learn. What, then, is it that we do need to learn?

"The negative precepts of the natural law," the encyclical reminds us, "are universally valid. They oblige each and every individual, always and in every circumstance. It is a matter of prohibitions which forbid a given action *semper et pro semper*, without exception, because the choice of this kind of behavior is in no case compatible with the goodness of the will of the acting person, with his vocation to life with God and to communion with his neighbor " (*VS* 52.1). The examples given are from Jesus' reaffirmation of the Decalogue (Mt 19:17–18): "You shall not murder, You shall not commit adultery, You shall not steal, You shall not bear false witness" (*VS* 52.3). What we are told in these and other passages is that we cannot adequately characterize— adequately, that is, for practical life, let alone for theory—that good toward the achievement of which we are directed by our nature and by Providence, except in terms which already presuppose the binding character of the exceptionless negative precepts of the natural law. And correspondingly we cannot characterize adequately that in our natures which alone makes us apt for and directed toward the achievement of that good except in the same terms. Unless our passions, habits, motives, intentions, and purposes are ordered by the negative as well as the positive precepts of the natural law, they will not be ordered toward our own good and the good of others. For the negative precepts structure or fail to structure our relationships with others as well as our characters. "They oblige everyone regardless of the cost, never to offend in anyone, beginning with oneself, the personal dignity common to all" (*VS* 52.1).

Obedience to these negative precepts is, then, enabling, both individually and communally. It frees us from a variety of hindrances and frustrations that would otherwise bring to nothing the pursuit by each of us of our own positive good and that of others. And they can be universally apprehended by rational persons as at once required and enabling, for they are "valid for all people of the present and the future, as well as those of the past" (*VS* 53.1). They belong to "the permanent structural elements" of human beings. What God commands of us in commanding these precepts is therefore what we already knew or could have known for ourselves as required for our good. What God asks of us, both in the Old Law and in its reaffirmation by Jesus Christ, is what, if we were adequately rational, we would ask of ourselves. God's commands are to be and do what will restore us to our freedom, and the Church's teaching concerning the divine commands has the same aim and content. "Hence obedience to God is not, as some would believe, a heteronomy" (*VS* 41.1). We are not to have divided wills, divided minds, or divided hearts.

The use of a Kantian idiom in this passage is instructive. For the encyclical is both in agreement and in disagreement with Kant. It is in agreement in understanding the negative precepts of the moral law as exceptionless prohibitions. It is in disagreement in its assertion that human reason needs to be instructed and corrected by this revelation of God's law. For not only is it the case that what God commands coincides with what is demanded of us by our own rational natures—that is something to which Kant could have assented—but to act in some particular way, just because God commands us so to do, is always to conform our wills to the good will, knowing that what his goodness requires of us is what goodness requires of us. So the "self-determination" of human beings is compatible with a "theonomy" of the reason and will, since "free obedience to God's law effectively implies that human reason and human will participate in God's wisdom and providence" (*VS* 41.2). But this is not the only difference from Kant.

According to Kant, we are to do our duty by obeying the moral law for its own sake. The doctrine of the encyclical is that we are also to obey that law for the sake of the further good of ourselves and of others. The natural law teaches us what kinds of actions we need to perform, what kinds of actions we need to refrain from performing, and what kinds of person we need to become, if we are to achieve our own final end and good and to share with others in achieving our final end and good. In achieving that good we shall be perfected, something possible for us sinful human beings only by grace. And what we shall lose, if we fail to achieve it, will, Jesus taught us, be God himself "who alone is goodness, fullness of life, the final end of human activity and perfect happiness" (*VS* 9.3). "*To ask about the good*, in fact, *ultimately means to turn toward God*, the fullness of goodness" (*VS* 9.3).

What this underlines is that the conception of a final good for human beings is that of a good that cannot be weighed against any other, a good whose loss could not be compensated for by any other. It is not merely that of some good which contingently happens to outweigh all other goods, so that one might intelligibly ask about it how far it outweighs them and whether or not some combination of other goods might not possibly outweigh it. But if obedience to the precepts of the natural law, including the negative exceptionless precepts, is necessary for the achievement of a final good of this kind, is indeed partly constitutive of a life whose choices are directed toward that good as its end, then it makes no sense to ask whether some particular violation of one of those negative precepts might not be justified, because some good to be brought about by that particular violation in these circumstances on this occasion would or might outweigh the good to be achieved by conformity to that particular precept. The notion of outweighing cannot have this kind of application.

It may be instructive to consider—the example is mine, not that of the encyclical—the difference between St. Thomas Aquinas's view of why I may not be guilty of murder, even if, in the course of defending myself as a private person from a murderous onslaught by someone else, I happen to kill the aggressor, and a utilitarian view of why in those same circumstances I may not be guilty. The utilitarian will weigh the consequences of my undertaking an effective defense of myself or others—let us suppose that we are dealing with a case in which the only available effective defense will as a matter of fact result in the death of the aggressor—against the consequences of my failing to do so. If, as will commonly be the case, the benefit to be produced by an effective defense will in fact outweigh the harm of killing the aggressor, then, so the utilitarian will conclude, it will be right for me to mount an effective defense and I will do no wrong, if I intend, because of having so concluded, to kill the aggressor as the means of producing this balance of benefit over harm.

Aquinas's view is importantly different (*STh* II–II, q. 64, a. 7). I may not, whatever the predictable outcome in terms of a balance of benefit over harm, *intend* the death of the aggressor. What I may and should intend is only to defend myself—or other innocent persons—by using the minimum force necessary, even if in the course of so doing I do have to act so as to bring about the aggressor's death. The intentional killing of another by a private individual is prohibited by the natural law as a wrong that cannot be outweighed by any benefit whatsoever.

One recurrent source of error here has been too simple a view of what some of the negative precepts of the natural law require and a consequent misunderstanding of how certain practical conclusions follow from them. For some negative precepts of the natural law have a certain complexity. Consider the act of theft. "The primary and decisive element for moral judgment is the object of the human act, which establishes whether it is *capable of being ordered to the good and ultimate end, which is God*" (*VS* 79.2). St. Thomas first identifies the object of the act of theft as to take possession of what is the property of another where what is taken is a thing possessed (and not the other's person or some part of it) and to do so secretly (this distinguishes *furtum*, theft, from *rapina*, robbery). But a right understanding of what the precept of the natural law forbidding theft requires is therefore impossible without a right understanding of the concept of property. To own something is not, as in some views, to have inviolable rights over it. Owners hold their property as stewards for those in need, and in cases of extreme and immediate need, need which can only be met by taking what is otherwise to be regarded as your property, I do no wrong in taking what, because of that need, has become my property as much as yours, common property, and my taking is not rightly to be called theft or robbery, even if you have not consented to it (*STh* II–II, q. 66, a. 7).

Compare this mode of argument once again with an erroneous method which might in some particular situations lead to the same practical conclusion. A utilitarian might suppose that what has to be done is to weigh the good of upholding property rights against that of aiding this particular individual in need, in each case taking the relevant set of consequences into account, and perhaps arriving at the conclusion that, on balance, good will be maximized by aiding the needy individual. Two *prima facie* moral principles are in conflict, and the utilitarian's conclusion resolves the dilemma by appeal to the principle of utility. But of course some change in contingent circumstances, such that the upholding of property rights became of greater and more urgent importance, might well lead by the same utilitarian mode of argument on another occasion to the conclusion that the needy person should be allowed to starve to death. The consistent utilitarian has to deny that it could be right to hold that no one should ever be allowed to starve to death when there are any resources available to prevent this, whatever the consequences. But just what the utilitarian denies, the natural law affirms.

So even when in particular cases and circumstances what the negative precepts of the natural law enjoin does coincide with what a
consequentialist would prescribe, they do so on a basis that is deeply
at odds with all notions of weighing and balancing consequences or
of giving proportionate weight to different considerations. It is not of
course that there are not greater and lesser goods. To do evil is always
to prefer a lesser good to a greater. But the good at stake in all situations in which obedience or disobedience to the natural law is in question is such that no other can be weighed against it. Hence, when the
encyclical explains the mistake made by those consequentialists and
proportionalists who have supposed that somehow or other some
good can be weighed against the evil of violating some particular
negative precept, this identification of error is not just one more ad-
dendum to an exposition of God's law, whether understood as the
natural law or as received through revelation from Moses and Jesus
Christ. It is rather that recognizing that and why this is an error is itself
a *sine qua non*, a necessary condition, of any well-founded understanding of the natural law and of our human relationship to it.

This is also true of a different, but not unrelated, error concerning the intentions of agents. It has been sometimes supposed that an
intention or purpose can be good prior to and in independence of the
character of the actions in which it is embodied, and that the goodness of that intention or purpose can make the acts that flow from it
good, independently of their character in respect of the precepts of the
natural law. Here the mistake is to suppose that the agent's willing,
expressed in the formation of its intentions and purposes, can derive
its goodness or badness from any source except the object of the act
deliberately chosen in that willing. The object of each particular action is the proximate end of that action embodied in that action, and
unless that action so characterized accords with the precepts of the
natural law, the action cannot be good and the willing cannot be good
either. And to will badly, as to act badly, is to fail in the achievement
of human freedom. In making this claim about freedom *Veritatis splendor* challenges a good deal of what is commonly received nowadays
as wisdom.

There is in the dominant moral culture of our particular time and
place a widespread and influential conception of human beings as
individuals who initially confront a range of possible objects of rational desire, a range of goods, among which each of them has to make

his or her own choices, and which each individual has to order for himself or herself, in accordance with his or her set of preferences. It is in accordance with those choices and that rank ordering that individuals formulate their principles, attempting in so doing to arrive at agreement with other rational persons, so that each in affirming and implementing his or her own preferences and choices may do so in a way consonant with those of others. Hence it is on the basis of individual preferences and choices that values and norms, including those of morality, come into being and from those preferences and choices that they derive their authority. Different versions of this view have been presented in the idioms of more than one type of philosophical theory. But the view itself is tacitly presupposed by many people who are quite unaware of themselves as having any philosophical commitments. And such people have often come to believe that this purported ability to create moral values and norms is central to their freedom. Their choices and preferences are to be treated as sovereign, and their liberty consists in the exercise of this sovereignty. Hence any assertion of the objective authority of norms and values seems to constitute a serious threat. During the hearings on the nomination of Clarence Thomas to the U. S. Supreme Court, Senator Joseph Biden expressed a fear "that natural law dictates morality to us, instead of leaving matters to individual choice" (*The Washington Post*, September 8, 1991). But this conception of moral freedom as a power in each of us to make our own fundamental premoral choice of moral norms and values is illusory and deceptive.

What freedom is for human beings depends upon what their capacities are, upon what difference it makes to them how they set about actualizing those capacities, and upon what success they are able to have in so doing. To have become free is to have been able to overcome or avoid those distractions and obstacles which frustrate or inhibit the development of a capacity for judgment by standards whose rational authority we are able to recognize for ourselves and for action in accordance with such judgment. To have failed to become free is to have rendered oneself subject to frustration or inhibition in respect of such development. And the exercise of choice as such may contribute as easily and as often to failure as to success in becoming free. What we all have to learn is how to make right choices, on the basis of judgments that are genuinely rational and genuinely our own, so that our choices contribute to the development and exercise of our capacities. The virtue which we need if we are to become capable of right choice is the Aristotelian virtue of *phronesis, prudentia.* The acquisition of that virtue is impossible without a recognition of the rational authority of the precepts of the natural law, most of all perhaps of the negative exceptionless precepts. Thereby we become able to choose in a way that is not self-frustrating, but liberates our capacities for judgment and action directed toward our good. This is why the negative precepts are what I called them earlier, enabling, and why acknowledgment of their rational authority is a constitutive element of human autonomy. But just how is this so? We can usefully begin by considering first how they structure our relationships to others and then how they correspondingly structure our relationship to ourselves and so our selfhood.

We find ourselves engaged with others in a variety of ongoing institutional and informal enterprises and projects, through which we and they seek to achieve a variety of goods, goods of enduring relationships in the family and in friendship, goods of productive work, of artistic activity and scientific enquiry, goods of leisure, goods of communal politics and of religion. In each of these projects and types of activity, individuals have to learn how to discern and to order the specific goods of each area and how to make those choices through which they can be achieved. How those goods are understood and what means there are for achieving them will of course vary a good deal from culture to culture. What will not vary is twofold: the need for a presupposed understanding that such goods will contribute to the achievement of the human good and the need for recognition of a set of requirements which enable human beings to benefit from the disciplines of learning. Those universal and invariant requirements specify the preconditions for the kind of responsiveness by one human being to others which makes it possible for each to learn from the others' questioning. They are the preconditions of a kind of rational conversation in which no one need fear being victimized by others as the outcome of their engagement with those others. Without acknowledgment of them, implicit or explicit, there would be lacking the basis for rational conversation about goods and about the good and for rational cooperation in achieving good and the good either within cultures or between cultures. They are definitive therefore of what human beings share with one another by nature, as rational beings. And they are in fact the requirements imposed by the precepts of the natural law.

What is true of relationship with others also holds of our relationship with ourselves. The same preconditions necessary for rational conversation with others are necessary also for rational deliberation with and by myself. My ability to learn from my own experiences in a way that will conduce to the achievement of my good depends upon my adopting a certain standpoint toward myself, a standpoint in which I am able to evaluate myself as a rational agent with, so far as possible, the same objectivity that I would evaluate another. Truthfulness, the courage of endurance and the courage of patience, a considerateness and a generosity which avoid both mean-spiritedness and self-indulgence are as necessary in my treatment of myself as they are in my treatment of others. And the minimal requirements of those virtues are none other than the precepts of the natural law.

If, then, conformity to the precepts of the natural law is a precondition of the kind of learning, both for oneself and in relationship to others, which develops maturity of rational judgment, any attempt to locate human freedom in a freedom to make choices which are prior to and independent of the precepts of the natural law is bound to be not only theoretically mistaken but also practically misguided. Theoretically those who accept such a view understand law as primarily a constraint upon, rather than an enabling condition of freedom. And this is why they suppose that acknowledgment of the natural law is incompatible with freedom. As the encyclical puts it, they posit *"an alleged conflict between freedom and law,"* supposing that individuals and social groups have a *"right to determine what is good or evil"* (*VS* 35.3). Their belief has practical consequences. It leads them on to a reformulation of moral rules, so that no moral rules are held unconditionally and unqualifiedly. The rule about truth-telling, for example, becomes "Never tell a lie, except when . . ." and there then follows a list of types of exception, a list which will vary from person to person and group to group, except that all their lists are apt to end with an "etc.," and as with the rules about truth-telling, so also with other moral rules. The social and political consequences are those described in Sections 100 and 101 of the encyclical.

What this erosion of rules is always apt to lead to is a surrender of human relationships to competing interests, economic interests which, if not shaped by temperateness and justice, will reduce persons "to use-value or a source of profit" (*VS* 100, quoting the *Catechism of the Catholic Church* 2414), political interests which, if not likewise shaped, will threaten integrity and legality. These are evils not only of totalitarianism. They may also result from "an alliance between democracy and ethical relativism" (*VS* 101.1), a relativism according to which each individual is treated as free to decide upon his or her own moral rules.

One strong contention of the encyclical is that the only barrier to such an erosion and its consequences is a recognition of the objective authority of the precepts of the natural law, a recognition not only of the significance of the content of the natural law but also of its function in structuring human nature. Each individual human being is a unity of body and soul, and the body is to be understood in terms of this soul-informed unity. Bodily inclinations are of moral significance, and bodily movements give expression to meanings. Human bodies are more than physicochemical and biological structures, although they are both these things. This conception of the body as primarily a bearer of meanings links Aristotelian themes in the philosophy of mind and body with perspectives developed within Polish phenomenology by, among others, Karol Wojtyla, and also of course by a variety of followers of Husserl there and elsewhere, most notably perhaps by Merleau-Ponty but also, earlier and as strikingly by Edith Stein. It is "in the body," the encyclical declares, following both St. Thomas and Stein, that the person discovers those "anticipatory signs," which are "the expression and the promise of the gift of self" (*VS* 48.3). Moral direction therefore is not something to which the body is merely subjected as something alien and external. Physical activity is intelligibly structured toward the ends of the whole person, something that is rendered invisible by any reductive physicalism. It is the whole human person as a unity of body and soul which is ordered to its ends by the natural law, when the human being is in good functioning order. The truth that it is by being so ordered that the person is enabled and empowered—a bodily enabling and empowerment–is among those truths without a grasp of which an understanding of freedom cannot be achieved (*VS* 50).

The concept of truth here invoked is, in some sense of that variously employed adjective, a realist one. Our judgments about how it is right for us to act and about how human nature is structured have authority only in virtue of their conformity to standards independent of and prior to judgment, desire, choice, and, will, standards of truth as well as of rational justification. Conscience has no authority in and by itself, but only insofar as its subjective deliverances conform to those objective standards. "Once the idea of universal truth about the good, knowable by human reason, is lost, inevitably the notion of conscience also changes" (*VS* 32.2). And it is not just that conscience is thereby accorded a false self-sufficiency and a misleading authority, important although that is (*VS* 32). There is also a consequent failure in our self-knowledge, a failure to identify and to recognize that in our human nature which makes our freedom a real possibility, and beyond this sometimes a denial of the reality of a determinate human nature. An inadequate conception of truth is thus not just a source of failure in semantics or epistemology. Both the relationship of our understanding of truth to our understanding of freedom and the relationship of our capacity for achieving truth to the actuality of freedom make it crucial for moral philosophy and also for moral theology that we should have an adequate conception of truth. But the required standard of adequacy is of course compatible with more than one philosophical theory of truth.

What is required is that truth should be understood to be something other and something more than warranted assertibility. What we take to be warrantedly assertible is always relative to the standards of warrant presently upheld in our particular time and place, in our particular culture. But in asserting that something is true, we are not talking about warrant or justification, but claiming rather that this is in fact how things are, whatever our present or future standards of warrant or justification may lead us to state or imply, that this is in fact how things are, not from the point of view of this or that culture, but as such. Such assertions of course often turn out to be false, but once again what they turn out to be is not false-from-a-point-of-view, or false-by-this-or-that-set-of-standards, but simply false. Without this culture and-standpoint-transcending aspect of the true and the false, those twin concepts could not play the part that they do in our lives. Without them we could not be the culture-transcending rational animals that we are.

Of course it is only in terms provided for each of us by our own culture that human beings can initially formulate whatever truths we may apprehend about human nature and about the natural law. And it is from the resources provided by our own culture that we first set about trying to provide "*the most adequate formulation*" for those truths (*VS* 53.3). But insofar as the conception of human nature which we arrive at is indeed that of human nature as structured by the natural law, we will have succeeded in transcending what is peculiar to our own or any other culture. It will have become a conception of that which "is itself a measure of culture," of that in human beings which shows that they are "not exhaustively defined" by their culture and are not its prisoner (*VS* 53.2). So once again a connection between truth and freedom appears. Just as we are not to be explained as wholly determined by our physical and biological make-up, so we are not merely products of our cultural environment, but actual or potential creative shapers of it, precisely insofar as we can evaluate its perspectives in terms which are nonperspectival, the terms of truth.

What I have tried to do so far is no more than to sketch the philosophical content of *Veritatis splendor*, and I hope that something at least of the coherence and the complexity of that content has emerged. But if the encyclical is not to be seriously misrepresented, another dimension needs to be added. Someone might well remark that if and insofar as the encyclical is philosophy, it does indeed have one characteristic property of philosophy: every thesis thus presented is one treated as contestable within contemporary academic philosophy and denied by the protagonists of one or more influential philosophical standpoints. Moreover nothing in the encyclical's presentation is going by itself to change the philosophical convictions of any of those engaged in the debates of contemporary moral philosophy. The question therefore arises: Is anything achieved by the encyclical other than a salutary reminder both to Catholic philosophers and to others of some of the philosophical commitments and presuppositions of Catholic Christianity? The answer is: A good deal more is achieved, both at and beyond the level of philosophy, for the encyclical not only spells out the philosophical commitments and presuppositions of Catholic Christianity, it also explains just why these commitments and presuppositions are going to be regarded as contestable, at what points their rejection is of the greatest significance, and what the intellectual and moral costs of such rejection are. It does so by presenting us with what is in effect a theology of moral philosophy embedded in a theology of the moral life.

The starting point for the reflections which yield that theology is a meditation on the conversation of Jesus with a rich young man in the nineteenth chapter of Saint Matthew's Gospel (*VS* 6–27). We are to recognize in that young man "every person who, consciously or not" (*VS* 7.1) poses to Christ the Redeemer questions about morality which are in fact questions about the meaning of one's own life. This is a form of unquiet questioning, present in everyone, to which each significant action and decision implicitly or explicitly proposes an answer. The rich young man makes explicit both the question and his own answer. Jesus redirects the young man's questioning from the law to God, who is not only the author of the law, but is himself the final end of the law, "the final end of human activity" (*VS* 9.3). What is required of the rich young man, and so correspondingly of each of us, is that he give up everything to God, so that by holding back nothing, he will acknowledge that God, the supreme good, his supreme good, cannot be weighed against any other good. He must go beyond mere conformity to the law to a kind of obedience which understands the point of the law as an expression of God's love. But it is not in the young man's power to achieve this by himself. That is a possibility opened up to him and to others "exclusively by grace" (*VS* 24.1), grace which Jesus offers as a gift to the young man, who, even though he has observed all the Commandments, "is incapable of taking the next step by himself alone" (*VS* 17.1). But the young man refused Jesus' invitation and "went away sorrowful, for he had many possessions" (Mt 19:22). What did the young man lose by preserving his attachment to his possessions? *Veritatis splendor* does not answer this question directly in the sections which bring this initial scriptural meditation to a close. But in an important way the whole of the rest of the encyclical constitutes an answer to it.

Unless, unlike the rich young man, we respond to God's offer of grace by accepting it, we too shall be unable fully to understand and to obey the law in such a way as to achieve that ultimate good which gives to such understanding and obedience its point and purpose. But unless we can understand and obey the law adequately, we will be unable to recognize the truth concerning our own nature and to realize its potentiality for an exercise of rational freedom through which we can perfect our individual and communal lives (*VS* 38–40). This inability would constitute a loss in ourselves of that which is of most value to ourselves and to others. What we have to learn from the story of the rich young man is that attachments to what it seems to us that we cannot bear to lose (in his case his possessions) if they come between us and the possibilities that obedience to the law and grace together open up for us–that is, if they come between us and God–result in a far more radical loss to and of the self. But what has this to do with the philosophical parts of the encyclical?

Each of the errors about the natural law and its relationship to the human good identified in the encyclical is a dangerous obstacle to the achievement of right understanding of and fruitful obedience to the law. It is not too much to say that each represents an attachment comparable to the rich young man's attachments to his possessions. But how can this be so? I have so far presented these errors very largely as philosophical errors—although I have at certain points gone a little further than this—and we are generally unaccustomed in our culture to think of philosophy as having so interesting a potentiality as that for moral danger. But in fact those errors identified in the encyclical which I catalogued earlier are not only philosophical mistakes. They are the articulation at the level of moral philosophy, at the level, that is, of rational and reflective argument, of everyday practical, moral errors and ones that are peculiarly influential in our own particular culture. They can be usefully classified under three headings. And in each of the three types of case particular mistakes are symptomatic of some more general habit of mind and practice.

First, then, there are those mistakes which derive from distorted conceptions of the freedom and autonomy of the individual self, mistakes which involve a repudiation of the Kantian standpoint just as much as of the Thomistic. One expression of these conceptions is attachment to some notion of the self as constituted in key part by its prerational and premoral choices, an attachment sometimes expressed in resentment and indignation that moral standards should be thought to have any other authority than those choices. From this point of view, claims about the objectivity of the natural law are construed as attempts at an alien imposition upon the self of something that it has not chosen. Another expression of this distorted view of the self is the conferring upon the individual conscience of a sovereign independence of any standards external to its own judgments. Both these distortions are commonplaces of the justifications for actions and judgments often offered in the everyday life of our culture, in families, in workplaces, and in schools. What each presupposes is a denial of just that connection between the objectivity of the law and the autonomy and freedom of the self which is asserted in the encyclical. And therefore any philosophical theorizing which seems to afford sufficient rational grounds for denying this connection lends dangerous credibility to everyday error.

Secondly, there are those mistakes which derive from the tendency in our culture to conceive of all practical situations as ones in which it is appropriate for rational agents to weigh benefits and costs, and in which every benefit and every cost can be weighed against every other, so that each may achieve for himself or herself the greatest possible, or at least a satisfactory, balance of benefits over costs. This generally has two bad consequences. If and whenever changing social circumstances alter the balance of costs and benefits, so that what was hitherto a profitable principle for me to live by becomes an unprofitable one, then it also becomes, in this view, rational and right for me to exchange that principle for another. So it comes about that no principles are held unconditionally, no commitments are unqualified. But insofar as this is so, human relationships are fundamentally altered. Unconditional trust in another becomes a form of moral superstition. Temporariness becomes a crucial feature of the moral life and the virtue of integrity–of a willingness and an ability to stand by one's central commitments whatever the consequences–becomes thought of not as a virtue, but as a piece of moral irrationality. So a consistent consequentialism in everyday life would entail the loss of what is from the standpoint of the natural law a constitutive virtue of the mature self.

Another consequence of this same attitude, according to which all rational decision issues from this kind of calculation of benefits and costs, is that what is in fact incommensurable is too often treated as though it were commensurable. When this is so, what is presented in the guise of rational calculation in fact conceals, usually unwittingly, an underlying set of evaluative judgments of quite another kind. The apparently rational may thus disguise, and often enough does disguise, arbitrariness of preference and power. And the self is once again injured by such concealment and deception.

To this someone may respond that I—and by implication the encyclical—seem to have contradicted myself. I insisted a little earlier, as does the encyclical, that the precepts of the natural law are to be obeyed whatever the consequences. But now I am emphasizing, as also does the encyclical, the bad consequences of certain errors which both derive from a disregard for and serve to obscure the character of the natural law. How can I first deny the relevance of consequences and then assert it? The answer is that consequences are wholly irrelevant to the prohibitions of the negative precepts of the natural law. The rational justification of those precepts is not a matter of the consequences of disobeying them, and to justify my actions and omissions by reference to what those precepts forbid is not to appeal to consequences. Among the positive precepts of the natural law, however, is that we should all have an abiding concern for the flourishing of our families, our social and political order, and our culture. Here right action does involve the promotion of certain consequences and the avoidance of others so far as that is possible. Some goods in these areas are indeed greater than others. Hence derives the moral relevance of the consequences for familial, social, and cultural life of widespread disobedience to and confusion concerning the natural law. There is no inconsistency.

It is just this type of concern for the condition of our culture, as well as for individuals, which receives expression in the encyclical's insistence that for any culture to flourish those whose culture it is must recognize the need to call upon those intellectual and moral resources which belong to human beings as such and not only to what is specifically its own. The belief that our only resources are those provided by and specific to our own particular culture and the corresponding belief that the highest standards that we can know are the highest standards of that culture sometimes present themselves in our own culture in the form of a crude relativism. But even the sophisticated who disown any such relativism in theory often behave in practice as if something very like it were true, by their attitude to alien cultures, engaging with those cultures only on assumptions that take for granted the superiority of the dominant standards of our own culture. So far too often, for example, North Americans treat human beings everywhere as though it could be taken for granted that they are primarily consumers of whatever the most advanced technology is able to supply.

This attitude allows people to conceal from themselves what they are and have become, for they lose sight of any standard more fundamental than those upheld in their own culture by which important aspects of that culture might be judged defective. And without an adequate acknowledgment of the natural law, which provides just such a standard, we can have no sound basis for the kind of conversation with the representatives of alien cultures in which we might learn how to see ourselves from their point of view and so learn further about ourselves. Such failure can "eliminate awareness of one's own limits and of one's own sin" (*VS* 105.1) and so lead to a further deprivation of the self. We can avoid such failure not only by calling upon what is already ours, but also by recognizing what is to be learned from a variety of other traditions, "the great religious and sapiential traditions of East and West, from which the interior and mysterious workings of God's Spirit are not absent" (*VS* 94).

Relativism is, then, a third type of error identified in the encyclical; it appears both in everyday life and as a contending position in the enquiries of moral philosophy. The importance that attaches to the identification of all three kinds of error is thus both moral and intellectual. And if moral philosophers are to dispose themselves rightly in relation to those errors, they need not only what can be afforded by their own enquiries, but much more than this, that grace necessary for the redirection and restoration of the self of which the Gospel speaks. Each of these three kinds of error turns out to be an attachment to something which in the end deprives us not only of our good, that is, of God, but also of something crucial in ourselves, something without which we will become incapable of achieving that which alone in the end gives point and purpose to our activities. One central moral and theological lesson of the encyclical is that without understanding of and obedience to God's law, we become self-frustrating beings.

Yet if this is so, if, that is to say, both our moral lives and our philosophical enquiries are bound to be ultimately frustrated unless we are able to learn what the Gospel has to teach, then it would be tragic and seemingly paradoxical if what interposed itself between us and the Gospel, obscuring what the Gospel has to say about these errors, was some aspect of the discipline of Catholic moral theology. The history of Catholic theology suggests, however, that this can indeed happen and in two ways. One is by some theologians making themselves independent of authoritative Catholic teaching, so that for premises derived from that teaching they substitute premises of their own. And this is most notably and harmfully the case when they try to make themselves the authority which declares what authoritative Catholic teaching is. The other is by theologians deriving from such premises particular erroneous conclusions. How the pope and the bishops should respond is for them and, happily, not for me. But were they to have failed to respond, this would itself be a failure quite as great as that of any theological error. Even so, the significance of theological errors becomes somewhat different when those errors providentially provide matter and occasion for a declaration of the truths of the Gospel. One way of missing the point of *Veritatis splendor* would be to tie its reading too closely to the work of those particular moral theologians whose writings may have been the occasion for its composition. For quite apart from any errors that they may have committed, *Veritatis splendor* is and will remain a striking Christian intervention in moral debate, at once authoritative teaching and a voice in that continuing philosophical conversation between Christianity and modernity to which Pascal and Kierkegaard, Newman and Barth and von Balthasar, have all been contributors. *Veritatis splendor* continues the same evangelical and philosophical conversation with secular modernity, and the appropriate initial response of each of us to it should concern our own past and present defects and errors rather than those of others. There is much work to be done.

II. Issues

Veritatis splendor and the Theology of Natural Law*

Russell Hittinger

I. Introduction

This paper discusses the problem of natural law *ad intra*, within Catholic moral theology.[1] Although it includes a few very general remarks about public moral discourse in the conclusion, it has almost nothing to say about any particular issue of justice in the public sphere. It proffers no "natural law" answers to what judges ought to do or how the budget deficit ought to be resolved or the moral perspective that ought to guide welfare funding. Furthermore, although the paper might reinforce the suspicion of Evangelical Protestants that there is something both attractive and repellent about Catholic uses of natural law, the paper does not try to convince Protestants on any specific disputed issue.

Rather, the paper endeavors to tell a story about how the concept of natural law became a serious problem in modern Catholic moral theology, and how the papal encyclical *Veritatis splendor* responds to that problem. My account will be very imperfect indeed, for it will be necessary both to tell a story and to make a number of distinctions along the way, allowing each in turn to illuminate the other. It is difficult enough to do both, and more difficult to do so in the brief compass afforded by this paper.

II. An Initial Set of Distinctions

In his 1958 lectures at the University of Chicago, later published under the title *The Tradition of Natural Law: A Philosopher's Reflections* (1965), Yves R. Simon remarks that the subject of natural law

* Delivered at the Ethics and Public Policy Center, Washington, D.C., on March 7, 1996; published in *A Preserving Grace: Protestants, Catholics, and Natural Law*, ed. Michael Cromartie (Grand Rapids, Mich.: Wm. B. Eerdmans Publishing Company, 1997). Permission to reprint has been granted by the Ethics and Public Policy Center.

"is difficult because it is engaged in an overwhelming diversity of doctrinal contexts and of historical accidents. It is doubtful that this double diversity, doctrinal and historical, can so be mastered as to make possible a completely orderly exposition of the subject of natural law."[2] A "thorough analysis of natural law," he goes on to say, requires "an elaborate technique and sharp philosophical instruments."[3]

But to what should the instruments be applied? what is a theory of natural law a theory of?

In the first place, natural law can be regarded as an issue of propositions or precepts that are first in the order of practical cognition. In this view, an account of natural law endeavors to bring into focus those reasons for action which are "first." Thus, when the theorist reconnects debate about justice back to first principles, from which the mind can lay out properly considered and argued conclusions, he can be said to have (or practice) a theory of natural law. In the second place, natural law can be regarded as an issue of nature or human nature, in which case natural law is not only a problem of epistemology and logic, but a problem of how practical reason is situated in a broader order of causality. Third, natural law can be approached not only as order in the mind or in nature, but as the ordinance of a divine lawgiver.

Discourse about natural law can gravitate toward any one or combination of these foci: natural law in the mind, in things, and in divine providence. If one reads contemporary literature on the subject, it quickly becomes evident that there is little or no agreement as to how the three foci ought to be integrated. For there is no general agreement about what should count as proper problem, much less what counts as proper philosophical instruments.

Rather than engage in an endless survey of the methodological problems, I shall begin with an assertion. The theologian is (or ought to be) chiefly concerned with the third of these foci: namely, natural law as an expression of divine providence. As Karl Barth said in *Church Dogmatics*, "Ethics [is] a Task of the Doctrine of God."[4] Whatever else Barth said or thought about the subject of natural law, the proposition that moral theology is a task of the doctrine of God is incontestable. The Christian theologian is interested in who God is, and what God does, as he reveals himself.

Who we are, and what we do, are questions which can be asked and pursued outside of theology. To be sure, the theologian will be interested in how those questions are asked and pursued by the gentiles. Catholic and Protestant theologians have different attitudes toward these strands (Balthasar says "fragments") of moral inquiry and behavior separated from the living Word of God. Catholic theologians perhaps have been tempted to overestimation, while Protestants have been inclined to underestimation. But *qua* theologian, the main focus for the theologian is, as Barth said, the doctrine of God.

III. Historical Reflections

Until recently the proposition that natural law is chiefly a theological issue was uncontroversial in Catholic moral theology. Natural law in the human mind or in nature were regarded as distinct, but not architectonic, foci. Let us first consider two passages from the Church Fathers.

In the second century Tertullian took up the problem of divine governance prior to the written Law. Like so many other of the patristic theologians of both the East and West, Tertullian argued that the law given to Adam (Gn 2:17) was the natural law. "For in this law given to Adam we recognize in embryo all the precepts which afterwards sprouted forth when given through Moses." After reciting the ten precepts of the Decalogue, Tertullian concludes that the first law is "the womb of all the precepts of God"—a "law unwritten, which was habitually understood naturally, and which the fathers kept."[5] Which of the patriarchs? Tertullian mentions Noah, Melchizedek, Enoch, and Abraham.

This teaching is simple and familiar. Our first parents were given an unwritten law, expressing the rule of law itself: men govern only by sharing in divine governance. Adam and Eve, who understood the law *naturaliter* (naturally), did not keep it. But the patriarchs before Moses adhered to the unwritten law. In this brief passage, Tertullian alludes to natural law in the mind and in nature. His principal interest, however, is the economy of divine laws. As to what men knew or did *post peccatum*, Tertullian commits himself only to saying that the patriarchs were counted "righteous, on the observance of a natural law."[6]

In the fourth century Gregory of Nyssa proposed:

> that human nature at its beginning was unbroken and immor-
> tal. Since human nature was fashioned by the divine hands and
> beautified with the unwritten characters of the Law, the inten-
> tion of the Law lay in our nature in turning us away from evil
> and in honoring the divine. When the sound of sin struck our
> ears, that sound which the first book of Scripture calls "the
> voice of the serpent," but the history concerning the tables calls
> the "voice of drunken singing," the tables fell to the earth and
> were broken. But again the true Lawgiver, of whom Moses was
> a type, cut the tables of human nature for himself from our
> earth. It was not marriage which produced for him his "God-
> receiving" flesh, but he became the stonecutter of his own flesh,
> which was carved by the divine finger, for the Holy Spirit came
> upon the virgin and the power of the Most High overshadowed
> her. When this took place, our nature regained its unbroken
> character, becoming immortal through the letters written by his
> finger.[7]

Like Tertullian, Gregory of Nyssa alludes to natural law in the
mind. The "intention of the Law," he writes, "lay in our nature in
turning us away from evil and in honoring the divine." This is the
traditional notion of a *lex indita*, a law instilled in the mind, which
later patristic and medieval theologians would call *synderesis*.[8]
Gregory also speaks of the order of the human nature. Yet it is clear
that Gregory's focus is set upon what God does: first in ordering
man by nature, second in disciplining men through the written law,
and finally in re-creating men through the mystery of the Incarnation and Redemption.

These two passages are typical of the patristic thinking on natural law. Issues of epistemology and human nature are distinct, but
not architectonic foci. Nor even is moral theology (in our modern
sense) the main focus. Rather, theology proper, the doctrine of revelation, organizes their perspective. Chief among the theological
themes are (i) the economy of divine laws, (ii) the manner in which
Christ recapitulates not just Moses but Adam, (iii) and generally,
getting the story right, which is to say, thinking rightly about Scripture.[9]

As early as the Second Council of Arles (473), the "law of nature" (*lex naturalis*) was defined as "the first grace of God."[10] Beginning in late antiquity, theologians transformed the nomencla-

ture of the lawyers to bring it in line with Christian theology. The *Corpus iuris civilis* divided law generally according to *ius naturale*, *ius gentium*, and *ius civile*.[11] The word *lex* was reserved not just for written law (according to the Institutes, *scriptum ius est lex*), but was associated especially with imperial pronouncements.[12] The *Lex Iulia*, for example, was the Julian Act.[13] This usage was also adopted by the canonists. *Lex*, Gratian states in the *Decretum*, is a written statute, a *constitutio scripta*; and a *constitutio*, he goes on to explain, is "what a king or emperor has decided or declared."[14] In St. Thomas's *Summa theologiae*, the *iura* are classified as *leges*. So, rather than the *ius naturale* we not only get *lex naturalis*, but a classification of law according to *diversae leges*: e.g. *lex aeterna*, *lex nova*, *lex Mosaica*, *lex membrorum*, *lex humana*, *lex vetus*, etc.[15] The term *lex*, which the lawyers reserved for a written edict issued by an imperial lawgiver, had become for theologians a usage emphasizing the divine origin of all law, whether it be instilled in the heart or imparted by written or oral arts.

As regards the being and cause of the natural law, the theological tradition moved steadily away from any anthropocentric or merely naturalistic conception of the *ius naturale*.[16]

The thought of Thomas Aquinas, of course, has become nearly synonymous with "Catholic" doctrine of natural law. It would take volumes to dispel the modern misperceptions and misrepresentations of his natural law theory. Many misperceptions are due to the fact that Thomas, more than the patristic theologians, articulated the epistemological and natural foci with some philosophical precision. Those discussions in Thomas are often lifted out of context, and then debated as though they were completely independent of theology.

I have no intention of trying to dispel all of the misperceptions at their proper level of detail and complexity. Two points, however, need to be made. First, nowhere in his writings is natural law defined in anything but theological terms. Indeed, in answer to the objection that it was needless reduplication for there to be both an eternal and a natural law, Thomas responds: "this argument would hold if the natural law were something diverse from the eternal law, whereas it is nothing but a participation thereof."[17] Natural law is never (and I must underscore "never") defined in terms of what is first in the (human) mind or first in nature.[18]

Although his modern readers have little inclination to discrimi-
nate among the three foci, or to reflect upon how they are themselves arranged in an order of priority and posteriority, Thomas
understood what is at stake in arriving at a proper definition. The
fact that we first perceive ourselves discovering or grasping a rule
of action does not mean that the human mind is first in the causal
order, or in the ultimate order of being. For example, the judge who
discovers a rule does not confuse the cause of discovery with the
cause of the rule—unless, perchance, they are one and the same
cause. In the case of natural law, Thomas defines the law from the
standpoint of its causal origin (viz. what makes it a law), not in
terms of a secondary order of causality through which it is discovered (viz. the human intellect). Without the order of priority and
posteriority, we shall have either nature or the human mind as the
cause of the law—not the cause of knowing or discovering, but the
cause of the law itself. Such would destroy the metaphysical continuity between the various dispensations of divine providence.
For if God is to govern, he will have to supersede, if not destroy,
the jurisdiction (allegedly) constituted by human causality. Insofar as the natural law is regarded as the foundation of the moral
order, and insofar as that is thought to be caused (and not merely
discovered) in some proper and primary way by human cognition,
God will have to unseat the natural law. Almost all of the modern
theories of natural law seek to relieve that conflict in favor of what
is first in the human mind. Thomas understood what is at stake in
giving definitions, and was exceedingly careful not to confuse what
is first in human cognition with what is first in being.[19]

In the second place, as we saw earlier, Tertullian used the adverb *naturaliter* (naturally) not to characterize the law, but rather
to describe how it is known. Nature is not the law, but the mode
of knowing it. This Latin adverb would eventually find its way into
the Vulgate translation of Romans 2:14–15 as to what the *gentiles*
know or do without benefit of divine positive law. Thomas
Aquinas frequently uses the same term in order to emphasize the
mode of divine promulgation.[20] Natural law is *lex indita*, instilled
in the human mind by God, moving the creature to its proper acts
and ends. As for his estimation of the efficacy of natural law in the
human mind, Thomas never wavered from the judgment that only
the rudiments (or the *seminalia*, "the seeds") are known by the

untutored mind. With regard to the *gentiles* mentioned in Romans 2:14 ["who having not the Law, did naturally (*naturaliter . . . faciunt*) things of the Law"], St. Thomas points out that the words *naturaliter* and *faciunt* indicate that St. Paul was referring to *gentiles* whose "nature had been reformed by grace" [*per naturam gratia reformatam*]. Any other interpretation, Thomas warns, would be Pelagian.[21]

Thomas is well known for having insisted upon the *de iure* possibility of affirming the existence of God by natural reason. His estimation of the de facto condition of the human mind led him to make the cautious statement: "known by a few, and that after a long time, and with the admixture of many errors."[22] More to the point, however, Thomas explicitly and emphatically denied that the philosophers were able to translate such scraps of theology into virtuous acts of religion. None of the pagan theologies satisfied the natural, not to mention supernatural, virtue of religion.[23]

In his last recorded remarks about subject of natural law, made during a series of Lenten conferences in 1273, Thomas's judgment is even more stern: "Now although God in creating man gave him this law of nature, the devil oversowed another law in man, namely, the law of concupiscence. . . . Since then the law of nature was destroyed by concupiscence, man needed to be brought back to works of virtue, and to be drawn away from vice: for which purpose he needed the written law." As the new, critical Leonine edition confirms, the words are *destructa erat*—"was destroyed."[24]

How can he say that natural law is destroyed in us? First, he certainly does not mean that it is destroyed in the mind of the lawgiver. As a law, natural law is not in nature or the human mind, but is rather in the mind of God. The immutability of natural law, he insists, is due to the "immutability and perfection of the divine reason that institutes it."[25] Insofar as natural law can be said to be "in" things or in nature, it is an order of inclinations of reason and will by which men are moved to a common good. While the created order continues to move men, the effect of that law (in the creature) is bent by sin. Not so bent that God fails to move the finite mind, for the fallen man is still a spiritual creature, possessed of the God-given light of moral understanding, but bent enough that this movement requires the remediation of divine positive law and a new law of grace.[26] In fact, Thomas held that God left men in such a condition—between the time of the fall and the Mosaic law—in order to chastise men.[27] The so-called "time of natural law," which refers of course to the historical and moral condition of man, not the precepts of the natural law itself, is not normative for Thomas's ethics. And it was the effort to make that condition normative that marks the modern project.

IV. Modern Ideology

In the modern era the theology of natural law is moved to the periphery and usually eclipsed altogether. The epistemological and natural foci become architectonic. The new sciences adopted the method of resolutive analysis and compositive synthesis. The appearances of nature are analytically reduced to the most "certain," which is to say, the most predictable elements: namely, modes of quantity (size, shape, velocity, etc.). Then, by the method of compositive synthesis, the quantities can be rebuilt as mathematical objects. This method was applied across physics to humane matters. In *De Homine*, Hobbes, for example, takes man as he is a thing of "mere nature," and reduces the appearances to stable and predictable matters of quantity. Once we analytically reduce man to such quantities, we do not find Presbyterians and Catholics; rather, we find a stimulus-response mechanism that endeavors to augment its power. What is first, then, are natural laws as "lower" laws rendering men amenable to the law of the sovereign. In *De Cive*, man is rebuilt according to rules which are true laws. Hobbes explains: "Politics and ethics (that is, the sciences of just and unjust, of equity and inequity) can be demonstrated a priori; because we ourselves make the principles—that is, the causes of justice (namely, laws and covenants)—whereby it is known what justice and equity, and their opposites injustice and inequity are."[28]

Hobbes, of course, was a materialist. But this method of reduction and recomposition was not tied to materialist doctrines. Continental Rationalism and Idealism also deployed methods of reduction to what is first in the mind, from which reality can be constructed, modeled, predicted. Upon the reduction, Hobbes could only find "lower" laws; other Enlightenment thinkers purported to find first principles of justice and equity. Whatever the differences, the trademarks are certainty and predictability, gauged according to what is first in cognition.

Yet the main reason for the eclipse of the theology of natural law was the theologico-political problem. What better way to solve the theologico-political problem than to imagine men appealing to no authority other than what is first in the mind? Virtually all of the Enlightenment "state of nature" scenarios make this move. In Hobbes, Locke, Rousseau, and Kant, man is considered in an "original" position, under the authority of no pope, prince, or scripture. If there is a God, he governs through no mundane authority. Authority will have to make its first appearance in the covenants of individuals constrained to reach a consensus on the basis of what is (or seems) self-evident. The twelfth century summist Johannes Faventinus declared: "The streams of natural rectitude flow into the sea of natural law, such that what was lost in the first man is regained in the Mosaic law, perfected in the Gospels, and decorated in human customs."[29] The modern myth of the "state of nature" rejects this scheme of divine pedagogy—not directly, but indirectly, by rendering it superfluous to the quest for first principles of the political order. Indeed, the "state of nature" was meant to be a secular substitute for the story of Genesis. It never was a pure science of morality, but rather a merely useful one, designed for the political purpose of unseating the traditional doctrine of natural law.

The fact that a proposition is pellucid, cognized without logical need of a middle term (e.g., "life is good," which can be grasped without some set of theological inferences or authorities), is supposed reason enough to conclude that logical independence means ontological independence; and the "state of nature" mythology had the aim of representing that independence. Since no orthodox Christian theology holds that God and his orders of providence and of salvation crop up as what is first in untutored cognition, the forcing of natural law into the myopia of that one focus is bound to destroy moral theology on the reefs of half-truths. The half-truth is that there are principles of practical cognition which are proximate to the natural functioning of the intellect. They are only the beginning (the *seminalia*) of practical reason. When, however, the starting points are made autonomous, the human mind declares independence not only from the deeper order of divine tutoring, but also from the tutoring afforded by human culture, including human law.

This is why natural rights, for so many modern advocates, turn out to be nothing other than immunities against the order of law. Thus what began for the Christian theologians as a doctrine explaining how the human mind participates in a higher order of law is turned into its opposite. The natural law becomes "temporal," the temporal becomes "secular," and the secular becomes the sphere in which human agents enjoy immunity from any laws other than those they impose upon themselves.

For a time, Catholics were not confused by the new ideologies of natural law, for they were expressed by political movements vehemently hostile to the Church. Once, however, political modernity became the "normal" state of affairs, and once the Church found a way to respond to modernity in something more than a purely reactive mode, it was almost inevitable that the new conceptions of natural law would begin to color moral theology.

V. Modern Catholic Thought

Catholic moral theology could not remain unaffected by modern conceptions of natural law. As I said, there is a superficial congruity between the tradition and modernity. Both (in various ways) hold that there is a moral order first in the mind, and that some problems can be reasoned without immediate introduction of premises drawn either from revelation or from a fully worked-out cosmology of nature. This overlap of traditions on this specific point is apt to be misleading. Thomist, Cartesian, and Kantian conceptions of what it means to be "first" in the mind express very different understandings of practical reason, and how practical reason is situated with regard to what is "first" in nature and in ultimate order of being.

But when the focus on what is first in the mind is conjoined with the desperate modern need for consensus, it becomes easy for Catholic uses of natural law theory to cross into something new. The use of natural law by moral theologians has always been Janus-faced. On the one hand, it can be used to express specifically theological propositions about divine providence. On the other hand, it can be used to ground or mount arguments about particular disputed issues of conduct.

In modern times, we observe a steady drift toward the latter concern; and with it, a gradually diminishing sense of the sapiential context afforded by theology proper. Nowhere can this be seen more clearly than in the tradition of modern social encyclicals. As to things which have been declared contrary to nature and/or reason, a short list includes: dueling, Communism, divorce, contraception, Freemasonry, in-vitro fertilization, and contract theories of the origin of political authority. And this is not to mention the bevy of rights and entitlements which have been declared to be owed to persons under the rubric of justice *ex ipsa natura rei*, by the very nature of the thing. Read carefully, the encyclicals assume that all three foci (law in things, in the mind, and decreed by divine providence) are legitimate, and in principle integrated in moral theology. Compared to his successors, Leo XIII was especially careful to make the distinctions which kept divine providence in the picture.[30]

It is not my intention to cast doubt on any particular assertion about natural law or natural rights in these official documents. The problem (for our purposes here) is not particular judgments about the morality of dueling or contraception, but the possibility that the encyclical uses of natural law create the misleading impression that on any vexed issue the minds of the faithful and the gentiles can be directed by appeal to elementary principles of natural law. The moral picture of a baptized agent becomes difficult to distinguish from that of the unbaptized, which is not surprising, since so many of the encyclicals deal with political and economic crises. Thus we have the Church reaching into its treasury of wisdom, pulling out the right answer, without adequately displaying the wisdom, and sometimes without showing how the chain of arguments is grounded in anything other than Church authority.

Humanae vitae suffered especially in this regard. Some rather thin strands of argument about natural functions are terminated in one direction in the authority of the Church to interpret the natural law. Not surprisingly, Pope John Paul II devoted much of his pontificate to filling out the picture, beginning with a book-length set of allocutions on the proper exegesis of Genesis.

In any case, the teaching method of trimming arguments to fit what is first in cognition, buttressed perhaps with appeals to what is first in the chain of legal command (the papal office), would eventually yield diminishing and disappointing results, not only for the gentiles, but for the faithful–especially the moral theologians. By almost insensible steps, it was easy to fall into the habit of regarding discourse about natural law as an instrument of persuasion, the truth of which becomes measured by its success in garnering assent.

Take, for example, Cardinal Maurice Roy's 1973 remarks on the "Occasion of the Tenth Anniversary of the Encyclical *Pacem in terris.*" Addressing himself to Pope Paul VI, Cardinal Roy has this to say about the encyclical's references to natural law:

> Although the term "nature" does in fact lend itself to serious misunderstandings, the reality intended has lost nothing of its forcefulness when it is replaced by modern synonyms. . . . Such synonyms are: man, human being, human person, dignity, the rights of man or the rights of peoples, conscience, humaneness (in conduct), the struggle for justice, and, more recently, "the duty of being," the "quality of life." Could they not all be summarized in the concept of "values," which is very much used today?[31]

Interestingly, on John XXIII's remark that peace is "absolute respect for the order laid down by God,"[32] Roy observes: "But here again, this word jars the modern mentality, as does, even more, the idea that it summons up: a sort of complicated organic scheme or gigantic genealogical tree, in which each being and group has its predetermined place."

Eager to reinforce truths proximate to the human mind (or, perhaps, those least proximate to the chain of church authority), even the phrase "order laid down by God" seemed (to Roy) too theologically strong. Whereas earlier generations of theologians addressed the gentiles by emphasizing the relationship between moral order and divine providence, a new generation of Catholic theologians were being taught (inadvertently) that the rudiments of moral order ought to be discussed without any reference to divine governance, or, for that matter, to created nature. Modern gentiles, it seems, cannot bear the burden of even the weakest theological discourse.

To give credit where it is due, it must be said that the Church was thrust into the position of having to teach, *ad extra*, on precepts of the moral order which are in principle proximate to the human

mind. That nations or individuals must not murder, rape, and plun-
der are not propositions uniquely or exclusively theological. Many
of the precepts advanced in papal encyclicals have been held by
men of goodwill who do not explicitly assent to the doctrines of
Christianity or the Catholic Church. The Catholic Church has always regarded itself as a consensus-builder among the peoples and
nations.

The high tide of the overestimation of natural law discourse
was the post-World War Two era, when the Church was eager to
reinforce the right lessons of the war. Western modernity found
itself recoiling from legal positivism, and moving honestly (if tem-
porarily) to reform its polities on the basis of ideas about human
dignity and natural rights. Catholic philosophers and theologians
like Jacques Maritain and John Courtney Murray did remarkable
work trying to show how the Catholic tradition should seize the
moment.[33] The concrete experience of the war and its aftermath
renders the gentiles teachable, notwithstanding their disordered
theories about the moral order. In retrospect, we see that there was
an overestimation not only of what the gentiles know, but what
they were willing to do with their knowledge. Perhaps the most
bizarre overestimation of common ground was Cardinal
Bernardin's recommendation that Catholic lawyers ought to adopt
the natural law theory of Ronald Dworkin.[34] From another point of
view, we could say that there was a drastic underestimation of the
Church's teaching mission. In the literature and discourse of that
period, it is often difficult to say who was teaching whom.

Fifty years after WWII, in *Evangelium vitae*, the pope laments the
fact that the children of Locke and Rousseau have decided to reject the natural law foundations of civil government. The pope
writes:

> A long historical process is reaching a turning-point. The
> process which once led to discovering the idea of "human
> rights"—rights inherent in every person and prior to any
> Constitution and State legislation—is today marked by a
> surprising contradiction. Precisely in an age when the invio-
> lable rights of the person are solemnly proclaimed and the
> value of life is publicly affirmed, the very right to life is
> being denied or trampled upon, especially at the more sig-
> nificant moments of existence: the moment of birth and the
> moment of death (*EV* 18.3).

"[P]aradoxically," John Paul continues, what were once crimes now "assume the nature of 'rights,' to the point that the State is called upon to give them legal recognition." It is "sinister," the pope says, that states are "departing from the basic principles of their Constitutions." For by recognizing as moral rights the right to kill the weak and infirm, the "entire culture of human rights" (*EV* 18.5) is threatened. "It is a threat capable, in the end, of jeopardizing the very meaning of democratic coexistence.

Thinking it had seized upon a moment favorable to making common cause with the modern notions of human dignity and rights, the Church finds that the culture has retreated from the few things that seemed right about its own modernity. In any case, it is surely significant that most of the encyclical *Evangelium vitae* involves a detailed exegesis of the first four chapters of Genesis. The pope takes his audience back to the Scriptures. The gentiles need to be taught.

If the papacy overestimated the efficacy of the instruction *ad extra*, it underestimated the problems *ad intra*. Not only was natural law disembedded from moral theology, but moral theology was disembedded from the rest of theology. In his encyclical *Aeterni Patris* (1879), Leo XIII anticipated the problem of theology being done in piecemeal fashion, lurching from issue to issue, and resolved chiefly by the application of authority. He wrote: "For in this, the most noble of studies, it is of the greatest necessity to bind together, as it were, in one body the many and various parts of the heavenly doctrines, that, each being allotted to its own proper place and derived from its own proper principles, the whole may join together in a complete union."

Unfortunately, this ideal was not successfully realized prior to Vatican II. Perhaps the best account of the dwindling estate of moral theology prior to Vatican II is the recent book by Servais Pinckaers, O.P., *The Sources of Christian Ethics* (1995). Regarding the typical presentation of moral theology in the manuals used in seminaries, Pinckaers notes:

> Moral theology was divided into fundamental and particular sections. Fundamental moral theology included four chapters, covering human acts, laws, conscience, and sins. Particular moral theology, after a chapter on the theological virtues and their obligations, was generally divided according to the Ten

Commandments, to which were added the precepts of the Church and certain canonical prescriptions. The sacraments were studied in the light of the obligations required for their administration.[35]

If *ad extra*, doctrines of natural law were being used to produce conclusions to vexed moral issues among the gentiles, the tendency *ad intra* was its mirror image. The task of moral theology was one of laying out the premises from reason and church authority for the purpose of directing the legal dimension of marital and sacramental actions. Not only in the seminaries, but in the universities, the thought of St. Thomas was accorded great respect; yet it was extracted from the *Summa theologiae* in a way that favored the rationalistic elements of law. Almost everyone who teaches Thomas today would agree with Pinckaers that Thomas's thought was deeply misrepresented by isolating the first seven questions of the so-called Treatise on Law (*STh* I–II, qq. 90–97) from the questions on beatitude, virtue, and ultimately from the questions on the Old Law and the New Law.

The subject of natural law was placed in the most unfortunate position of being organized around two extreme poles. On the one hand, it represented the conclusions of Church authority; on the other hand, it represented what every agent is supposed to know according to what is first in cognition. We have Cartesian minds somehow under Church discipline.

The response was inevitable. In our time, there is a deep and ultimately irrational reaction against any depiction, much less any organizing, of the moral life in terms of law. Here, we cannot sort through all of the species of this reaction in contemporary moral theology. Earlier, we saw Cardinal Roy trying to construe "order laid down by God" in any way that might avoid the notion of a legal order. As we will see in due course, *Veritatis splendor* tries to moderate this reaction against the notion of conduct regulated by law. Yet, as a token of the very sort of reaction that it tries to moderate, it is interesting that the National Conference of Catholic Bishop's advertisement for the encyclical states that "It reverses pre-Vatican II legalism by speaking of the good and the bad rather than the forbidden and permitted, and by speaking about the invitation to live a moral life in God rather than the enforcing of laws or norms." This is precisely the simplistic attitude that the encyclical tries to overcome.

Before moving to *Veritatis splendor*, it is necessary to mention one particular reaction against law. It is the one that the encyclical takes the most pains to refute. We said that once natural law was disembedded from moral theology, and moral theology from theology, the concept was precariously stranded between two poles of authority: a chain of command somehow terminating in the authority of the Church, and a chain of propositions somehow terminating in the individual mind. Rather than fundamentally reconsidering this picture, casuists and confessors valiantly endeavored to relieve the burden of conscience. So, in the case of *Humanae vitae*, the conclusions of the natural law deriving the official chain of command seemed (to many) to conflict with what individual "reason" pronounced.

We should not be surprised that casuistry would not have the last word. Natural law itself would have to be reformulated to side with individual conscience. Through the sluice-gates of this problem would flow into Catholic moral theology the distinctively modern notions of natural law as individual autonomy. If this response went no further than to claim the competence of the individual to respond to divine providence (with the church being a non-authoritative support), then the story would have ended with a surprising "Protestant moment" for Catholic moral theology. But that is not where it ended. At least in contemporary moral theology, it ends with the claim of autonomy in the face of Providence: The Creator God exists, perhaps, but he does not govern.

For example, in his most recent book, Father Joseph Fuchs contends that: "When in fact, nature-creation does speak to us, it tells us only what it is and how it functions on its own. In other words, the Creator shows us what is divinely willed to exist, and how it functions, but not how the Creator wills the human being *qua* person to use this existing reality."[36] Fuchs goes on to assert that: "Neither the Hebrew Bible nor the New Testament produces statements that are independent of culture and thus universal and valid for all time; nor can these statements be given by the church or its magisterium. Rather, it is the task of human beings—of the various persons who have been given the requisite intellectual capacity—to investigate what can and must count as a conviction about these responsibilities."[37] In other words, God creates, but he gives no operating instructions.[38]

Father Fuchs asserts that: "One cannot. . . deduce, from God's relationship to creation, what the obligation of the human person is in these areas or in the realm of creation as a whole."[39] Regarding *Gaudium et spes*, where the human conscience is spoken of as a *sacrarium* in which we find ourselves responsibly before God—*solus cum solo*[40]—Fuchs states that the notion that "the human person is illuminated by a light that comes, not from one's own reason. . .but from the wisdom of God in whom everything is created. . .cannot stand up to an objective analysis nor prove helpful in the vocabulary of Christian believers."[41]

Father Fuchs's rejection of the council's teaching on the nature of conscience at least has the virtue of consistency. It follows from his own doctrine that while God creates, he does not govern the human mind. The human mind is a merely natural light, to which there corresponds a merely natural jurisdiction over ethics. In its work of discovering moral norms, the mind discovers the contextual proportions of good and evil, case by case as it were. Although Fuchs struggles to avoid the implication, it would seem that no general statute of positive law could concretely bind human conscience because it could never adequately measure the proportions of good and evil across cases and contexts. At best, law would be a summary of previous findings, which then functions as an indicator (rather than a norm) of present or future choices.

Hence, specifically on the issue of natural law, Fuchs insists that: "A classical understanding of natural law is basically a 'positivist' understanding of natural law (a static law 'written on nature'), and precisely does not offer genuine natural law as the living an active creaturely participation in God's eternal wisdom."[42] The traditional words are still present: e.g., "written on the heart," "participation in God's eternal wisdom." But they now mean something different, and in fact the opposite of the tradition in Augustine and Aquinas. For the older tradition, there is a clear distinction between the agency of the mind discovering or discerning norms and the being or cause of the norm. The human mind can go on to make new rules because it is first ruled. This, in essence, is the doctrine of participation as applied to natural law. Natural law designates for Fuchs, however, the human power to make moral judgments, not any moral norm regulating that power—at least no norm extrinsic to the operations of the mind. This is not a subtle departure from the tradition; nor more subtle than the difference between giving a teenager the keys to the car with a set of instructions, and just giving him the keys to the car.

VI. *Veritatis splendor*

The encyclicals usually have pastoral purposes. Fundamental principles are cited only insofar as is needed to address the problem at hand, or perhaps to remind the faithful of what everyone believes. *Veritatis splendor* takes a different approach. Noting that the Church has proposed moral teaching on "many different spheres of human life," Pope John Paul goes on to declare: "Today, however, it seems necessary to reflect on the whole of the Church's moral teaching, with the precise goal of recalling certain fundamental truths of Catholic doctrine which, in the present circumstances, risk being distorted or denied." (*VS* 4.2)

Veritatis splendor is not aimed at a consensus-building among the gentiles. It is addressed to the episcopacy. Moreover, it is important to bear in mind that the encyclical is not chiefly concerned with applied ethics, but with the foundations of moral theology (*VS* 4.2).

The first statement about the crisis over foundations concerns the authority of the Church: "the magisterium itself is considered capable of intervening in matters of morality only in order to 'exhort consciences' and to 'propose values,' in the light of which each individual will independently make his or her decisions and life choices." (*VS* 37.1)

If the crisis only concerned the authority of the Church, the pope would be putting moral theology into precisely the corner where the modern mind wants it: for it would look like the assertion of a this-worldly power to command; an assertion that is immediately answered by a counter assertion of the authority of individual conscience. The pope needs to show that being commanded by another is not merely the device of ecclesiastical powers and offices; it is not created by papal authority or by tradition.

The pope therefore reformulates the issue:

> [C]ertain moral theologians have introduced a sharp distinction, contrary to Catholic doctrine, between an ethical order, which would be human in origin and of value for this world alone, and an order of salvation for which only certain intentions and interior attitudes regarding God and neighbor would

> be significant. This has then led to an actual denial that there exists, in divine revelation, a specific and determined moral content, universally valid and permanent. The word of God would be limited to proposing an exhortation . . . which the autonomous reason alone would then have the task of completing with normative directives which are truly "objective," that is, adapted to the concrete historical situation. (*VS* 37.1)

Here, at last, we reach something fundamental for moral theology. Is the moral order a creature of divine providence, or does divine governance have to be added on to an already complete and autonomous human jurisdiction over morals? Here, we are not worrying about the morality of gambling or contraception. Rather, the problem is the condition(s) of the possibility of moral theology. If God only provides the "natural" conditions for human practical reason, giving the human mind a kind of plenary authority over all of the material norms, then God does not govern—except perhaps in the metaphorical fashion suggested by some of the Deists.

> Were this autonomy to imply a denial of the participation of the practical reason in the wisdom of the divine Creator and Lawgiver, or were it to suggest a freedom which creates moral norms, on the basis of historical contingencies or the diversity of societies and cultures, this sort of alleged autonomy would contradict the Church's teaching on the truth about man. It would be the death of true freedom: "But of the tree of the knowledge of good and evil you shall not eat, for in the day that you eat of it you shall die" (Gn 2:17). (*VS* 40)

Throughout *Veritatis splendor*, the pope tries to give all three *foci* of natural law their due:

1. An order of nature (the "truth about man").
2. The rudiments of which are "in principle accessible to human reason." (*VS* 74.4)
3. Which are expressions of divine providence.

At least in passing, he notes the relevance of (1) and (2) to the "demands of dialogue and cooperation with non-Catholics and non-believers, especially in pluralistic societies"(*VS* 74.4). Reflection on the good and evil of human acts and of the person who performs them is "accessible to all people" (*VS* 29). However, there can no mistaking the main emphasis of the encyclical, which concerns (3).

The question is how to give all three foci their due, while still showing their proper organization in theology. In the *Institutes*, John Calvin quotes St. Bernard of Clairvaux: "With propriety, therefore, Bernard teaches that the gate of salvation is opened to us, when in the present day we receive the Gospel with our ears, as death was once admitted at the same doors when they lay open to Satan. For Adam had never dared to resist the authority of God, if he had not discredited his word."[44]

The pope adopts a similar strategy of exposition, one that is dialogical from the very beginning. While never denying the fact that man enjoys natural starting points for grasping moral good and evil, the pope puts man into conversation with God; he interrupts the soliloquy.

Notice how the major chapters are arranged:

- In the first chapter the reader is situated along the road where the rich young man encounters Christ (Mt 19). The pope contends that questions about the good are essentially religious questions.

- In the second chapter the reader is resituated in the light of the original conversation between God and man in Genesis 2. Most of the discussion of natural law takes place in this context.

- In the third chapter the reader is turned toward the world, according to the theme of martyrdom and witness.

- In the conclusion the reader stands with Mary at the foot of the cross.

In the first chapter, he explains that the first and ultimate question of morality is not a lawyerly question. Unlike the Pharisees, the rich young man does not ask what the bottom line is, from a legal standpoint. Rather, he asks what must be done in order to achieve the unconditional good, which is communion with God. Christ takes the sting out of law, not by annulling it, but by revealing the Good to which it directs us. Remove or forget the Good, and it is inevitable that law becomes legalism.

The Scripture relates that the young man went away sad, for he had many possessions. But the modern audience is more apt to turn away sad when faced with the teaching that there is a moral law that is indispensable, and indeed which binds authority itself. The pope points out that all issues of circumstance, culture, place, and time notwithstanding, certain actions can never be made right, and that no human "law" can make them right. Just as from the scales and axiomatic measures of music there can come a Beethoven sonata or a Penderecki twelve-tone composition, so too from obedience to the Commandments there opens the possibility of a creative, fluid, and completely realized human liberty. The point of learning the scales is not mindless repetition; the point is to make beautiful music. No doubt, a piano teacher who focused only upon the scales would be a simpleton, a legalist as it were. But a piano teacher who neglected to call the pupil's attention to the scalar rudiments would not be worthy of the name teacher. Musical order does not, and indeed cannot, begin merely with human spontaneity and creative improvisation. The same is true in the domain of moral action. Anyone who would set up an opposition between law and freedom, and then take the side of freedom, not only underestimates the need for law, but misrepresents the nature of freedom.

The story of the rich young man, of course, shows the essential unity of the Law and the Gospel. In *Veritatis splendor* the pope also spends considerable effort dealing with a related theme: namely, the unity of the two tables of the Decalogue. "*Acknowledging the Lord as God,*" he says, "*is the very core, the heart of the Law,* from which the particular precepts flow and toward which they are ordered" (*VS* 11.1). Each precept, he continues, ". . .is the interpretation of what the words 'I am the Lord your God' mean for man" (*VS* 13.2).

"To ask about the good," in fact, "ultimately means to turn towards God," the fullness of goodness. Jesus shows that the young man's question is really a "religious question, and that the goodness that attracts and at the same time obliges man has its source in God, and indeed is God himself" (*VS* 9.3).[54] Georges Cottier, the Dominican theologian of the papal household, has underscored the importance of this point in the encyclical: ". . . awareness of the self as an image of God is at the root of moral judgments, beginning with the norms of the moral law. . . . The image is turned toward its Archetype and is the origin of a desire for union with it and assimilation to it. The natural law makes known to our reason the essential goods to which we must tend in order to reach God, who is the supreme Good."[46]

In the second chapter, the pope takes the discussion of the foundations of the moral order back to the original situation in Genesis 2. This is the patristic common place for the discussion of natural law. Ever since his catechesis on the Book of Genesis, given during his weekly audiences in 1979–80 (published under the title of *Original Unity of Man and Woman*) the pope has returned over and over to the first four chapters of Genesis.[47]

> Some people . . . disregarding the dependence of human reason on Divine Wisdom . . . have actually posited a "complete sovereignty of reason in the domain of moral norms regarding the right ordering of life in this world. Such norms would constitute the boundaries for a merely "human" morality; they would be the expression of a law which man in an autonomous manner lays down for himself and which has its source exclusively in human reason. In no way could God be considered the Author of this law, except in the sense that human reason exercises its autonomy in setting down laws by virtue of a primordial and total mandate given to man by God. These trends of thought have led to a denial, in opposition to Sacred Scripture (cf. Mt 15:3–6) and the Church's constant teaching, of the fact that the natural moral law has God as its author, and that man, by the use of reason, participates in the eternal law, which it is not for him to establish" (*VS* 36.3).

Turning to the injunction in Genesis 2:17, the pope writes:

> By forbidding man to "eat of the tree of the knowledge of good and evil," God makes it clear that man does not originally possess such "knowledge" as something properly his own, but only participates in it by the light of natural reason and of Divine Revelation, which manifest to him the requirements and promptings of eternal wisdom. Law must therefore be considered an expression of divine wisdom. (*VS* 41.2)

The natural condition of man is one of participation in a higher norm. Man has liberty to direct himself because he is first directed by another.[48]

The pope makes use of a number of authorities to express the idea of natural law as "participated theonomy."[49] He refers to Psalm 4:6 ("Let the light of your face shine upon us, O Lord"), emphasizing that moral knowledge derives from a divine illumination (*VS* 2.1); from Romans 2:15 ("The *gentiles* who had not the Law, did naturally the things of the Law"), he calls attention to the idea that is not just by positive law that humans are directed in the moral order *(VS* 12.1, 46); from Gregory of Nyssa, he cites the passage that autonomy is predicated only of a king *(VS* 38.1); from St. Bonaventure, he cites the dictum that conscience does not bind on its own authority, but is rather the "herald of a king" *(VS* 58). The very existence of conscience, the pope argues, indicates that we are under a law that we did not impose upon ourselves.[50] Conscience is not a witness to a human power; it is a witness to the natural law. And this is only to say that the natural law is a real law which cannot be equated with our conscience. It was precisely this equation, the pope notes, that beguiled our first parents, when the serpent in Genesis 3:5 said they could be as gods. What does it mean to be as gods? It means that the human mind is a measuring-measure, having plenary authority to impart the measures of moral good and evil.

The pope also notes that the topic of natural law has been too readily detached from the economy of divine laws and pedagogy.

> Even if moral-theological reflection usually distinguishes between the positive or revealed law of God and the natural law, and, within the economy of salvation, between the "old" and the "new" law, it must not be forgotten that these and other useful distinctions always refer to that law whose author is the one and the same God and which is always meant for man. The different ways in which God, acting in history, cares for the world and for mankind are not mutually exclusive; on the contrary, they support each other and intersect. They have their origin and goal in the eternal, wise and loving counsel whereby God predestines men and women "to be conformed to the image of his Son" (Rom 8:29). God's plan poses no threat to man's genuine freedom; on the contrary, the acceptance of God's plan is the only way to affirm that freedom.(*VS* 45.2)

It is surely a token of the disrepair of Catholic moral theology that the bishop of Rome would have to remind the episcopacy, and through them, the moral theologians, that natural law does not constitute a sphere of immunity (a kind of cosmic tenure for moral theologians) from the plan of divine laws.[51] But once again, what the pope has to grapple with in this respect is not only decades of neglect *ad intra*, where the theme of natural law was detached from the fundamental principles of theology, but also the history *ad extra*, where natu-

ral law and natural rights betokened that ground of liberty in which
men find themselves under no mundane authority. This secular myth,
which was developed as a counter to Genesis, is contrary to the most
fundamental principles of Christian theology.

However the Church might find a common ground of discourse
with the gentiles, it cannot be done on the basis of the that counter
myth. Of course, some truths about the nature of man and the
structure of moral reasoning are, as the pope says, "in principle
accessible to human reason." He does not discredit the effort of
modern polities to affirm human rights and to place moral limits
upon the power of the state.

Having duly noted the existence of principles proximate to human
reason, the pope emphasizes two things. They correspond, in turn, to the
two other foci of natural law: natural law in the mind, and in nature.

First, he reminds the reader of the wounded human condition
that needs to be repaired by Christ:

> What is more, within his errors and negative decisions, man
> glimpses the source of a deep rebellion, which leads him to re-
> ject the truth and the good in order to set himself up as an ab-
> solute principle unto himself: "you will be like God" (Gn 3:5).
> Consequently, freedom itself needs to be set free. It is Christ
> who sets it free: He "has set us free for freedom" (cf. Gal 5:1).
> (*VS* 86.2)

Second, he insists that human reason, endeavoring to construct the
conditions for human fulfillment, needs revelation and grace.

> Only in the mystery of Christ's Redemption do we discover
> the "concrete" possibilities of man. It would be a very seri-
> ous error to conclude . . . that the Church's teaching is essen-
> tially only an "ideal" which must then be adapted, propor-
> tioned, graduated to the so-called concrete possibilities of
> man, according to a "balancing of the goods in question."
> But what are the "concrete possibilities of man"? And of
> which man are we speaking? Of man dominated by lust or
> of man redeemed by Christ? (*VS* 103.3)

VII. Conclusion

What can Evangelical Protestants learn from this story? They might
conclude that Karl Barth was right.

> It [moral theology] is in agreement with every other ethics
> adduced to the extent that the latter is obviously aware

explicitly or implicitly—of its origin and basis in God's command; to the extent that it does not seek authorization before any other court; to the extent that it actually attests the existence and validity of this principle. But it cannot and will not take it seriously to the extent that it tries to deny or obscure its derivation from God's command, to set up independent principles in face of autonomies and heteronomies which comprise the theonomy of human existence and action, to confront divine ethics with a human view of the world and of life which is supposed to have its own (if anything) superior value, and to undertake the replacement of the command of the grace of God by a sovereign humanism or even barbarism.[52]

It would be tendentious, of course, to suggest a meeting of the minds between Barth and *Veritatis splendor*. But on this one point of theonomous ethics, there is more than a merely facile similarity. By way of negation, we can agree that the modern, secular construction of natural law is contrary to the Gospel. It is as destructive within the house of Catholic moral theology as it was in the Protestant denominations, who passed through the challenge of Deism and liberalism a century before the Catholic Church.

In a certain respect, the degrading of Catholic moral theology is more cruel because Catholicism has staked more on this issue of natural law than Protestantism. The repair will also be more complicated for Catholics, among other reasons, because the Catholic tradition has regarded the two foci of natural law in the mind and in things as having (some) intelligibility for those who know little or nothing of the revelation of Jesus Christ, and who have not given any effort to reconnecting them back to the architectonic perspective of divine providence. These foci cannot be brushed away under the rubric of the "epistemology of sin," as some Protestants are wont to do. Moreover, the Catholic Church has endeavored to address problems of justice in the temporal order according to principles immediately proximate to it.

The problem, for Catholics, is how to do all of this without on the one hand creating the misleading impression *ad extra* that these proximate principles are the end of the story, and without on the other hand reducing *ad intra* its own moral theology to a habit of extroversion—to having a merely worldly opinion about disputed issues in the temporal order, which opinion is then configured to conform to the consensus (if any) among the gentiles.

Today, especially in the United States, Evangelical Protestants find themselves reconsidering the issue of natural law. Their interest seems to be occasioned by two things. First, the political success of Evangelical Protestantism has made it necessary to frame an appropriate language for addressing civil politics and law. Second, the Evangelicals find themselves having to dialogue with Catholics, with whom they share many common interests in matters of culture and politics—interests which would seem amenable to natural law discussion. Even though it is true that many Protestants today are chiefly interested in use of natural law *ad extra*, as a way to speak to the "world," the lesson they might learn from recent Catholic moral theology runs in the other direction. For assuming the legitimate and persistent need of the Christian churches to address worldly issues of justice and morality, it is easy to lose control of this discourse, so that natural law makes moral theology superfluous, and even impossible.

It seems to me that the expression "natural law" ought to be avoided whenever possible in the Christian address to the world about worldly things. I realize that this is practically impossible, but I shall give the reasons anyway.

Catholics, and most Protestants, will agree that there is a sphere of moral discourse about public matters that can be distinguished from sermonics and catechetics. The question is whether we should refer to the moral discourse in this sphere as "natural law." Of course, we believe it is the natural law that renders the gentiles amenable to the rudiments of moral discourse. In view of the traditional Catholic understanding of this matter (still put forth in the new *Catechism of the Catholic Church*),[53] we believe that what the gentiles know is an effect of divine pedagogy, whether the gentiles know that or not. Christians do not need to teach or to construct the first rudiments of the "natural law," for this much is not the effect of human pedagogy in the first place. God, not our discourse, constitutes human creatures as moral agents. The basis of moral order will not stand or fall on whether, or to what extent, we use the words "natural law."

The problem is not whether the gentiles are moral agents, but rather the meanings they assign to the rudiments they possess by virtue of the natural law. In modern times, the rudiments have been gathered into ideologies of natural law or natural rights which are not only false, but are expressed in the form of a belligerent universalism. In our country, there is a long tradition of political rhetoric about natural rights. Sadly, today most uses of this rhetoric are degraded, signifying the expansion of individual liberty on terms which are either non-moral or contrary to the moral order. Even John Courtney Murray insisted that the rhetoric was historically rooted in ideologies of the Enlightenment that ought to be corrected by a true account. Indeed, Murray's account of the American consensus includes explicit theological propositions about the relationship between moral order and divine providence. If there is a widespread dissent from these propositions, the basis for a public philosophy will collapse.[54]

Father Murray would have been mortified, but perhaps not completely surprised, by the spectacle of that collapse in our times. In 1991, on the eve of the Senate hearings on the nomination of Clarence Thomas to the Supreme Court, Senator Joseph Biden took the position that the Judiciary Committee should explore whether Judge Thomas held a "good" or "bad" theory of natural law. A bad theory of natural law, in Biden's view, would seek to expound a "code of behavior . . . suggesting that natural law dictates morality to us, instead of leaving matters to individual choice."[55] A good theory, on the other hand, would support individual rights of immunity against morals legislation on matters of personal sexual conduct and abortion. The natural law teachings in recent papal encyclicals would have to be regarded as "bad" natural law.

For public purposes, it is more prudent to ridicule than to argue with positions like Biden's. But the problem remains. Christians in search of a sphere of public moral discourse discover that they no longer live in the age of Jefferson and Lincoln. The moral discourse of the public sphere abounds with the rhetoric of natural law, to be sure; but it is terribly degraded. The most serious setbacks in our political and legal order have been done in the name of natural law, abortion rights being the most evident, but by no means the only, case in point. How then do Christians correct the ideologies in which natural law is ensconced without going on to discuss those very things which public discourse is supposed to avoid? How can Christians avoid the task of having to actually reconstitute the sphere of public moral discourse? If Christians wish to do so, I can see no alternative than to restore natural law rhetoric to its true and adequate premises. At the very least, we should return to the older American custom of speaking of "higher law." This usage, employed by Martin Luther King Jr., has the advantage of semantics which indicate the more than human ground for the public moral order.

The Church Fathers referred to pagan learning as the gold of Egypt, which could be melted down from the idols. But the modern ideologies of natural law and natural rights are quite different. For the moderns took the theological notion of natural law and re-shaped idols. If it is necessary to take public discourse where it stands, and by the arts of the dialectic and rhetoric to move it away from the idols, it must be done very cautiously. When the Christian theologian plays with the modern rhetoric of natural law, he should know that he is playing with something more than fire. *Ad extra*, he is apt to underestimate the anti-theological meanings of modern natural law (essentially, man as a free agent without God), meanings which are easily reinforced if the rhetoric is not corrected; *ad intra*, he is liable to bring the idols back into the house of moral theology.

Both of these problems are addressed in recent encyclicals. To conclude, let us return to John Paul II's example. As I pointed out earlier, the pope vigorously supports the modern experiment in constitutional democracy and human rights. But once he discerned that the rhetoric of natural rights was being used to justify killing the unborn and infirm, he took his readers in *Evangelium vitae* back to the Book of Genesis. The gentiles need and deserve the whole truth, even in order to preserve the rationality embedded in their own "secular" experiment. As for the use of natural law within moral theology, *Veritatis splendor* reintegrates natural law into the dogmatic theology of revelation and Christology. It seems to me that these two encyclicals, one aimed *ad extra*, the other *ad intra*, get the problem of natural law situated just about right.

Endnotes

1. Thanks to Steve Long, Robert Tuttle, and Keith Pavilschek, who made useful suggestions and criticisms of earlier drafts of this paper.
2. Yves R. Simon, *The Tradition of Natural Law: A Philosopher's Reflections*, ed. Vukan Kuic, intro. by Russell Hittinger (New York: Fordham University Press, 1992 reprint), 5.
3. Ibid, 15.
4. Barth, *Church Dogmatics* II/1, 36.
5. Tertullian, *Adv. Iudaeos*, cap. 2 (PL 2–2:599, 600), *"quasi matrix omnium praeceptorum Dei. . . non scriptam, quae naturaliter intelligebatur."*

6. A millennium later, Thomas Aquinas would also refer to the time between the fall and the Law as the time of the law of nature, when God left men to what little they could glean from the original law in order to curb their pride (*STh* I–II, q. 98, a. 6). As for who knew and abided by the natural law, Thomas says the patriarchs, who were men of faith. Commenting on the figurative meaning of the sacrifices in the Jewish ceremonies, Thomas tries to draw together the phases of revelation in Christology:

> The figurative cause is that the bread signifies Christ Who is the *panis vivus* [living bread], as stated in Jn 6. He was indeed an ear of corn, as it were, during the state of the law of nature, and in the faith of the patriarchs; he was like flour in the doctrine of the Law of the prophets; and he was like perfect bread after he had taken human nature; baked in the fire, that is, formed by the Holy Spirit in the oven of the virginal womb; baked again in a pan by the toils which he suffered in the world; and consumed by fire on the cross as on a gridiron. (*STh* I–II, q. 102, a. 3, ad 12)

For Thomas's estimation of Abraham, see infra note 21.

7. Gregory of Nyssa, *The Life of Moses*, II, trans., intro., and notes by Abraham J. Malherbe and Everett Ferguson (New York: Paulist Press, 1978), 215–16.
8. Note the similarity to Thomas's formulation of the first precept of law in *STh* I–II, q. 94, a. 2: "*Bonum est faciendum et prosequendum, et malum vitandum,*" "the good is to be done and pursued, and evil resisted." Thomas calls it the *primum praeceptum legis*, the first precept of law.
9. Regarding debates *ad extra*, the patristic theologians tend to worry about rival Jewish or Gnostic accounts of divine governance. Gnostics asserted that the "law" in Genesis 2:17 was a dietary (and hence a positive) law of the Demiurge, the same deity that shows up later in Jewish Scriptures giving more positive (and usually dietary) laws. Against the rabbis, Christian apologists contended not only that there is law after the Mosaic law, but that the *lex nova* restores a law antecedent to Sinai.
10. "*per primam Dei gratiam, id est per legem naturae*" (DS 336).
11. *Instit. Justin.* I.2
12. Ibid. I.2.3.
13. Ibid. IV.18.4.
14. *Decretum Gratiani* I. D. 1, can. 3, 4.
15. *STh* I–II, q. 91.
16. The new *Catechism of the Catholic Church* gathers all law together under the rubric "moral law," the various species designating modes of divine pedagogy. CCC 1950–52.
17. *STh* I–II, q. 91, a. 2, ad 1.
18. It is an understandable, but regrettable, mistake to focus exclusively on *STh* I–II, q. 94. Here, indeed, Thomas speaks of natural law in terms of what is first in the mind and first in nature. He makes no reference to God. But in q. 94 he is not defining the natural law; the *ratio formalis*—what it is, and what makes it law—is discussed in qq. 91 and 93. Question 94 takes up the *ratio materialis*: natural law as an effect in the creature.
19. *STh* I–II, q. 93, a. 2.
20. *STh* I–II, q. 90, a. 4, ad 1.
21. *In II Rom.*, lectio 3 (215–16). St. Thomas notes that unless we distinguish between these two classes of gentiles, Romans 2:14 would be open to a Pelagian reading of these two words *naturaliter* and *faciunt*. In *STh* III, q. 1, a. 6, St. Thomas contends that the election of Abraham and the dispensation of the law to Moses presupposed the restoration of knowledge of the sovereign of the natural law: "He was pleased to choose Abraham as a standard of the restored knowledge of God and of holy living [in quo forma esset renovatae notitiae Dei et morum]."
22. *STh* I, q. 1, a. 1.
23. *STh* II–II, q. 94, a. 1.
24. Thomas Aquinas, *Collationes in Decem Praeceptis*, I, line 27, edition critique avec introduction et notes, par Jean-Pierre Torrell, in *Revue des sciences philosophiques et theologiques* 69 (1985), 5–40, 227–63.
25. *STh* I–II, q. 97, a. 1, ad 1.

26. *STh* I–II, q. 89, a. 6.
27. *STh* I–II, q. 98, a. 6.
28. Thomas Hobbes, *De homine*, 10.5.
29. *"Flumina honestatis redeunt ad mare iuris naturalis, quod ita processit, ut quod in primo homine paene perditum est, in lege Mosaica revelaretur, in evangelio perficeretur, in moribus decoraretur"* (Johannes Faventinus, *Summa*, Brit. Mus., MS Royal 9 E. vii, fol. 2, c. 2).
30. For example, *Diuturnum*, issued on June 29, 1881, three months after the assassination of the Russian Czar Alexander II, who was killed on the very day that he signed a new liberal constitution, directly criticizes the secular ideologies of natural law.
31. Cardinal Maurice Roy, "Occasion of the Tenth Anniversary of the Encyclical 'Pacem in terris'" (April 11, 1973), no. 128, in Joseph Gremillion, *The Gospel of Peace and Justice* (New York: Orbis, 1976), 557.
32. *Pacem in terris*, 1.
33. Yves Simon was a conspicuous exception. He worried that the problem of natural law in our times is not so much the need to defend the idea against its cultured critics, but rather to prevent it from being ensconced in ideologies formed under the practical pressure of responding to the various intellectual and institutional felonies of modern life.
    Our time has witnessed a new birth of belief in natural law concomitantly with the success of existentialism, which represents the most thorough criticism of natural law ever voiced by philosophers. Against such powers of destruction we feel the need for an ideology of natural law. The current interest in this subject certainly expresses an aspiration of our society at a time when the foundations of common life and of just relations are subjected to radical threats. No matter how sound these aspirations may be, they are quite likely to distort philosophic treatments. For a number of years we have been witnessing a tendency, in teachers and preachers, to assume that natural law decides, with the universality proper to the necessity of essences, incomparably more issues than it is actually able to decide. There is a tendency to treat in terms of natural law questions which call for treatment in terms of prudence. It should be clear that any concession to this tendency is bound promptly to cause disappointment and skepticism. (Simon, *The Tradition of Natural Law*, 23)
34. Joseph Cardinal Bernardin, "Seeking A Common Ground on Human Rights," *De Paul Law Review* 36 (1987), 159–65.
35. Servais Pinckaers, O.P., *The Sources of Christian Ethics*, trans. Sr. Mary Thomas Noble, O.P. (Washington D.C.: The Catholic University of America Press, 1995), 298–99.
36. Josef Fuchs, *Moral Demands and Personal Obligations*, trans. Brian McNeil (Washington, D.C.: Georgetown University Press, 1993), 100.
37. Ibid., 55.
38. The majority of Paul VI's Commission for the Study of Problems of the Family, Population, and Birth Rate issued a report urging that the Church change her teaching on contraception. The authors of the majority report at least had the honesty to state clearly their theological premise. They reasoned that although the sources of human life are from created nature, the rules for the choice and administration of that natural value fall to human jurisdiction. "To take his own or another's life is a sin," the Majority Report contended, "not because life is under the exclusive dominion of God but because it is contrary to right reason unless there is question of a good or a higher order."
39. Fuchs, *Moral Demands*, 39.
40. "Deep within his conscience man discovers a law which he has not laid upon himself but which he must obey. Its voice, ever calling him to love and to do what is good and to avoid evil, tells him inwardly at the right moment: do this, shun that. For man has in his heart a law inscribed by God. His dignity lies in observing this law, and by it he will be judged. His conscience is man's most secret core, and his sanctuary. There he is alone with God whose voice echoes in his depths" (*Gaudium et spes* 16).

41. Fuchs, *Moral Demands*, 157.
42. Ibid., 40.
43. The subtitle reads: *De fundamentis doctrinae moralis ecclesiae,* "Concerning the Foundations of the Church's Moral Teaching."
44. John Calvin, *Institutes of the Christian Religion,* trans. from the Latin by John Allen, in 2 vols. (Philadelphia: Presbyterian Board of Christian Education, 1936), I, ii.1, at 270.
45. See Karol Wojtyla, *Love and Responsibility,* trans. H. T. Willetts (San Francisco: Ignatius Press, 1981), 223: "For 'a religious man' means not so much 'one who is capable of religious experiences' (as is generally supposed) as above all 'one who is just to God the Creator.'"
46. Georges Cottier, O.P., "Morality of a human acts depends primarily on object chosen by will" (*L'osservatore Romano* 6 [February 9, 1994], 11).
47. E.g., in *Laborem exercens* and *Evangelium vitae.*
48. In Scholastic parlance, the human reason is a measuring measure (*mensura mensurans*) only insofar as it is first a measured measure (*mensura mensurata*).
49. "Others speak, and rightly so, of theonomy, or participated theonomy, since man's free obedience to God's law effectively implies that human reason and human will participate in God's wisdom and providence" (*Veritatis splendor* 41.2).
50. "The judgment of conscience does not establish the law; rather it bears witness to the authority of the natural law and of the practical reason with reference to the supreme good, whose attractiveness the human person perceives and whose commandments he accepts" (ibid. 60).
51. In the *London Tablet* Bernard Häring rejected *Veritatis splendor,* basing his objection (in part) on a right of conscience grounded in natural law. See *National Catholic Reporter* November 5, 1993.
52. Barth, *Church Dogmatics* II/1, 36, "Ethics as a Task of the Doctrine of God," 527.
53. See supra, note 16.
54. John Courtney Murray, S.J., *We Hold These Truths* (New York: Image Books, 1964), 53.
55. Sen. Joseph Biden, "Law and Natural Law," *Washington Post* (September 8, 1991). Senator Biden, it can be recalled, voted against the confirmation of Robert Bork because, among other reasons, Bork expressly rejected judicial uses of natural law. Against Bork, Biden declared: "I have certain inalienable rights because I exist."

The Truth about Freedom: A Theme from John Paul II*

Avery Dulles, S.J.

For Lord Acton, according to Gertrude Himmelfarb, liberty was no mere social arrangement recommended by convenience but was on the contrary "the highest ideal of man, the reflection of his divinity."[1] Another great historian of the concept of freedom, Mortimer Adler, writes that "there is perhaps no philosophical idea which has had so much impact on political action."[2] For centuries, he points out, the world has been divided by rival conceptions of freedom. Whether liberty consists in doing what one likes or in doing what one ought makes an overriding difference in practice. A great cleavage exists between those who absolutize freedom and those who hold that true freedom can only be freedom in the truth.

The rootedness of freedom in the truth has been a constant and central theme in the writings of John Paul II. Already in 1964, as a young bishop at Vatican II, Karol Wojtyla, as he was then called, criticized the draft of the declaration on religious freedom because it did not sufficiently emphasize the connection between freedom and truth. "For freedom on the one hand is for the sake of truth and on the other hand it cannot be perfected except by means of truth. Hence the words of our Lord, which speak so clearly to everyone: 'The truth will make you free' (Jn 8:32). There is no freedom without truth."[3]

Again in his first encyclical *Redemptor hominis* (1979) John Paul II quoted the words of Christ, "You will know the truth, and the truth will make you free." He added: "These words contain both a fundamental requirement and a warning: The requirement of an honest relationship with regard to truth as a condition for authentic freedom, and the warning to avoid every kind of illusory freedom,

* Delivered at the Acton Institute, Grand Rapids, Michigan, on February 1, 1995. Permission to reprint has been granted by the Acton Institute.

every superficial unilateral freedom, every freedom that fails to enter into the whole truth about man and the world."[4]

In his encyclical *Veritatis splendor*, the pope rejects a series of ethical systems that propose novel criteria for the moral evaluation of human action.[5] Despite their variety, he declares, these systems are at one in minimizing or even denying the dependence of freedom upon truth. This dependence, he says, finds its clearest and most authoritative expression in the words of Christ, "You will know the truth, and the truth will make you free" (*VS* 34.3).

The pope's philosophy of freedom runs counter to the value-free concept so prevalent in contemporary culture, perhaps especially in the United States. Many people today would say that freedom and truth are wholly separable, since anyone is free to affirm the truth and abide by it, to ignore the truth, or even to deny it and act against it. If freedom were bound by the truth, they ask, how could it be freedom? In the course of his discussion of freedom and law in *Veritatis splendor*, the pope proposes his answer to questions such as these.

I. The Concept of Freedom

Before undertaking to answer these difficulties, we would do well, I believe, to take a close look at the meaning of the term "freedom," which has different implications at the natural and the personal levels.

At the lower level, that of nature, freedom means the absence of physical constraint. A balloon rises freely when nothing obstructs it; a stone falls freely when nothing impedes it. A dog is free if it is let off the leash so that it can follow its impulses. To be free, in this sense, is to act according to an inner inclination. To be unfree is to have that inclination frustrated.

At the higher level, distinctive to persons, freedom demands, in addition, the absence of psychological compulsion. My freedom as a person is limited to the extent that instinct or passion compels me to act in certain ways—for example, to flee from danger or flinch with pain.

If my motives could never transcend my individual self-interest or the collective self-interest of my group, I could never be truly free. I could always be manipulated and compelled act in specific ways by fear of punishment or hope of reward. Just as animals can be drawn by dangling a carrot in front of their noses, or by wielding a whip, so a child can be induced to behave in certain ways by the prospect of gratification or the fear of pain. Unable to escape from the determinism of instinct or appetite, we could be forced to act by threats and promises.

One of the benefits of training and discipline is to enhance our zone of inner freedom. By education and exercise we develop the motivation and character that enables us to resist physical and especially psychological pressures. Some learn to go for long periods without sleep, to abstain from food, or to endure intense physical pain without abandoning their resolve. Such persons have greater freedom than others. They have a larger zone of inner self-determination.

In determining my own course of action, I cannot dispense with motives. If choices were completely arbitrary, freedom would be meaningless and in the last analysis impossible. In my free actions I follow what I apprehend as good and worthy of being chosen, but the choice is not forced upon me. I consent to the attraction because my reason approves of it. In acting freely, I experience myself as the source of my own activity and as responsible for the results. My actions recoil to some degree on myself, and so make me to be what I am. Thus the freedom to determine one's activity is at the same time self-determination. The present pope explains this at some length in his major work, *The Acting Person*, and in various philosophical essays written before he became pope.[6]

In *Veritatis splendor* John Paul II quotes St. Gregory of Nyssa on the royal dignity that pertains to those who have this kind of dominion over themselves. "The soul shows its royal and exalted character ... in that it is free and self-governed, swayed autonomously by its own will. Of whom else can this be said, save a king?"[7] According to the pope, freedom does not attain this royal dignity until it rises to the level of making choices that perfect the dynamism of the human spirit toward the divine, following motives that solicit its free adherence. To this effect the pope quotes from Vatican II: "God willed to leave them [human beings) 'in the hands of their own counsel' (cf. Sir 15:14), that they would seek their Creator of their own accord and would freely arrive at full and blessed perfection by cleaving to God" (*Gaudium et spes* 17; *VS* 38.1). As I have said, we possess this freedom only when we go beyond individual and collective selfishness and reach out to that which reason perceives as objectively good and true. Our freedom is not diminished but expanded and fulfilled when we employ it to bring about a true good. This, again, is the teaching of Vatican II:

> Human dignity requires one to act through conscious and free choice, as motivated and prompted personally from within, and not through blind impulse or merely external pressure. People achieve such dignity when they free themselves from all sub-servience to their feelings, and in a free choice of the good, pursue their own end by effectively and assiduously marshaling the appropriate means. (*GS* 17; *VS* 42)

Because the moral law, as known by reason, does not constrain us, it leaves us physically and psychologically free either to obey or to violate it. But if we reject the true good, we inevitably yield to the passions and instincts of our lower nature and thereby undermine our authentic freedom. To act freely against the truth is to erode freedom itself.

Michael Polanyi, the great philosopher of science, speaks in much the same terms as John Paul II. He writes:

> While compulsion by force or by neurotic obsession excludes responsibility, compulsion by universal intent establishes responsibility. . . . The freedom of the subjective person to do as he pleases is overruled by the freedom of the responsible person to act as he must.[8]

Lord Acton has often been praised for his statement that freedom is "not the power of doing what we like, but the right of being able to do what we ought."[9] As this definition indicates, Acton is concerned not so much with the philosophical as with the political definition of freedom. Those who have a constitutional right to do as they ought are politically free, and if they are not physically or psychologically impeded from following the moral imperative, they are also free in the philosophical sense of the word.

II. Freedom and Altruism

In his paper "The Personal Structure of Self-Determination," from which I have already drawn some ideas, John Paul II makes a further inference, based on the relational character of the person. Every person, he maintains, is both a being willed by God for itself and at the same time a being turned toward others. To be isolated from others is a form of self-imprisonment. We become most truly human in the measure that we go out of ourselves and give ourselves for the sake of others. This "law of the gift," as the pope calls it, is inscribed deep in the dynamic structure of the person as fashioned in the image of the divine.[10] He confirms this insight by quoting from Vatican II: "The human being, who is the only creature on earth that God willed for itself, cannot attain its full identity except through a disinterested gift of self" (*GS* 24). The citizen serves the common good out of a free commitment or devotion. Those who love God serve him freely, and if they refuse that service they undermine the freedom that love has given them. Those who obey the Commandments out of fear are not fully free, but they fall into even deeper slavery if they disobey God in order to gratify their own impulses. The truly free person is one who does what is good out of love for goodness itself.

Thinkers who consider the law of God to be a hindrance to human freedom have been misled into regarding obedience as a form of heteronomy or self-alienation, as though God were a hostile power imposing terms on humanity as a defeated enemy. In fact, God's law proceeds only from benevolence toward creatures whom God loves. The moral law is intended to safeguard human dignity. Human freedom and divine law conspire to the same end.

In this connection John Paul II speaks of "theonomy." Rational knowledge enables us to participate in the light of eternal wisdom, which is expressed in the divine law. In obeying God's law, I incline myself before his divine majesty and at the same time follow my deepest vocation as a creature. In the pope's own words, "Law must therefore be considered an expression of divine wisdom: by submitting to the law, freedom submits to the truth of creation. Consequently one must acknowledge in the freedom of the human person the image and the nearness of God, who is present in all (cf. Eph 4:6). But one must likewise acknowledge the majesty of the God of the universe and revere the holiness of the law of God, who is infinitely transcendent: Deus semper major" (*VS* 41.2).

The supreme exemplars of freedom, for John Paul II, are the martyrs. They are the heroic persons who are so committed to the known good that they stand up under pressures that would overcome the will power of most others. Given the choice between denying their principles and losing their lives, they freely lay down their lives and thereby give witness to the truth. Jesus, who freely laid down his life for our sake, sets the pattern for martyrs.

The martyrs represent an achievement of freedom beyond the capacities of the great majority of men and women. They inspire us by their example to rise above the more limited measure of freedom that we can claim for ourselves. For the theology of freedom it is important to recognize that the freedom with which we are born is frail and limited. John Paul II compares it to a seed that must be cultivated. Some degree of freedom is an essential part of the reflection of God that is constitutive of human nature, but our freedom is incomplete. Wounded as we are by original sin, we often prefer limited and ephemeral goods to those that are pure and abiding. We are even tempted to assert our freedom against our Creator, as if freedom could exist without regard for truth. God's redemptive action in Christ helps to liberate us from this illusion. As Paul writes in Galatians 5:1, "For freedom Christ has set us free" (*VS* 86.2). Since Christ himself is the truth (Jn 14:6), it is also correct to say that the truth sets us free (cf. Jn 8:32).

III. Freedom and Law

It is partly in revealing the law that God liberates his people. Already in the Old Testament, God brought the tribes of Israel out of bondage and united them to himself through the Sinai Covenant, which contained the basic precepts of the moral law. That covenant was perfected by the New Law of the Gospel, which Scripture describes as an interior law "written not with ink but with the Spirit of the living God, not on tablets of stone but on tablets of human hearts" (2 Cor 3:3, quoted in *VS* 45.1, with additional references to Jeremiah and Paul).

As a new and interior law, the Gospel teaches us both by enlightening our minds and by instilling a love and affection for the truth. The divinely given attraction toward the true goal of human existence, which is none other than God himself, does not impede our freedom of choice, since it inclines us toward the very thing that right reason would select. The inner instinct of grace heals our rebellious wills and inclines us to do as God wills. In so doing, it removes an obstacle to freedom—our innate tendency to pursue the immediate and apparent good rather than the ultimate and true good. It brings us closer to the final condition of the blessed in heaven, who cannot do other than love God, but who do so freely because they see how lovable God is.

IV. Freedom and Conscience

In speaking of the interior law of the Gospel imprinted by God on the human heart, I am inevitably raising the question of conscience, which is a subject of considerable confusion in our day. John Paul II remarks that the idea of conscience has been deformed by modern thinkers who have lost the sense of the transcendent and are in some cases atheistic. These thinkers often depict conscience as a supreme and infallible tribunal that dispenses us from considerations of law and truth, putting in their place purely subjective and individualist criteria such as sincerity, authenticity, and being at peace with oneself (*VS* 32). In opposition to this trend, John Paul II shows in *Veritatis splendor* that conscience is an act of intelligence that adheres to objective norms. The freedom of conscience is secured by its conformity to truth.

The classical biblical text on conscience, quoted by John Paul II, is Romans 2:14–16: "When Gentiles who have not the law do by nature what the law requires, they are a law unto themselves, even though they do not have the law. They show that what the law requires is written on their hearts, while their conscience also bears witness and their conflicting thoughts accuse or perhaps excuse them" (cf. *VS* 57).

The meaning of this dense and complex passage is clarified by a paragraph from Vatican II that John Paul II also quotes:

> In the depths of his own conscience man detects a law which he does not impose on himself, but which holds him to obedience. Always summoning him to love good and avoid evil, the voice of conscience can when necessary speak to his heart more specifically: 'Do this, shun that.' For man has in his heart a law written by God. To obey it is the very dignity of man; according to it he will be judged (cf. Rom 2:14–16)." (*GS* 16, quoted in *VS* 54.1)

According to these authoritative texts, conscience is not a purely subjective and autonomous principle; it is in no way opposed to the truth of God's law, which is its ground. Its judgments always presuppose the first principle of practical reason, the obligation to do good and avoid evil.

Paul, as we have seen, describes conscience as an unwritten law inscribed by God on the human heart. St. Bonaventure spells out this relationship more explicitly. In a text quoted by John Paul II he writes: "Conscience is like God's herald and messenger; it does not command things on its own authority, but commands them as coming from God's authority, like a herald when he proclaims the edict of a king. This is why conscience has a binding force."[11]

In the history of Catholic theology, John Henry Newman is outstanding for having clarified the relationship between conscience and God. Conscience, he writes in his Letter to the Duke of Norfolk, is the voice of God in the nature and heart of man.[12] In his *Grammar of Assent* Newman speaks of conscience as "our great internal teacher of religion."[13] It "teaches us not only that God is but what He is; it provides for the mind a real image of Him, as a medium of worship."[14] Newman then goes on to explain how it discloses God as lawgiver, judge, and rewarder. In a justly famous paragraph he declares: "Conscience is the aboriginal Vicar of Christ, a prophet in its informations, a monarch in its peremptoriness, a priest in its blessings and anathemas."[15]

Newman contrasts this true and traditional conception of conscience with what he calls its modern counterfeit. While some philosophers attack the very concept of conscience as a primitive and irrational force, the popular mind, in advocating the rights of conscience, really seeks to assert human self-will, without any thought of God at all. Conscience thus becomes "a license to take up any or no religion." For Newman, on the contrary, conscience is a stern monitor and is essentially bound up with the acknowledgment of God. "Conscience has its rights because it has duties."[16]

Building on passages such as these, John Paul II is able to show that, far from being a power to make one's decisions autonomously and creatively, conscience binds us to the law of God, to whom conscience is responsible. He then goes on to remark that conscience is neither adequate nor infallible as a source of moral guidance. Because it attests to a higher intelligence and will to which it is subject, it arouses a concern or anxiety to find out what course of action is here and now required of the individual to do good and avoid evil.

Conscience impels one to seek authoritative direction. Newman eloquently points out the providential role of the Church is supplying this need. In his Letter to the Duke of Norfolk he writes:

> All sciences, except the science of Religion, have their certainty in themselves; as far as they are sciences, they consist of necessary conclusions from undeniable premises, or of phenomena manipulated into general truths by an irresistible deduction. But the sense of right and wrong, which is the first element in religion, is so delicate, so fitful, so easily puzzled, obscured, perverted, so subtle in its argumentative methods, so impressible by education, so biased by pride and passion, so unsteady in its flight, that, in the struggle for existence amid the various exercises and triumphs of the human intellect, this sense is at once the highest of all teachers; yet the least luminous; and the Church, the pope, the Hierarchy are, in the Divine purpose, the supply of an urgent demand.[17]

Conscience, therefore, is in no way opposed to the use of external sources of traditional and revealed wisdom. It seeks help from authority in forming its judgments. Far from being an exception to the general rule that freedom is oriented toward objective truth, the experience of conscientious decision-making confirms the rule that, as the pope expresses it, the freedom of conscience is never freedom *from* the truth but always and only freedom *in* the truth (*VS* 64).

V. Freedom and Vocation

I have tried thus far to establish that freedom is meaningless and self-destructive if it is not used in the service of what is truly good. A freedom that dispenses itself from concern with truth could only be a false and illusory freedom. But it does not follow that the whole course of our life is prescribed in advance by an objective order of truth that excludes any originality and creativity on our part. In most situations we are faced with a choice between several competing goods. Just as I am free to order peas or carrots at dinner, or to wear a plain or striped shirt, so, on a larger scale, I am at liberty to choose any occupation, profession, or walk of life that is honorable in itself and consonant with my abilities and temperament. It would be a mistake to imagine that there would be only one acceptable course of action. Without prescribing everything in advance, God invites us to make creative decisions, in consonance with the moral law.

In this connection one must consider the idea of vocation. God may invite us, without compelling us, to do more than duty requires. In his meditation on the call of the rich young man at the beginning of *Veritatis splendor*, John Paul II points out the distinction between obedience to the Commandments, which is required for salvation, and a particular vocation, which may enable an individual to attain more perfect freedom. Many spiritual writers hold that the rich young man, whom Jesus urged to give away his goods to the poor, was not strictly required to perform this generous act. He could presumably have saved his soul by continuing to observe the Commandments, as he had been doing for years. Ordinarily, at least, the vocation to the life of the evangelical counsels does not come as a command but as a gracious invitation. Although we cannot achieve perfect freedom without accepting the highest possibilities opened up to us by God's grace, we are morally free to do all that God does not forbid.

VI. The Free Society

Up to this point I have focused on the freedom of the individual. In the final section of this paper, I should like to turn to the free society. It is more difficult to see how a society can be directed by truth unless the convictions of many of the members are overridden, in which case the society can hardly be called free. John Paul II, acutely conscious of this problem, offers some important considerations that I shall attempt to summarize.

The free society rests on the supposition that the members are endowed with inalienable rights. If the rights of individuals were conferred by the state or by the society, they could be removed by human power, and the way would be open to tyranny. As the authors of our Declaration of Independence recognized, the Creator himself has given human beings an inalienable right to life, liberty, and the pursuit of happiness, though of course the exercise of these rights has to be regulated with regard to the common good.

Alluding to the biblical and patristic doctrine that human beings are made in the image of God, the pope contends that the human person, as the visible image of the invisible God, is by nature the subject of rights that no individual, group, class, nation, or state may violate. Where the transcendent source of human dignity is denied, the way lies open for totalitarianism and other forms of despotism, in which naked power takes over, so that the interests of a particular person or group are imposed on the rest of society.[18]

As the pope goes on to explain, authentic democracy is possible only on the basis of a rule of law and a correct conception of the human person. "If there is no ultimate truth to guide and direct political activity, then ideas and convictions can easily be manipulated for reasons of power. . . . In a world without truth, freedom loses its foundation and man is exposed to the violence of passion and to manipulation, both open and hidden" (*Centesimus annus* 46.2).

But an objection still arises. People are not free unless they can determine their own form of government and participate in the making of their own laws. Thus it would seem that if they are not at liberty to deny the transcendent truth, they are not really free. On a purely political definition of freedom, we may concede that a people is free to institute slavery or to adopt a totalitarian form of government, but in so doing they damage or destroy their own freedom. An abiding freedom requires a consensus based on transcendent truth. Just as individuals forfeit their own freedom when they try to liberate themselves from moral norms, so the society surrenders its freedom if it fails to respect the personal dignity of its members.

The concept of public consensus is not always rightly understood. According to a widely prevalent view, it is simply a majority opinion, which may be based on fashion or emotion, or an ideology, based on the self-interest of a class. John Courtney Murray, in his masterful work, *We Hold These Truths*, explains that according to the classical tradition of political thought, consensus is a very different thing: it is a doctrine or judgment that commands public agreement because of the merits of the arguments in its favor.[19]

Public consensus, according to Murray, transcends sheer experience and expediency; it is basically a moral conception. Those who articulate it are the ones whom Thomas Aquinas called the "wise" (*sapientes*)[20] and whom George Washington called "the wise and honest."[21] The ability to discern what laws and policies best safeguard the dignity and rights of the citizens depends upon a careful inquiry in which intelligence is tutored by experience and reflection and guided by an instinct for the right and the good. The reason of the wise and the good is a responsible reason, concerned with fidelity to moral principle, and matured through familiarity with the complexities of the developing human situation.

The consensus, therefore, must be articulated by those who excel in practical wisdom; but in order to be a real consensus, it must also be accepted by the people. At the basis of the American experiment in ordered liberty, Murray explains, there are truths. "We the People" hold these truths and, showing "a decent respect for the opinions of mankind," declare them in public documents.[22] The American consensus consists not only in the general principles expressed in the Declaration of Independence but also in the more specific provisions of the Constitution and the Bill of Rights. These provisions likewise embody truths formulated by the wise and accepted by the people at large.

In the atmosphere of contemporary pluralism, there is a tendency to overlook the inviolable connection between freedom and truth, as though freedom implied a right to construct one's own moral universe without accountability to any higher agency. Václav Havel speaks in this connection of a deep moral crisis in the post-totalitarian society:

> A person who has been seduced by the consumer value system, whose identity is dissolved in an amalgam of the accoutrements of mass civilization, and who has no roots in the order of being, no sense of responsibility for anything higher than his or her own personal survival, is a demoralized person. The system depends on this demoralization, deepens it, is in fact a projection of it into society.[23]

Pope John Paul II, from a similar perspective, speaks of a "crisis of truth" (*VS* 32.2). All around us, says the pope, the saving power of the truth is contested, and freedom alone, uprooted from any objectivity, is left to decide for itself what is good and what is evil (*VS* 84). As he writes in *Centesimus annus*:

> Nowadays there is a tendency to claim that agnosticism and skeptical relativism are the philosophy and the basic attitude which correspond to democratic forms of political life. Those who are convinced that they know the truth and firmly adhere to it are considered unreliable from a democratic point of view, since they do not accept that truth is determined by the majority or that it is subject to variation according to different political trends. (*CA* 46.2)

Democracy, as Murray insisted, is more than a political experiment. It is a spiritual and moral enterprise, depending for its success upon the virtue of the citizens.[24] Political freedom is endangered if the institutions no longer serve the ends of virtue and if the people fail to discipline themselves. The crisis of society, therefore, is simply that of the individual writ large. Just as the freedom of the individual cannot stand without personal adherence to truth, so the free society cannot flourish without a virtuous citizenry, disposed to live out their identity as children of God and as brothers and sisters in a common humanity. The consensus must be nourished not by disordered passion but by an inner sense of responsibility to a higher law, interpreted by the wise and honest. Because so many of us live according to purely pragmatic standards of pleasure, wealth, and power, we are in danger of losing the moral and spiritual foundations on which our freedom rests.

The contemporary crisis of freedom, therefore, is at root a crisis of truth. Lord Acton perceived this more than a century ago. John Courtney Murray reached similar conclusions on the basis of his study of the American political tradition. In our own day, John Paul II has clearly demonstrated the inseparable connection between freedom and truth. In the course of his long career, he has eloquently and forcefully proclaimed the principles that must underlie every free society, including the American experiment of ordered liberty.

Endnotes

1. Gertrude Himmelfarb, *Lord Acton: A Study in Conscience and Politics* (Chicago: University of Chicago Press, 1952), 241.
2. Mortimer J. Adler, *Freedom: A Study of the Development of the Concept in the English and American Traditions of Philosophy* (Albany, N.Y.: Magi Books, 1968), 5.
3. Karol Wojtyla, Archbishop of Krakow, intervention of September 25, 1964, in *Acta synodalia Concilii Vaticani II, Period III*, vol. 2, pp. 530–32, at 531.
4. John Paul II, *Redemptor hominis* 12 (Washington, D.C.: United States Catholic Conference, 1979), 36.
5. Chapter 2 of *Veritatis splendor* deals with "The Church and the Discernment of Certain Tendencies in Present-Day Moral Theology," nn. 28–83.
6. Karol Wojtyla, *The Acting Person* (Dordrecht, Holland: D. Reidel, 1979), esp. 106–86; idem, "The Personal Structure of Self-Determination," chapter 13 of *Person and Community: Selected Essays* (New York: Peter Lang, 1993), 187–95.
7. Gregory of Nyssa, *De hominis opificio*, chap. 4; PG 44: 135; cf. VS 38, p. 61.
8. Michael Polanyi, *Personal Knowledge* (New York: Harper Torchbooks, 1964), 309. Italics in original.
9. Quoted by John Courtney Murray, *We Hold These Truths* (New York: Sheed & Ward, 1960), 36. Father Robert Sirico, C.S.P., President of the Acton Institute, has kindly sup-

plied me with the original source. Acton's statement, "Liberty is not the power of doing what we like, but the right of being able to do what we ought," appeared in *The Rambler*, January 1860, p. 146.

10. Wojtyla, *Person and Community*, 194.

11. Bonaventure, *In II libris sententiarum*, dist. 39, a. 1, q. 3, cond.; cf. *Veritatis splendor*, 58.

12. John Henry Newman, "Letter to the Duke of Norfolk" in *Newman and Gladstone: The Vatican Decrees*, ed. Alvan S. Ryan (Notre Dame, Ind.: University of Notre Dame Press), 128.

13. John Henry Newman, *Grammar of Assent* (Garden City: Doubleday Image, 1955), 304.

14. Ibid.

15. Newman, "Letter to the Duke of Norfolk," 130.

16. Ibid.

17. Ibid., 132–33.

18. John Paul II, Encyclical *Centesimus annus*, 44; Origins 21 (May 16, 1991): 1–24, at 17.

19. Murray, *We Hold These Truths*, chap. 4, pp. 97–123, at 105.

20. Thomas Aquinas, *STh* I–II, q. 100, a. 1, points out that to judge matters that require extensive consideration of different circumstances is the task of the wise, who then have the task of teaching the rest of the community.

21. Murray (*We Hold These Truths*, 111) gives no specific reference. Presumably he is thinking of Washington's statement, "Let us raise a standard to which the wise and honest can repair; the rest is in the hands of God" (speech to the Constitutional Convention at Philadelphia in 1787). Quoted from *A Treasury of Presidential Quotations*, ed. Caroline T. Harnsberger (Chicago: Follett, 1964), 300.

22. Murray, *We Hold These Truths*, 106.

23. Václav Havel, *Living in Truth* (London: Faber & Faber, 1987), 62.

24. Murray, *We Hold These Truths*, 36–37.

Desire for Happiness and the Commandments in the First Chapter of *Veritatis splendor*

Livio Melina
(translated by Margaret Harper McCarthy)

"The desire for happiness" and "the Commandments" seem to constitute two irreducible alternatives, representing a contrariety that separates the classical conception of morality from the modern. The choice that Catholic post-Tridentine handbook theology made to remove the treatise on happiness from moral theology and to focus on the Commandments appears unavoidable, even to contemporary moral theology. The perspective of the desire for happiness, which is thought to bind the ethical imperative to an empirical element that is indeterminate, subjective, and, above all, self-interested, has been eliminated from the ambit of moral thinking as incapable of guaranteeing the absolute and unconditional character of morality. This has been achieved by means of a philosophical critique[1] that appears not to have lost currency and persuasiveness. Moreover, from a theological point of view, the perspective of the desire for happiness seems unwittingly to risk turning God, the end of all, into the means of "my" self-realization.[2] Faithfulness to Biblical inspiration, rather than to an Aristotelian schema, seems necessarily to privilege the Commandments as the original form of morality.[3]

It is therefore surprising to note how the encyclical *Veritatis splendor*, in its evocative rereading of the dialogue between Jesus and the young rich man (in Mt 19:16–22), reintroduces the category of the "desire for happiness," characterizing it as proper content for moral inquiry. The encyclical also, however, associates this perspective with that of the Commandments when it cites the response of Jesus, who, after having invited the rich man to turn his gaze toward the One who alone is good, directs the young man to

observe the Decalogue. This is not simply a juxtaposition of different and mutually incompatible perspectives. While it is not obliged
to provide a theoretical and systematic justification, the papal
document does solicit attempts to grasp the constitutive connections that would provide for an integration of these two categories;
this is specifically the task of the moral theologian. Thus, when the
encyclical suggests that the question about happiness—as the question *"about the full meaning of life,"* and as prior to the question
"about rules to be followed"—is the "echo of a call from God who
is the origin and end of man's life" (*VS* 7.1), it situates itself within
the perspective of the renewal to which the Second Vatican Council called moral theology, which, in its theoretical exposition, will
have the task of illustrating "the lofty vocation which the faithful
have received in Christ, the only response fully capable of satisfying the desire of the human heart" (*VS* 7.1).[4]

This article intends to accept the invitation of the encyclical and
the council by thematizing the relation between the desire for happiness and the Commandments. Starting from the indications of the
first chapter of *Veritatis splendor*, moral theology is called to establish this relation at a fundamental level. I shall develop my reflection on this theme in three stages. In the first place, I shall present
an examination of the three terms at issue (desire, happiness, and
Commandments) with the intention of grasping the similarities and
dissimilarities between them. In the second place, I shall take up
the global context within which *Veritatis splendor* situates the relation between these terms, and which is provided by the link between freedom and truth. Finally, the specific theme of the first
chapter of the encyclical will be put into relief by displaying the
novel points of departure of the framework it presents.

I. Preliminary Consideration of the Terms of the Problem

A. "Desiderium"

Already the ancients associated the term "desire" with *sidera*,
the stars.[5] What does desire have to do with the stars? The original semantic environment seems to be the sacred language of
the oracles, hence, of an anxious search in the stars for some
sign of assurance that that for which the heart hopes will be

fulfilled. With respect to the verb *considerare*, which has the same root, desire would therefore be a moment of disappointment, the downward glance of a gaze originally turned toward the stars. In this way the characteristic ambiguity of desire may be appreciated. On the one hand, there results a compromise of its original yearning for the heavens (the infinite), hence a restless wandering among earthly objects, unable to find in them either an adequate satisfaction of its aspiration or a sure sign that the hope inscribed in one's heart will come true (this wandering has rightly been called the "nomadic character of desire").[6] On the other hand, one can observe that desire, although poised toward the finite, continues to bear within itself the memory of, and the nostalgia for, the infinite: in every one of our desires this *Sehnsucht* for the heavens remains as a secret yearning, never attained in the finite.

The category of desire, therefore, shows itself to be anthropologically revelatory of the creaturely indigence constitutive of the human being, a being thrown into the world with the original promise that his thirst for the infinite will be quenched, but who inevitably runs up against disappointment. If the reality that man encounters awakens the promise, it also painfully denies it, so that in the face of desire one is obliged to make a fundamental choice of attitude. One must either affirm and confirm the native promise of the heart, notwithstanding disappointments, maintaining an openness to the possibility of fulfillment (which is not brought about by any human "doing"); or one must renounce the promise of the infinite, and adapt to the finite. The reasonableness of the former attitude is evident in the fact that it does not entail a rejection or negation—as does the latter—of any element of human experience. Above all it does not require one to censure the most interesting and decisive element of the heart: the promise.[7] If, on the one hand, faithfulness to that promise requires the affirmation of the existence of an answer adequate to our desire, and if, on the other hand, realism excludes that such an answer be situated within the horizon of human doing, then it follows that the answer can only be given in the form of a gift from Another. The fulfillment of desire can only be believed and awaited, not projected and constructed as some work to be done.[8]

The great poet Dante has expressed with unsurpassable verses desire's original tension as well as its temptation to turn in on itself:

> Everyone confusedly apprehends a good in which the mind may be at rest and desires it, so that each strives to reach it, and if the love is sluggish that draws you to see it or gain it, this terrace, after due repentance, torments you for that. Other good there is which does not make men happy; it is not happiness, it is not the good Essence, the fruit and root of every good.[9]

The aspiration for total fulfillment dwells, in a confused manner, within the restless searching of the human heart, a heart that desires in every thing loved that final end that alone grants happiness. The ascent of purgatory is essentially the purification of desire because, freed from bonds of limited and apparent satisfaction ("pure and ready to mount to the stars"),[10] it can be assumed into the same movement by which God moves the universe; so, finally, it can there find its peace, contemplating "the Love that moves the sun and the other stars."[11]

From this comes the need for an education in desire. Such an education, by renouncing the immediate appeasement in the finite, once again orients the gaze and the tension of the heart toward the heavens, toward the star; the heart thereby recuperates its global horizon, the fullness of satisfaction. In order to be saved, then, desire needs to entrust itself to a promise of fulfillment, and to find a personal reference point that, in accompanying desire, allows for its purification.

B. Happiness

Wladyslaw Tatarkiewicz, in a classical study of the term "happiness,"[12] has shown its extreme semantical complexity. There seem, however, to be two principal conceptions of happiness that he brings to the fore. In the first place there is the modern conception ("happiness"[13]), which he interprets as satisfaction with one's own life, taken as a whole. What is in question here is a subjective perspective, in which the one unquestionable criterion for happiness is the judgment of the subject, who does not therefore have to distinguish between true and false happiness. The single criterion for this definition of happiness is psychological: the saturation of desire. In the second place, there is the classical conception (*eudaimonia* or *beatitudo*), which he takes as the perfection of life in the objective sense. In this view of things it is not only possible but also necessary to refer to objective and rational criteria in order to establish what is true happiness.

St. Augustine, in the *De Trinitate*, offers a definition of that which constitutes happiness in the objective sense: "A happy man is one who has all that he wants and, at the same time, wants nothing bad."[14] The two elements complete each other and serve to define happiness as the correspondence of the tending of the subject with the presence of its proportionate object. For happiness, in fact, the state of subjective satisfaction (having all that one wants) is not enough; rectitude of the will (not wanting anything bad) is also necessary. And here it is the object that decides: "it is the good that causes the happiness of the happy man." For the Doctor of Hippo, happiness has, therefore, an objective character: one can distinguish between true and false happiness on the basis of the object of the will, the Good.

For his part, St. Thomas Aquinas, in the *Summa*, places the criterion for the determination of true happiness within the subject: "To desire happiness is nothing other than to desire the satisfaction of the will."[15] He then affirms, however, that only the true good can satisfy the will *fully*. Here he recovers the totality of the horizon of desire, tied to the will (i.e., the appetite guided by reason), which preserves its openness to the infinite. For Thomas, too, happiness has an objective character, for it is connected with the goodness of the object; on just this basis the goodness of the subject and his happiness is defined. Beatitude has an objective meaning (*finis cuius*) and in this sense is identified with God, the *summum bonum* and final end. But beatitude also has a subjective meaning (*finis quo*), and in this sense it coincides with an activity of the subject.[16] To be truly happy, one must become the kind of person who loves the good, wherein true happiness is found, and in this way become himself good.[17]

At this juncture surfaces the theme of the structural disproportion between desire, which animates human action, and its object. Desire cannot be fulfilled by the possible objects of action: it is made for the stars. As Maurice Blondel has pointed out, between the *volonté voulante* (willing will) and the *volonté voulue* (willed will) there exists a structural disproportion,[18] which action attempts in vain to overcome. The desire for happiness, i.e., the desire for the complete fulfillment of the will in its openness, the secret spring of every action, must be guided by reason. At the same time, however, the truth about the Good is always beyond any rationalistic pre-comprehension that would attempt, prior to our actions, to seize it in a concept. It is therefore necessary to entrust oneself to *praxis*, to live action with a trusting "pre-sentiment" of complete fulfillment. Action seems to have to function as reason's guide in reason's tending toward its proportionate object. But action so understood takes the form of a practical "entrustment" to a promise, in order to receive its fulfillment as a "gift."

C. The Commandments

A conflict of principle between desire for happiness and the Commandments is necessarily implied by the legalistic conception of modern moral thinking[19] and by the correlative subjectivist conception of happiness. The Commandments, even if reabsorbed into the autonomy of an interior norm, continue to be opposed to desire, now reduced to the empirical sphere of the passions (Kant). This contraposition is not, however, the necessary consequence of classical ethics, provided this ethics is not interpreted in a "rationalistic" manner.

In the ethics of classical inspiration, and in particular in Thomistic ethics, the concept of *lex* is secondary and subordinate to that of *virtus*.[20] The law, which maintains an irreducible character of exteriority, but which at the same time is recognized in its intrinsic rationality, has as its aim the guidance of men toward virtue.[21] As such the law is reformulated and is understood to have as its finality the education of desire. In fact, we might say that virtue is desire educated to see the stars: appetite molded by reason, which maintains its intentional openness to the final end. Therefore the Commandments exist in function of an education of desire. So, on the one hand, they posit the external limits of its immediate satisfaction, in order to save its total openness; on the other hand, they forge its aspirations in conformity with their authentic ends. The Commandments deny our urges toward partial satisfaction so as to protect our secret and ultimate longing. Impeding the reduction of desire or its collapse into itself, the Commandments guide desire toward the stars.

The priority of virtue over the commandment is a decisive characteristic of the "ethics of the agent-subject" or "ethics of the first person" vis-à-vis the "ethics of the observer" or "ethics of the third person."[22] For the former, the agent subject is at the center, with his aspiration toward the good and toward happiness; for the latter, an external regulation of behavior, by means of norms and precepts, is at the center. *Veritatis splendor* explicitly makes the former framework its own when it affirms that in order to grasp the object that morally specifies action it is "necessary to place oneself *in the perspective of the acting person*" (*VS* 78.1). Moreover, this is also the orientation of its first chapter, which emphasizes as the origin of morality the question the young man puts to Jesus: "Master, what good thing must I do to obtain eternal life?" Precisely by starting with this question *Veritatis splendor* reintroduces the desire for happiness as the original experience and foundational principle of morality, within which the Commandments, in their turn, find their proper place and significance.

II. The Global Context of *Veritatis splendor:* The Connection between Freedom and Truth

Veritatis splendor situates the problem of the relationship between desire (for happiness) and the Commandments within the more comprehensive thematic of the *connection between freedom and truth* (*VS* 4 and 84), whereas that which connotes the specifically theological dimension of the problem, namely, the connection between faith and morality, is set in the background. This framework, centered on freedom, is characterized as "modern," for within it are gathered the most debated questions of contemporary moral reflection (*VS* 31). Nevertheless, freedom is reunited to truth from within (*VS* 34) as the condition of its authenticity. In order to grasp the significance of this contextualization, so decisive for the encyclical's perspective, it is necessary to consider the conception of freedom and truth proposed by the pontifical document.

A. Truth

The truth of which it speaks is not the object of a merely "speculative" knowledge, in which reason alone is at play. It is rather a matter of a *practical truth*: a truth on which one's personal life depends, a truth that is not only to be contemplated, but to be done, and that therefore is given to be known only in the form of a "re-cognition," i.e., only insofar as one's freedom is engaged with it.[23] In this regard, St. Thomas Aquinas speaks of a *veritas vitae*[24] as the complete correspondence, both interior and exterior, of the whole of man's being with divine truth; the individual virtues bring this correspondence to fruition within the specific ambits of their competence. At issue here is a principle of general rectitude, which sustains and grounds the whole of human existence, in conformity with the divine law.[25] Man assents to moral truth only by virtue of his freedom and with the whole of his being, which must be shaped by the virtues: "the virtuous man judges everything rightly, and in each thing the truth appears to him . . . he being the canon and measure of them."[26] It is precisely the decisive function accorded to the appetite in regard to moral knowledge that characterizes the classical position of Aristotle and St. Thomas Aquinas, and that differentiates them from every intellectualistic reduction of virtue to a merely executive role.[27]

Veritatis splendor discusses this theme in reference to conscience (*VS* 64), recalling the indispensable connaturality required for the knowledge of the concrete good and citing John 3:21: "He who does what is true comes to the light." But also in regard to the final end, happiness, the decisive criterion for its determination cannot but be *practical reason* (cf. *VS* 40).[28] It seems to me that the encyclical acknowledges this practical connotation of the decisive theme of truth when it notes that the moral question is a question *"about the full meaning of life"* (*VS* 7.1). This signifies quite a different thing from a purely theoretical or rationalistic truth; it expresses, rather, the relation established between a particular action and the whole. An action is meaningful only insofar as it becomes intelligible; and this is achieved when it is connected with the ultimate end of existence, and therefore with reality as a whole, understood as the expression of a divinely sapiential design. The moral question cannot be limited to "moralistic" terms, i.e., as the mere conformity of an action with a rule. Rather, it must be viewed more radically as a question about the identity of the person (*veritas vitae*), about the link that connects his action to his end, which gives meaning to his life. "There is a connection between the moral good and the fulfillment of his own destiny" (*VS* 8.1). In this tending toward truth, where what is in play is the meaning of one's life as a whole, even knowledge is attained only through the whole person, who must be in harmony with the good, and who, in the engagement of his freedom, risks by entrusting himself.

B. Freedom

The relativity of freedom to truth, according to the attestation of the Gospel—"the truth will make you free" (Jn 8:32)—also necessarily implies a reinterpretation of the modern conception of freedom. Freedom is not "indifference,"[29] but love for the true good. The theme of the desire for happiness is integrated into morality as the original and constitutive inclination of freedom, but this is oriented in turn by the judgment of reason. Reason regards the desire for happiness not as an empty psychological formula left up to subjective interpretation. Rather, desire is viewed as the tension toward the ultimate end of man's aspiring, guided by reason.[30] Desire, once it is brought fully back into the dynamic of freedom and morality, is not a naturalistic passion of only empirical and psychological relevance, but the conscious openness to the fullness of the horizon of the Good. At the root of all diffidence about desire and the natural inclinations is perhaps the prejudice of a reductivistic interpretation that places them at the level of merely sensible experience. What is decisive, therefore, is the rediscovery of their properly spiritual dimension: The desire for happiness is the expression of our *natura spiritualis* in its spontaneous aspiration for the true and the good.[31] Such a nature, theologically understood as a manifestation of the image of God, far from leading one to the particularism of sensible experience, opens the person to the universality of the spirit.

The *truth concerning the good* thus mediates between desire and its full satisfaction, between native aspiration and its final fulfillment. Freedom is animated by an aspiration restored and maintained in its original openness: the Commandments and the virtues have this purpose.

In conclusion, it may be useful to touch on the thesis of the philosopher Karol Wojtyla concerning the *truthful integration of desire*,[32] which can perhaps be identified as the underlying philosophical background to the encyclical, permitting us to grasp the meaning of this thematic. The freedom of man is made for the gift of self to the other; in this gift even desire is integrated, which, by submitting itself to the truth, agrees to acknowledge the primacy of the other and so to realize itself ecstatically. At issue here is a gradual process that assumes instincts, impulses, emotions, and sentiments, but that can bring about their integration only within the truth. The reference to the truth, in fact, conditions the authentic freedom of self-determination and permits a transcendence with respect to various forms of determinism. The virtues have a decisive role in this process, for they are precisely the formation of desire in the light of the openness to the truth.

III. Novel Points in the First Chapter of the Encyclical

In the first chapter of *Veritatis splendor* the connection between desire for happiness and the Commandments is grasped in the concrete dynamic of the encounter and dialogue between the rich young man and Jesus (Mt 19:16–22). This original perspective allows certain novel points to emerge—points that are important for the renewal of moral theology at its very foundation.

A. The Moral Life as "Encounter" with Jesus Christ

The moral path is grasped at its genesis as an "encounter" with Jesus (*VS* 7.2), an encounter in which the desire of the young interlocutor (but in him also human beings of all ages) is aroused with all of its force, as aspiration for eternal life, for the "fulfillment of his own destiny" (*VS* 8.1). It is on account of the "attractiveness of the person of Jesus," a promise intuited in his words and in his actions, that the question is reawakened with all of its openness.

In this way man's ethical dimension is situated within the concrete context of a personal relationship, a relationship that develops dialogically in history. From this is derived an emphasis on the fundamental value for moral theology of categories such as "vocation," "covenant," "promise," "trust," "companionship," "hope," and "gift." Such categories are well represented in the Sacred Scriptures, but for centuries have been obscured by the systematic moral theology of the handbooks; indeed, they have remained irrelevant even in the elaboration of post-conciliar normative ethics. The concentration on the Commandments, or on norms, has favored a reductive focusing of the debate on the autonomy of moral reason, which has overshadowed and rendered essentially pleonastic all reference to revelation and, in particular, to its contents.[33] The reinsertion of these contents into moral theology, under the auspices of *Optatam totius*, n. 16, requires not so much a reproposal of Holy Writ according to the modes of persuasive or "narrative" discourse (so fashionable today) as a fundamental reflection, on the basis of a phenomenology of the ethical experience of man as such, that grasps its transcendental categories in their structural connections[34] and, above all, that provides a properly theological hermeneutic, in reference to Christ. It is, in fact, in him, in the encounter with him, "true light which enlightens everyone" (Jn 1:9, cited in *VS* 1.1), that the solution can be found for the problem in theological anthropology so decisive today for moral theology, the problem concerning the relation between nature and grace.[35]

In the encounter with Jesus, desire is saved from its withdrawal into itself and lifted up toward a goal, in which one can find fulfillment in a form heretofore unknown. Christian revelation proposes a surprising and superabundant fulfillment of the desire for happiness; and this resolves the paradoxical tension between the necessity of finding an answer for living and acting reasonably and the impossibility of full satisfaction of this desire in this world. To linger with the metaphor that, beginning with the etymology of desire, accompanies the thread of our reflection, we could say that the stars have come to earth in order to encounter and save the errant and vagrant desire of man.[36]

At the same time, this encounter so full of promise, which occurred as an unexpected and unthinkable grace, demands the reformulation of the young man's original question. If one's expectation is to be fulfilled, one must accept that it be surpassed. From out of the sphere of human "doing," Jesus invites man to turn his gaze to the fount of goodness, to him who, being the absolute Good, constitutes the final end of action. Only in total and disinterested love for this end does moral initiative and the question of eternal life make sense. In the encounter with Jesus, the young man discovers the depth of his own desire; on the other hand, he is invited to let that desire be reformed through education, by means of the Commandments and the following of Christ. In fact, the encyclical underlines the fact that the dynamic of the dialogue, beginning with the ardor of love for the absolute and final good, continues to recall the Commandments, those "paths" toward the fulfillment of the desire for eternal life, and then the following of the very person of Jesus (discipleship), after having abandoned everything for him.

B. The Christological Dimension of the Commandments

"From the very lips of Jesus, the new Moses, man is once again given the Commandments of the Decalogue" (*VS* 12.2). Jesus confirms and proposes the Commandments to men of every age as the way and condition of salvation. In this way the connection between commandment and promise is established from within the relation of the *covenant*. In fact, since the time of the Old Testament, the context in which the Commandments are given to us has been that of the covenant:[37] they have the form of a gift offered by God out of love, and received by his people in trust on the strength of a promise. Through the commandment the people of Israel entrusts itself to its Lord, who will guard and bring its desire for happiness to fruition (cf. Dt 6:3). The commandment is the typical form of the education in desire that is realized by means of faith within the historical relationship of the covenant. The exterior dimension of obedience is lived in the attitude of trust. In sum, even the Commandments of the Old Covenant are a way of imitating God in his salvific action toward the people.

But, once again, the full form of the commandment is personal. *Veritatis splendor* reproposes the affirmation of St. Ambrose according to which *"plenitudo legis in Christo est,"* asserting that *"he himself becomes a living and personal Law"* (*VS* 15.2). In the face of man's desire there is no longer the abstract and impersonal expression of the law, but the concrete and personal form of Jesus, who, according to the Balthasarian formula, is "the concrete categorical imperative,"[38] since he lived his eternal filial obedience to the will of the Father in a human existence wholly the same as ours. In its definitive Christological dimension, the commandment is revealed to be in function of the imitation of Christ, and so in perfect and free conformity to that archetypal Image, in which and for which man was created.

The original vocation inscribed from the image of God encounters the wholly unprecedented eschatology of the Son made man: the human desire for happiness encounters a gratuitous reality exceeding every human expectation and project, a reality of fulfillment through participation in the life of the divine. Christ in his humanity becomes the "way," the synthesis of every preceding moral law, the definitive hermeneutic of every commandment.

In this way the dialectic of autonomy and heteronomy is also surpassed. "In Christ" the law is perceived as the expression of the will of the Father and embraced in a filial way; in the Spirit, while remaining *heteron* (something other) with respect to God, we are assumed gratuitously into a filiation that makes us also *heteros* (someone other). In the Spirit, the Christological commandment is interiorized and becomes the new law of love, without, however, completely eliminating on earth the exterior elements (cf. *VS* 53),[39] which are nevertheless subordinated in function to the interior element (*lex nova Spiritus Sancti*).

C. The Commandments in the Itinerary toward the Perfection of One's Personal Vocation

In *Veritatis splendor* the Commandments are seen not only as the way to the end (*VS* 12), but also as a stage leading toward the maturation of freedom (*VS* 13), or rather leading toward perfection (*VS* 17). Now, the perfection of freedom is realized in the "gift of self," in charity (*VS* 18 and 87). This is the imitation of God and has the measure of God. *VS* 18, connecting by way of interpretation Luke 6:36 with Matthew 5:48, places Christian perfection, the imitation of divine perfection, within mercy. Charity is the fullness of the law (Rom 13:10) and according to its Christological reference, it is the "new" commandment (Jn 13:34). In it is surpassed the presumed conflict between the (egotistical) quest for one's own happiness (*eros*) and the gratuitous dedication to "the glory of God" (*agape*) (*VS* 10.1).[40] The desire for happiness, whose objective value has been entrusted to and protected by the commandment, reveals and nourishes its ecstatic character: it becomes charity, which affirms Another.

For this reason beatitude and charity are ultimately one. It is this authentically Thomistic conception of happiness that liberates happiness from every suspicion of egotistical interest.[41] In fact, for Thomas beatitude is, on the one hand, an activity, the most perfect activity of a person who has reached the highest level of development possible for a human being; and this activity is identical with charity perfectly realized. On the other hand, charity, as friendship with God, is our happiness inasmuch as it is that type of life in which the original potentialities of man are actuated to the highest degree in the gift of self to God and to neighbor. Therefore the desire for happiness, which is an expression of creaturely indigence and the beginning of the moral journey, culminates in charity, which is the affirmation of an Other and the perfect availability to receiving its form. The paradox of the Christian moral life is that it is precisely through welcoming the initial need for fulfillment and in allowing oneself to be educated by the presence of God in Christ that the human being is guided beyond himself, to be fulfilled in the gift, receiving from God even his very capacity to love.

At the same time, the perfection of freedom is the fulfillment of the person in his unique and unrepeatable vocation (*VS* 17 and 85). In the call of the Good one can hear, in fact, the echo of a personal vocation (*VS* 7) that concerns the "fulfillment of his own destiny" (*VS* 8.1); this call is a journey of freedom, in which "the good of the person" is affirmed (*VS* 13.3). The per-

sonalistic visage of the moral life is evident, in an ever more decisive way, in the encounter with Jesus as the movement from
the Commandments to the following of his person.

It must also be said that the *sequela Christi*, proposed by the
encyclical as the "essential and original foundation of Christian
morality" (*VS* 19.2), fully protects the dimension of personal
singularity belonging to the truth of morality, a dimension
about which our contemporary mentality is particularly sensitive. The moral life does not consist only in the fulfillment of
the universal regulations contained in the Commandments;
more importantly, it is a matter of the realization of the person,
in his unique and unrepeatable vocation, which emerges from
the most personal encounter with Christ. The contingency of
the different calls implied by differing vocational circumstances
requires us to accord the virtue of prudence its full value. Prudence is *"in Christ,"* a real participation in his wisdom, which
through the gifts of the Spirit makes us attentive and sensitive
to every suggestion of the Friend and enables us to act according to the end gratuitously given us.[42]

D. The Ways toward the Fulfillment of the Desire for Happiness

The first chapter of the encyclical appears now, at the end of
this reflection, as the proposal of a moral itinerary that, taking
up the desire for happiness, reconciles it with its authentic and
original horizon (the stars) and opens it to the gratuitous fullness of the divine life.

The Commandments of God are the first "way" indicated by
Jesus for obtaining eternal life (*VS* 12). Inasmuch as they are a
negative "limit," they block false aspirations by turning desire
away from the dead-ends of the finite and by orienting it elsewhere, namely, toward the infinite object for which it is made.
The Commandments, however, are also and above all "a path
involving a moral and spiritual journey toward perfection, at
the heart of which is love" (*VS* 15.2). In this second sense the
Commandments are at the service of the practice of love (*VS*
17); they educate desire to open itself up to love.

Yet the truly great way to the fulfillment of the desire of life
is Jesus himself. Through the gift of the Spirit there is now the
possibility of following Christ, the "living and personal law,"

and fulfilling the Commandments—which represent partial stages leading up to that fullness which he is (*VS* 17).[43] Nonetheless, even under the regime of the New Law the Commandments remain necessary reference points, since we possess only the first fruits of the Spirit.[44] In any case, all of the paths converge in the end, so as to bring to fruition in the moral subject the intimate conformation of our desires to those of Christ (cf. *VS* 21).

The intrinsic link between the desire for happiness and the fulfillment of the moral life is indicated by the encyclical with the theme of the *Beatitudes* (*VS* 16), a theme that has been overlooked by modern moral theology, but that is well represented in the great theological tradition.[45] These mark the gratuitous anticipation of the end within Christian action: they are a foretaste of the eternal along the journey. *Veritatis splendor* recalls their Christological character (the Beatitudes *"are invitations to discipleship and to communion of life with Christ,"* since they are a *"sort of self-portrait of Christ"*) and their indication of a promise that opens up in the disciple hope for the fulfillment that will be realized fully in the future Kingdom. By following Christ, in the paradoxical form of obedience and the abandonment of everything, man's desire for happiness already mysteriously participates in that beatitude of the Kingdom of heaven to which he aspires and which is given him gratuitously.

Endnotes

1. Cf. Immanuel Kant, *Grounding for the Metaphysics of Morals*, trans. James W. Ellington (Indianapolis: Hackett Publishing, 1981), 7–43.
2. Cf. Hans Urs von Balthasar, "Homo creatus est," in *Homo creatus est*, vol. 5 of *Skizzen zur Theologie* (Einsiedeln: Johannes Verlag, 1986), 9–26.
3. Cf. G. Angelini, *Il senso orientato al sapere: L'etica come questione teologica*, in G. Colombo, ed., *L'evidenza e la fede* (Milan, 1988), 387–443, esp. 414–19.
4. Cf. The Decree on Priestly Formation, *Optatam totius*, n. 16.
5. Cf. A. Ernout - A. Meillet, *Dictionnaire étymologique de la langue latine: Histoire des mots* (Paris: C. Klincksieck, 1932), 897; *Thesaurus linguae latinae*, vol. V, pars I, D (Leipzig: B. G. Teubner, 1909–34), 697–710. The ancients to whom one should refer are: Paul. Fest., 75; Prisc., Gramm. II, 274, 19; Isid., Orig. 10, 76. The original meaning deduced from the etymology is: "amissum vel absentem requirere," "libido absentem videndi."
6. F. Botturi, *Desiderio e verità: Per un'antropologia cristiana nell'età secolarizzata* (Milan, 1985), 12426.
7. These anthropological perspectives are evocatively outlined by L. Giussani in his writings, particularly in *Morality: Memory and Desire*, trans. K. D. Whitehead (San Francisco: Ignatius Press, 1986) and in *The Religious Sense*, trans. J. Zucchi (San Francisco: Ignatius Press, 1990).

8. Cf. Angelini, *Il senso orientato*, 416.
9. Dante Alighieri, *La Divina Commedia, Purgatorio*, Canto XVII, vv. 127–35: "Ciascun confusamente un bene apprende / nel qual si quieti l'animo, e disira: / per che di giugner lui ciascun contende. / Se lento amore in lui veder vi tira, / o a lui acquistar, questa cornice, / dopo giusto pentér, ve ne martira / Altro ben è che non fa l'uomo felice; / non è felicità, non è la bona / essenza, d'ogni ben frutto e radice." The English translation given here and throughout this article is that by John D. Sinclair (New York: Oxford University Press, 1961). I owe the suggestion of this citation once again to L. Giussani, *Si può vivere così? Uno strano approccio all'esistenza cristiana* (Milano, 1994), 67, in the context of a particularly interesting meditation on freedom (62–79). For a study on *desìo* in Dante's work, see M. Camisasca, *Riflessioni de medio corso* (Forlì, 1994), 19–33.
10. *Purgatorio*, Canto XXXIII, v. 145: "puro e disposto a salire alle stelle."
11. *Paradiso*, Canto XXXIII, v. 143–5: "Ma già volgeva il mio disìo e il velle, / sì come rota ch'igualmente è mossa, / l'amor che move il sole e l'altre stelle" (but now my desire and will, like a wheel that spins with even motion, were revolved by the Love that moves the sun and the other stars).
12. W. Tatarkiewicz, *Analysis of Happiness*, trans. Edward Rothert and Danuta Zielinskn (The Hague: M. Nijhoff, 1976), 1–36.
13. The author employs the English word here.—Trans.
14. St. Augustine, *De Trinitate*, XIII, 4, 7–9, 12.
15. St. Thomas Aquinas, *STh*, I–II, q. 5, a. 8.
16. Cf. *STh*, I–II, q. 1, a. 8.
17. Cf. P. J. Wadell, *The Primacy of Love: An Introduction to the Ethics of Thomas Aquinas* (New York: Mahwah, 1992), 44–62.
18. M. Blondel, *L'action (1893): Essai d'une critique de la vie et d'une science de la pratique*, 3rd ed. (Paris: Presses Universitaires de France, 1973), 132.
19. Cf. G. Grisez, "Legalism, Moral Truth and Pastoral Practice," in T. J. Herron, ed., *The Catholic Priest as Moral Teacher and Guide* (San Francisco, 1990), 97–113. For a historical judgment on the question of legalism in the post-tridentine handbook tradition, see L. Vereecke, *Da Guglielmo d'Ockham a Sant'Alfonso de Liguori: Saggi di storia della teologia morale moderna (1300–1787)* (Rome, 1990) and S. Pinckaers, *Les sources de la morale chrétienne: Sa méthode, son contenu, son histoire* (Fribourg, 1985), 258–82; English translation (ET) by Sr. Mary Thomas Noble, *The Sources of Christian Ethics* (Washington: Catholic University of America Press, 1995), 254–79.
20. Cf. G. Abba', *Lex et virtus: Studi sull'evoluzione della dottrina morale di San Tommaso d'Aquino* (Rome, 1983). See also two other recent interpretations of Thomist ethics: E. Schockenhoff, *Bonum hominis: Die anthropologischen und theologischen Grundlagen der Tugendethik des Thomas von Aquin* (Mainz: Matthias-Grunewald-Verlag, 1987); M. Rhonheimer, *Praktische Vernunft und Vernünftigkeit der Praxis: Handlungstheorie bei Thomas von Aquin in ihrer Entstehung aus dem Problemkontext der aristotelischen Ethik* (Berlin: Akademik Verlag, 1994).
21. St. Thomas Aquinas, *STh*, I–II, q. 107, a. 2: "Finis vero cuiuslibet legis est ut homines efficiantur iusti et virtuosi."
22. This shift of the principal point of view according to which ethics is elaborated and which indicates a decisive fracture between ancient and medieval ethics on the one hand and modern ethics on the other, has been articulated by S. Hampshire in his study of 1949, reprinted in A. MacIntyre and S. Hauerwas, eds., *Revisions: Changing Perspectives in Moral Philosophy* (Notre Dame: University of Notre Dame Press, 1983) and by E. Pincoffs in his "Quandary Ethics," *Mind* 80 (1971): 552–71.
23. In this regard, see my *La conoscenza morale: Linee di reflessione sul Commento di San Tommaso all'Etica Nicomachea* (Rome, 1987). On the subject of conscience see also E. Schockenhoff, *Das umstrittene Gewissen: Eine theologische Grundlegung* (Mainz, 1990), 115–33.

24. *In IV Sent.*, d. 46, q. 1, a. 1; *STh*, I, q. 16, a. 4, ad 3; II–II, q. 109, a. 2, ad 3; II–II, q. 109, a. 3, ad 3. Contrary to E. Schockenhoff's argument in *Das umstrittene Gewissen* (90–91, 129–33), the *veritas vitae* is not for Thomas set against the *veritas doctrinae* as a merely self-referenial factor of personal authenticity. Life is "true" when it brings about that to which it is ordained by the divine intellect and reflects therefore that fundamental divine truth, which is at the heart of the truth, be it the truth of life, or the truth of doctrine.

25. Cf. R. Cessario, *The Moral Virtues and Theological Ethics* (Notre Dame: University of Notre Dame Press, 1991), 21.

26. Aristotle, *The Nicomachean Ethics*, III, 4, 1113a, 29–35.

27. Cf. Cessario, *The Moral Virtues*, 79–90.

28. Cf. Abbá, *Felicità, vita buona e virtù*, 45.

29. Cf. Pinckaers, *Les sources de la morale chrétienne*, 329–54; ET, 327–53.

30. Cf. M. Rhonheimer, *La prospettiva della morale: Fondamenti dell'etica filosofica* (Rome, 1994), 45–49.

31. Servais Pinckaers has opportunely attracted attention to this in his *La morale catholique* (Paris, 1991), 71–88.

32. K. Wojtyla, *Love and Responsibility*, trans. H. T. Willetts (San Francisco: Ignatius Press, 1981), 114–18; *The Acting Person*, trans. A. Potocki (London: D. Reidel, 1979), 231–34.

33. Cf. W. Kerber, "Limiti della morale biblica," in K. Demmer and B. Schüller, eds., *Fede cristiana e agire morale* (Assisi, 1980), 129–43; J. Endres, "Genügt eine rein biblische Moraltheologie?" *Studia Moralia* 2 (1965); J. Fuchs "Christian Morality: Biblical Orientation and Human Evaluation," *Gregorianum* 67/4 (1986): 745–63. For a panoramic view of the current debates and problematics in fundamental moral theology, see my *Morale: tra crisi e rinnovamento: Gli assoluti morali, l'opzione fondamentale, la formazione della coscienza* (Milan, 1993), 7–39.

34. Cf. Angelini, *Il senso orientato al sapere*, 420–25.

35. Cf. the articles of R. Tremblay on *Veritatis splendor*: "Le Christ et la morale selon l'Encyclique de Jean Paul II *Veritatis splendor*," *Lateranum* 60 (1994): 29–66; "Jésus le Christ, vraie lumière qui éclaire tout homme: Réflexions sur l'Encyclique de Jean Paul II *Veritatis splendor*," *Studia Moralia* 31 (1993): 383–90.

36. Cf. St. Leo the Great, *Sermo XXIII, III in Nativitate Domini*, 3: PL 54, 199–203.

37. Cf. J. L'Hour, *La morale de l'Alliance* (Paris, 1985, originally published in 1966).

38. H. U. von Balthasar, *Neuf thèses pour une éthique chrétienne* (Bologna, 1979), 612–45.

39. Cf. St. Augustine, *De Spiritu et littera*, PL 44, 201–46, CSEL 40, IV, I; St. Thomas Aquinas, *STh*, I–II, qq. 106–8; E. Kaczynski, *La legge nuova: L'elemento esterno della legge nuova secondo San Tommaso* (Rome, 1974).

40. Cf. Balthasar, "Homo creatus est," 9–26.

41. On this theme see R. Guindon, *Béatitude et théologie morale chez St. Thomas d'Aquin* (Ottawa: Editions de l'Universite d'Ottawa, 1956); P. J. Wadell, *Friendship and the Moral Life* (Notre Dame: University of Notre Dame Press, 1989), 120–41.

42. Cf. R. Cessario, *The Moral Virtues*, 60, 76–79.

43. The Christocentric perspective of morality and the elements for a possible Christological integration not only of the Commandments of the Old Law but also of Natural Law are offered in I. Biffi, "Integralità cristiana e fondazione morale," *Scuola Cattolica* 115 (1987): 570–90, as well as in G. Chantraine-A. Scola, "L'évenement Christ et la vie morale," *Anthropotes* 1 (1987): 5–23, and in R. Tremblay, *L'"Homme" qui divinise: Pour une interprétation christocentrique de l'existence* (Montreal, 1993).

44. Cf. St. Thomas Aquinas, *Super ep. ad Romanos*, c. XII, lect. I (Turin: Marietti, 1953), n. 971.

45. See St. Augustine, *De sermone Domini in monte*, PL 34, 1229–1308, CC 35; St. Thomas Aquinas, *STh*, I–II, q. 69. Opportunely, S. Pinckaers has directed attention to this theme in *Les sources de la morale chrétienne*, 144–94; ET, 134–90.

Intrinsically Evil Acts and the Moral Viewpoint: Clarifying a Central Teaching of *Veritatis splendor*[1]

Martin Rhonheimer

I. Introduction: Distinguishing Choices and their Objects from Further Intentions and Consequences

Many Catholic moral theologians have asserted during the last few years that to know what a person really does each time he or she is acting and, consequently, to qualify morally this concrete doing, one must take into account all the further goals for the sake of which this person chooses what he concretely does. Equally, so these theologians contend, a balance of all foreseen consequences should be established to make out whether a determinate behavior is the right or the wrong thing to choose. Therefore, according to this view it will always be impossible to qualify as morally evil according to its species—its "object"—the deliberate choice of certain kinds of behavior or specific acts, apart from a consideration of the intention for which the choice is made or the totality of the foreseeable consequences of that act for all persons concerned. (*VS* 79.1)

The encyclical *Veritatis splendor* rejects this view of so-called "teleological" ethical theories[2] as incompatible with the existence of describable concrete actions which are "intrinsically evil," that is, which are evil "*always and per se*, in other words, on account of their very object, and quite apart from the ulterior intentions of the one acting and the circumstances" (*VS* 80.1). Consequently, this view finally is judged as incompatible with the existence of absolutely (without exception) binding, prohibitive (or negative) moral norms; that is, with so-called "moral absolutes."

The encyclical clearly distinguishes the object of a concrete choice, and the corresponding action, from ulterior intentions with

which a choice is made. It seems to me that one of the central problems implied in thus distinguishing choices and their objects from
further intentions may be formulated as follows: *What precisely* is
qualified when an action or freely chosen behavior is qualified as
"morally evil" *by virtue of its very "object"*? This point, I think, must
be carefully elucidated if we want to talk reasonably about concrete
actions, or choices of determinate behaviors, being morally evil by
virtue of their very object, i.e., *independent* of further intentions. If
we could not sustain the distinction between the "object" and "ulterior   intentions"   of   a   concrete   choice,   adherents   of
"consequentialism" or "proportionalism" could successfully deny
being implicated in the encyclical's criticism of these positions.

In order to answer the above question, however, another very
important assertion of the encyclical must not be overlooked. After having affirmed, in n. 78, that "the morality of the human act
depends primarily and fundamentally on the 'object' rationally
chosen by the deliberate will," the text of the encyclical adds the
following remark:

> In order to be able to grasp the object of an act which speci-
> fies that act morally, it is therefore necessary to place one-
> self *in the perspective of the acting person*.

And this is so, the encyclical continues, for the following reason (the emphasis is mine):

> The object of the act of willing is in fact a *freely chosen* kind
> of behavior. . . . By the object of a given moral act, then, one
> cannot mean a process or an event of the merely physical
> order, to be assessed on the basis of its ability to bring about
> a given state of affairs in the outside world. Rather, that
> object is the proximate end of a deliberate decision which de-
> termines the act of willing on the part of the acting person.
> (*VS* 78.1)

The above quoted rejection which follows in the encyclical (*cf.*
VS 79) in fact is formulated in quite a sophisticated way (e.g., it refers both "object" and the predicate "morally evil" to "*choice* of
behavior" and not simply to "behavior")[3] This sentence, repeated
in n. 82, remains the doctrinal core of the whole encyclical and one
of the cornerstones of its argument. And it seems to me that no
teleological ethical theory—be it consequentialist or proportionalist—can reasonably deny being affected, indeed, hit in the

heart, by this rejection. For it is characteristic for all teleological ethical theories that they consider senseless any distinction between objects and further intentions, as well as that they reject the possibility both of judging wrong a chosen action independently from all the foreseen consequences, and of speaking on this level as such about moral evil.

During the following exposition I will, without referring much to the text of the encyclical, simply expose how—according to my views which owe so much to the work of many others—the encyclical's teaching should be understood. I not only intend to follow Aquinas's ethical theory but also to render explicit some implicit presuppositions in the field of action theory that are necessary to render fully intelligible both Aquinas's account of moral objects as such and its pertinence for our present problem.[4]

I shall first clarify the term "object" as used in practical reasoning (Section 2). I then clarify the basic perspective in which we have to consider our problem, the perspective of intentionality, showing how problematic it is when an ethical theory distinguishes moral from non-moral goods (Section 3). This opens the way to speak properly about the object of a human act, which of course is fundamental for knowing what precisely is qualified when an action is qualified as "evil by virtue of its object" (Section 4). In the longest section (5), I will challenge the distinction between right-making properties and good-making properties of an action; I argue for a virtue-oriented rather than norm-or rule-based ethics, showing why only the former is able really to explain why there are in fact some intrinsically evil acts. In Section 6, I shall show how intentionality explains the *rational* structure of what we call the object of a human act. Finally, in Section 7, I will add some remarks about how to integrate my analysis into the general frame of a natural law theory.

II. Objects of Actions as Objects of Practical Reason

According to Aquinas, every action intended by the will is a *"bonum apprehensum et ordinatum per rationem,"* a "good understood and ordered by reason."[5] Clearly human acts are specified by different objects; every potency has its own specific object, which is its proper end. However, the human act is morally specified only by an "object in so far as it is related to the principle of human acts, that is reason."[6] One must, therefore, guard against identifying the object which provides the moral specification of an act with "things" or the natural ends of single potencies. As Germain Grisez has put it,

> human acts have their structure from intelligence. Just inso-
> far as an action is considered according to its naturally given
> structure, it is to that extent not considered as a *human act*—
> i.e., as a moral act—but rather as a physiological process or
> as instinctive behavior. Action with a given structure and
> acts structured by intelligence differ as totally as nature dif-
> fers from morality. Nature has an order which reason can
> consider but cannot make and cannot alter. Morality has an
> order which reason institutes by guiding the acts of the will.[7]

The object which provides the moral specification is always the object of a human act *just insofar* as it is an act of a *human* being. Without the act of practical reason which relates to any object in a specifically *moral* way, there is neither a human act nor a personal meaning of such acts. To speak of the "object of an action" is to speak of the content of an *intentional* action. That is to say, the morally relevant object of an action is the content of an act *insofar as* it is the object of an *intentio voluntatis* (whether this is on the level of the choice of concrete, particular actions, or on the level of intending *further* ends for the sake of which a concrete action is chosen as a means). With this we see that every object is equally the object of the practical reason which orders and regulates, the fundamental rule or measure of which is the natural law. Only in this way do both the various natural ends of human potencies and the *usus rerum exteriorum* become integrated into the personal *suppositum* in a cognitive-practical way. They thus become objec-tified in their intelligibility, which renders possible the recognition of their morally objective meaning.

III. The Perspective of Intentionality and the So-called Non-Moral Goods

The *bona propria*, i.e., the proper goods toward which the individual potencies are ordered as ends—considered in their ontic structure, independently from their being potencies of a human person, that is, considered on the level of their *"genus naturae"*—are not yet moral goods which are as such morally significant (they are no *bona debita* for the acting person as such).[8] But calling them "non-moral" goods seems to be equally erroneous. One simply cannot make moral judgments on the level of *"genus naturae."* However, to call these proper goods of potencies "nonmoral goods" is actually a moral qualification, since it is possible only from an ethical perspective. To be ethical, a perspective must take account of the acting subject's intentional relation to acts and ends. To affirm that the ends of natural inclinations are nonmoral goods or non-moral values is to assert that they do not possess an inherent *"proportio ad rationem."* This would mean that they were exactly *as inclinations "indifferentes ex specie,"* in St. Thomas's language, or that these inclinations, acts, and ends are morally indifferent not only if we consider them abstractly in their *"genus naturae,"* but also if we conceive them as forming part of the human *suppositum.* Again, this would mean that only *further* circumstances or intentions of the acting subject *by which* he acts on these inclinations and performs the acts proper to them would have a moral qualification, while the inclinations themselves would not.

To look at natural inclinations and their ends in an abstract-ontic way is, however, neither ethically nor anthropologically an adequate way of considering them. It simply can never lead to a morally qualifying judgment, and this is precisely what the assertion means which states that they are "indifferent" (*"adiaphora"*) or non-moral goods.[9] It is not the ends of these inclinations which are non-moral, but rather the abstract way of considering them which is non-moral. The problem springs from looking at natural inclinations simply as *natural* inclinations, inclinations of the *"genus naturae"* abstracted from the actual human person.[10]

This means that inclinations, their proper acts, and ends are falsely looked at as "data," "facts," and "state of affairs," from the perspective of an outside observer, rather than as inclinations of an intellectually and thus willingly striving person. As such, every human being experiences his inclinations as *his* inclinations, as something that he willingly and intentionally *pursues.* This, precisely, is not recognizable from the viewpoint of an outside observer.

From the viewpoint of the external observer, we also say that birds build nests because the outcome of a bird's gathering different materials and executing determinate bodily movement is in fact a nest. But do birds really build nests? That is, do they perform the *action* of "building a nest"? For this they should *intend*, in gathering materials, the goal of building a nest; they should gather materials, move, and work *for the sake of* building a nest. Moreover, they even should also intend the "why" of building the nest, e.g., "to protect their offspring." With good reason we assume that they indeed are not doing this.[11] A human person, however, who strives for self-preservation or for the care of his offspring, and who performs corresponding actions, does not only "arrive at" preserving his life, etc.; rather, he also *intends* it *in* his actions. He does something *for the sake of* preserving himself and caring for his offspring, and this "for the sake of" is a content of his *will*. Self-preservation and care for offspring are, in this case, objects of an intending will, guided by reason. And as such, the corresponding goods (self-preservation, care for offspring) are much more than the resulting *states of affairs* of "self-preservation" or "protection of offspring." It rather is a practical principle that guided a freely chosen act and its intentional content, a content that determines as an intelligible good the agent's will.[12] These contents of intentionality (self-preservation, care for others, and similar things) are *already on the level of natural inclination* a "good" of a striving *human person* and, therefore, "good for man" in the context of the person as a whole. It is precisely this which we call a "moral good." "Moral goods" are the contents of *acts of the will*. And the contents of acts of the will are precisely that which we call, from a moral viewpoint, their *objects*.

We can conclude that to call the ends pursued by natural inclinations "non-moral" goods signifies, in the final analysis, a moral qualification (or "dis-qualification") based on the *"genus naturae"* of these inclinations and their corresponding acts. This, however, is an illicit *transgressio in aliud genus* and, therefore, results in a conclusion easily recognizable as a sort of "naturalistic fallacy." The naturalistic fallacy is based on a failure to see that the *"genus naturae"* and the *"genus moris"* are not derivable one from the other.[13] The fallacy occurs when one adopts a morally qualifying predicate on the level of *"genus naturae."* But "moral indifference" actually is such a predicate. Equally, "morally right" is a morally qualifying predicate. It is a predicate which proportionalists adopt for actions on the basis of the resulting balance of non-moral goods which can be foreseen.

In this context the Stoic doctrine of the *adiaphora* is sometimes invoked:[14] Life, health, beauty, property, social status, honor, etc. are not, one says, goods which determine a person's being a good person. This depends exclusively on the goodness of the will. I would argue in the following way against this attempt to defend consequentialism by invoking this Stoic teaching: The Stoic doctrine only intends to differentiate the sphere of being from the sphere of acting. Indeed, whether somebody is a good or a wicked person does not depend on the state in which he happens to find himself or the state in which he happens to arrive *independently* from his willing as an acting subject. "Good" and "evil" as objects of practical reason and intentional striving, however, are not at all states of affairs, in which the acting subject happens to find himself. As soon as the agent relates practically to goods/bads as life, health, physical integrity, truth, property, it is no longer possible to call those goods or bads *adiaphora*, indifferent things or "extra-moral" goods; for the practical relation itself involves, with regard to them, one willingly taking a position on the basis of a judgment of practical reason; and it is precisely this which determines the quality of the *will* as a good or an evil will. So precisely insofar as a good is a *practical* good (or object of a free will oriented to action) it *cannot* be a non-moral good because *it is impossible that the will relates to "good" in a non-moral way* (not even to a piece of bread practically judged and chosen as "to be eaten here and now"). The Stoics wanted only to emphasize that moral goodness consists in an attitude of indifference with regard to any good other than virtue itself. So they intended to render praxis itself indifferent as far as it relates to these goods called *adiaphora*. The important thing, the Stoics affirmed, is to be virtuous, which means to live in *apathia* with regard to indifferent goods. Consequentialists and proportionalists, however, are not Stoics. For they assert that precisely in the sphere of these "indifferent goods" man has to take responsibility for optimizing these goods (and minimizing the bads), and that this is the basic criterion of the rightness of an action. That means that they also consider the *practical* relation to single *adiaphora* as "morally indifferent" (while Stoics want to render insignificant this practical relation) and that only the action, which optimizes them, is morally right. This, however, is a thesis in the field of action theory which is profoundly problematic.

IV. "Object" in the Perspective of Human Actions

This problematic consists in confusing the viewpoint of the "first person" (the agent's perspective) with the viewpoint of the third person (the observer's viewpoint). To a large extent, these two perspectives correspond to two quite different concepts of human action: the intentional and the causal-eventistic concept.[15] The latter looks at actions "from outside" and sees them as *events which cause determinate effects*. Events which cause effects, however, are not yet actions (it could, for example, be an earthquake). From such a perspective, "acting" can only be *reconstructed*, as it were, by interpreting the foreseen connection between act-event and its effect as being the reason for which a rational subject has performed this particular act. An action would be explained precisely when it was possible to indicate those *reasons* which the agent might have had for performing the action. The same applies to its moral qualification: The action itself and its effects are simply events or states of affairs (that is, non-moral realities). Only those reasons which an agent might have for causing through the action-event x the effect y (the state of affairs) are morally qualifiable; this, however, only as "morally right or "morally wrong." This, I should add, is more a qualification of effects (of y) and their desirability than a qualification of the actions (of x) by which these effects are brought about.

For example, the action-event x brought about by A could consist in causing (in what way does not matter) the death of P. The caused state of affairs will be "death of P." Only the reasons for the desirability of P's death (in the context of a balance of other goods and bads) would determine whether "to do x" is right or wrong. Such a reason may be, e.g., the foreseeable consequences of A's doing x for *all* concerned (i.e., also the effects of doing x with regard to the life of Q, R, S, T as a consequence of A's doing x; e.g., in a case of hostage-taking and blackmail).

What here, however, is entirely put aside is precisely the acting person as a subject which *intends* something *in* doing x; the acting subject, therefore, which performs x *for the sake of* causing P's death (with the *purpose* of killing him). That is: What is put aside is the *choice* of "killing-P " as a setting of A's will against the life of P. This also means: What is put aside is A's taking a position with regard to a specific *person* to which he owes, as to his fellow-man, this and that. This act of choice can adequately be seen only by looking at human actions in the perspective of the first person: From such a viewpoint there are not only two states of affairs (an action-event and its resulting effect), but also the act of *intending* P's death. This intentionality (which here is a choice, the choice of an action) cannot be reduced to "causing the state of affairs of P's death." Otherwise there would be no difference between what an earthquake "does" and what an acting person does: the object and intentional content of "causing P's death" means to set one's will against the life of P (=against P in the dimension of what fundamentally is good for him) and this positioning of one's will constitutes a specific relation between the acting person and P. The content of this "taking a position" shapes the agent's will and is, as such, the content of a free will, and is good or evil wholly *independently* of other (foreseeable) resulting states of affairs which might be brought about as a consequence of A's abstaining from killing P (as, for example, saving the lives of Q, R, S, T).

From an observer's viewpoint there is therefore no difference between "causing P's death" and "killing P," that is, "doing something *for the sake of* causing P's death." From the observer's viewpoint we may say in the same way "John killed ten persons" and "The earthquake killed ten persons" (as we affirm "The bird built a nest"). What we cannot say in either case from this particular perspective is: Besides the ten killed persons, there is also a *murderer*. In the case of the earthquake this would be simply nonsense; in the case of John, however, it *could* well be the case that he is, in fact, a murderer. But it will never be possible to justify such a differentiation from the observer's viewpoint (otherwise we should equally admit that an earthquake at least *could* be something like a murderer). In reality, however, "to kill P" is not simply "to cause P's being dead," but rather it is *to choose, to intend, to want* P's death (for the sake of *whatever* further end). Those practical goods which are objects of our actions (and here P's death is, for the agent, a practical good, the content of his action) are never such objects simply in their natural, ontic value-quality as states of affairs, but rather as objects of an act of the will guided by reason. That is why objects of actions—precisely *because* of their being objects of a human action—are goods in a *moral* sense. As said before: *bonum apprehensum et ordinatum per rationem.*

Therefore, *practical* reason, which is embedded in appetite, and the corresponding moral reflection never relate to the "bona propria"—the particular goods of single natural inclinations—as mere state of affairs on the level of their *"genus naturae"*; as such they *cannot* be objects or contents of the natural inclination of a *human person* who relates to them appetitively, by will informed by reason. For whom is self-preservation ever simply something given, a good only to be taken into account or a mere state of affairs, no matter how desirable? For whom is it ever a non-moral good, that is, a good which does not concern him as a person striving for the fulfillment of his being? As it was said, the ontic-natural aspect of these goods or ends is a *posterior* abstraction which abstracts them from the context of practical self-experience; so this purely natural aspect is a *reduction* of the proper intelligibility of these goods.

The goods of natural inclinations are never simply a set of given facts, and man is not simply the sum of various inclinations. They rather constitute the proper practical self-experience of persons as *a certain kind* of being. They form a whole, grasped by intelligence as "my" being. So, the practical self-experience of man as naturally striving for goods is precisely what constitutes the *identity* of a person as a *human* person: every inclination and its proper good are experienced as correlated to *my own* striving and not as something alien to me, as, e.g., nature which surrounds me, the world in which I am placed, my environment.[16] This "good-for-me" as object of a reason-guided will, as intelligible human good, is the content of true self-love which, through the golden rule (a rule of reason and as such a rule of the structural principle of justice based on acknowledgment of others as equal to me), leads to the command "Love your neighbor as you love yourself."

This kind of self-experience reflects the original ontological or anthropological integration of different natural parts of the human *suppositum*. On the basis of a metaphysic of the *suppositum*, such an experience is open for a deeper explanation. So it becomes obvious that each natural inclination by its very nature possesses, in the context of the person as a whole and precisely as an inclination *belonging* to a human person, a meaningfulness which from the beginning transcends the mere *"genus naturae."* This transcendence is destroyed or at least obscured by an abstract view which detaches these inclinations from their original context as inclinations of a human person. In a moral objectivation, the "natural meaning" of each natural inclination is precisely a *personal* meaning which must not be identified with its "*genus naturae.*"

The proper work of natural reason—the acts of which are always acts of a person—consists in grasping the transcendence of particular goods, exactly on the basis of the fact that they are integrated into the whole of the human *suppositum* as *intelligible goods*. As such an experienced intelligible whole of goods they form the "Self." In its natural act, which corresponds to a natural inclination to virtue, i.e., to a life guided by reason, reason comprehends these particular goods as *human* goods and therefore as fundamental practical goods of the person. These goods constitute our identity, the consciousness of *who we are* (I and the others) and fundamentally shape the will in respect of "the good for man."

V. The Fallacious Distinction between Right-Making Properties and Good-Making Properties of an Action

Moral philosophers who defend—however divergent be their approaches—a consequentialist position (a teleological ethic) usually are much concerned with emphasizing a fundamental difference between the "moral *rightness*" (or the "right-making properties") and the "moral *goodness*" (the "good-making properties") of an action.[17] The first, they say, concerns the question about the properties which render an action right or wrong; the second is related to those properties of an action insofar as it springs from a free *will*. By way of balancing goods and bads, only the question about the "rightness of types of actions" is meant to be resolved. And this, it is asserted, is the question which properly belongs to normative ethics. The question, however, about what makes the will of the acting subject a "good" will does not, according to their view, depend on whether an action is right or wrong but rather, e.g., on whether one acts out of benevolence toward other persons, out of love of justice, with a will to fairness or to respecting the other's conscience, with a "Christian intentionality," etc.

Of course in a sense this is rather obvious. It is true in the sense that an involuntary, and thus not imputable, error about what one has to do—in this sense a wrong action—may not hinder the will of somebody who acts in this way from being a good will, even as it does the wrong thing, e.g., a will which, in fact, intends justice even if it does not do the just thing. The corresponding action, then, would be at the same time morally good and wrong. The widespread acceptance of this distinction seems to be caused, to a large extent, by the possibility of this state of affairs. It is, however, a case in which the agent in reality does not choose and thus willingly perform the action which he *thinks* he is choosing and performing. It is, therefore, an exceptional case which, for analytical purposes, must be set aside until *after* having determined what basically causes the goodness and the rightness of actions; precisely, because of this, it cannot serve as a paradigm. To be able to justify a distinction between "right" and "good," we must start from the normal condition in which actions are chosen and performed, that is, from the condition that the agent chooses and thus willingly performs exactly the action which he *believes* he is choosing and performing.

Now, the predicates "right" and "wrong" are morally qualifying only insofar as we consider them as predicates for *human acts*. Certainly, a physician may perform an operation "rightly" (correctly, well, efficiently, competently, etc.); despite this, his way of acting may be qualified as "wrong" (e.g., if it is—in the first sense—a "well done" abortion). The first type of qualification concerns the technical aspect of the physician's acting, the second concerns the *moral* rightness of the choice of this action. In both cases we may, instead of "right" or "wrong," also call the action, respectively, "good" or "evil." The designation derives from the *perspective* in which we consider the action: Either we consider it from the technical perspective (the aspect of surgical techniques) or we consider it from a moral perspective (the aspect of its being the voluntary and deliberate action of a human person; this is the properly moral perspective). The second perspective includes the first (one cannot act in a morally right way without caring about one's technical competence). The distinction, however, between "*morally* right" and "*morally* good" seems to be off the point here. The only relevant distinction is the distinction between "*non-morally* (e.g., technically) right/wrong" and "*morally* right/wrong"; the second, however, is equal to (morally) "good" and (morally) "evil."

The position I am criticizing overlooks the fundamental difference between *praxis* and *poiesis*, taking its orientation from a "poietical" model of action.[18] It is indeed characteristic of technical actions that their (technical) rightness is distinguished from the goodness of the will of the person who performs a technical act. Aristotle, however, taught us that the goodness of a praxis (which is *eupraxia*) and the goodness of a moral agent (and this means his willful striving: *orexis*) is a specific kind of rightness (*orthotês*) : the rightness of *prohairesis*, of the *choice* of an action. Indeed, we can say that there exist fundamental structures of the rightness of desire which reveal themselves precisely through the *lex naturalis*. These structures determine—despite the legitimacy of a limited and well-defined balancing of goods—that certain actions are always wrong, precisely *because the desire or will involved in these kind of actions cannot be right. Yet a will which is not right is an evil will.* In this sense it is wrong to *choose* to kill a human person (that is: to set one's will against another man's life), whatever be the *further* intention or end for the sake of which this is chosen. To affirm that such a choice is not right (or wrong) means precisely to affirm that this is a disorientated choice of the will, that this is a type of action which *as such* (in itself) is *evil*. "As such" or "in itself" here signifies: independently from further intentions or foreseen consequences.[19] Such an action, springing from a corresponding choice, is evil because it shapes the will, rendering it an evil will, a will directed against "the good for man" (here from the perspective of justice). This precisely is what we designate "not right" or "wrong" in a *moral* sense.[20]

Hence, the distinction between right-making properties and good-making properties is in principle questionable. We always have to describe actions and behaviors as objects of *choices* and, therefore, as *intentional* actions. From such a perspective, however, the goodness of the will is regarded as depending on the goodness of freely chosen, *wanted* actions, which also includes the agent's willingly referring to the specific goal which constitutes the objective intentionality of this action (I will come back to this below). That is why acts of choice are always describable as forms of *rightness*, that is, of the rightness of desire or of the will. This enables us to indicate specific kinds of actions which are never to be chosen because they are not consistent with a good will, e.g., the choice of killing a person, whatever be the further intention. On the other hand, it is indeed possible to choose what is morally right with an evil intention; or to choose to do the morally wrong thing with a good will. Moral philosophers and theologians have always known this in the past, and it has traditionally been considered in ethics.[21]

Certainly many decisions, probably even the great majority of them, are legitimately worked out on the basis of weighing goods and consequences. This is particularly true for decisions taken in a wider social context (e.g. social, economical, scientific and research policy). But corresponding possibilities of action are, on the grounds of *moral reasons*, restricted. They are restricted by the condition that they be consistent with the fundamental "rightness of the will" on the level of concrete choices of actions. Here we encounter the kind of responsibilities which we are accustomed to expressing in so-called *absolute prohibitions*. On this level, the "right" and the "good" (or: the "wrong" and the "evil") basically are identical. Here, balancing goods and calculating possible consequences is *excluded*.[22]

It is one of the most important assertions of classical virtue ethics that there exist conditions for the fundamental rightness of actions which depend on basic structures of the "rightness of desire" and that it is therefore possible to describe particular types of actions, the *choice* of which always involves wrong desire. However, an ethic which understands itself—on the level of "normative ethics—as providing a rational discourse for the purpose of justifying moral *norms* (or rules) will never be able to acknowledge this. Norm-ethics are objectivistic in the sense that they *may not*, on the level of the concrete performance of actions, include in their reflection the acting subject and his willingly taking a position with regard to good and evil in choosing this or that particular action. Similarly they cannot pose the question about the rightness of desire, or about the truth of subjectivity, on the level of concrete choices of particular actions (*independently* from taking into account further intentions regarding the state of affairs or the weighing of consequences which foreseeably will be brought about by these actions or by refraining from them).

I concede it to be true, as has been argued,[23] that the traditional doctrine about the *fontes moralitatis as such* does not resolve problems of normative ethics; it rather presupposes these problems to be already resolved. For with respect to this approach, everything depends each time on what one considers to be the "object" of an action. Consequentialists will assert that to determine the object of a concrete action, one has to take into account its foreseeably resulting consequences for all concerned. In this sense, consequentialism does not deny the doctrine about the *fontes moralitatis*, it merely puts forward a specific solution about how to work out what the "object" of a particular action is.

Nevertheless this classical doctrine about "sources of morality" contains an undeniable assertion which, however, is implicitly denied by consequentialism. It is the assertion that, with regard to human action, it is possible each time to *distinguish* between (1) an "object" by which this action (and the agent's will) is already morally specified as "good," "evil," or "indifferent" *independently* from *further* intentions and (2) these further intentions. So the classical viewpoint holds that there are actions which are evil despite the best of intentions or despite the foreseen and intended outcomes precisely because the *choice* of this particular kind of action *through* which these laudable intentions are meant to be fulfilled must already be considered as morally evil. It will, however, never be possible to render intelligible this moral methodology on the grounds of an ethic which from the beginning is concerned with justifying moral norms. This is so because in such an approach the *distinction* between object and *further* intentions necessarily drops out of view. The only things that a norm ethic can produce in the way of an action theory are the particular occurrences (actions), on the one hand, and the consequences, brought about by them, on the other. If an agent *intends* the best consequences, then it is these which come to be designated the object of his act.

But this does not correspond to our ordinary experience as acting subjects and to the way we arrive at moral decisions; it rather has about it the air of casuistry. From the viewpoint of the acting subject we always encounter at least two intentionalities to be distinguished. If I break the promise of repaying somebody a determinate amount of money, causing by this his economic ruin because I, simultaneously, intend to prevent by this action the ruin of many others, I have *chosen* to break the promise given to my creditor *for the sake of* realizing an intention which is very laudable in itself. But here the object of choice (breaking the promise) is not less intentionally taking a position than the further intention (ben-

efiting others). The same applies to killing or lying with good further intentions.

Moral virtue is not only, as it is sometimes asserted, the will or
the free determination to do "the right thing" each time. Were it
like this, there would exist only one single moral virtue. Instead
moral virtue is the habitual rightness of *appetite* (of sensual affec-
tions, passions, and of the will, the rational appetite) related to the
various spheres of human praxis. An act which is *according* to virtue is an act which is suited to cause this habitual rightness of
appetite which produces "the good person." To keep one's promise is indeed such an act according to moral virtue.

Certainly, we can describe the action "to promise" from the
very beginning in an eventistic way, say, as a kind of uttering
words (a speech act) by which A causes in B the mental state of being certain that A will do x. One may for various reasons consider
it very beneficial that in a society there exists a practice of this sort.
So one will formulate a rule (or norm) according to which one is
bound to abstain from any performance which could deprive others from being certain that, whenever A performs the speech act
of "promising x," x will be brought about by A. The norm " never
break promises" means precisely "always abstain from weakening
the practice of promise-keeping." Even if one holds that the rightness of an action has to be determined exclusively on the basis of
its foreseeable consequences, one must equally consider that the
weakening of the practice of "promise-keeping" will be one of the
consequences—probably the most weighty one—to be included in
the balance. So, on the basis of such a rule-utilitarianism, one
should insist that one is always obliged to keep promises. Or more
precisely: one will not insist that promises have to be kept but
rather that the *rule* or *norm* "keep your promises" has to be *observed*.
This is an important difference (which will become clear immediately). The rule does not express the intrinsic morality of a type of
action but rather *constitutes* the reasonableness of a certain behavior on the grounds of the utility of the rule under which this behavior is subsumed and which is to be maintained by this behavior (for the benefit of society, of course). It is obvious that there
remains the possibility of conflict with other such rules ("conflicts
of obligations"); consequently the rule cannot be valid "absolutely." As a result we have to work out which rule has to be fol-

lowed in such a case: Either on the basis of a hyperrule, or by arguing in an act-utilitarian way. Utilitarian ethics thus tends to become a complicated attempt to resolve the problems of "norm-utilitarianism." Actually it becomes much more concerned with resolving the problems of utilitarian ethical theory than with resolving ethical problems.

It is quite clear that in all these cases an agent may very well do the right thing with an evil will, and sometimes the wrong thing with a good will (calculating or subsuming incorrectly or applying the wrong rule, though intending the overall benefit of society or of all concerned). Here, the discourse concerned with grounding norms and resolving cases of conflict of rules and obligations must be sharply distinguished from another discourse, the one concerned with the conditions of goodness and wickedness of appetite and will. This distinguishing does not, however, reflect the requirements and the structure of moral action but merely the requirements which arise from the particular characteristics of a norm-ethic. As said before, with such arguments one does not resolve *ethical* problems, but at most, if at all, the intrinsic problems of a particular ethical theory.

In reality, as acting subjects, we neither observe nor follow norms or rules, nor do we work out our decisions each time exclusively on the basis of foreseeable consequences for all those affected by our actions. Instead, human action realizes itself in the context of definite moral relationships, the relationships between concrete persons (fellow men, friends, married persons, parents and children, superiors and subordinates, employer and employee, creditor and debitor, physician and patient, partners in a contract, persons who live in a particular community, etc.).[24] Here, it is always concerned with what we *owe* to others, with the question of right and of good will toward particular fellow-men, with the question of responsibilities toward concrete persons.

Let us consider again the example of promise-keeping. Above we have defined "to promise" ("eventistically") as an utterance by which A causes in B the mental state of being certain that A will do x. However, the bringing about of B's mental state of being convinced that A will do x is not necessarily a promise; it could also be a menace, an announcement or a reassurance (what is really *meant* by a speech act like "You can be sure that tomorrow morning I'll come and see you"?). The above eventistic description of promising contains everything except the element which confers on this speech act the quality of being a promise. This it will be only if A wants to *confer on B a right or a claim* on A's doing x. So B's certitude that A will do x is grounded in a relation of *justice* caused precisely by the promissory act. Exactly this relation between A and B (that is: B's having a claim or a right on A's doing-x, and B's owing to A to do x)—a relation brought about by the speech act "I promise you"—that a norm "keep your promises" is nothing else than a more particular or specific version of the principle of justice to render each one what one owes him. The promissory act indeed creates a relationship between persons in which this general rationale of justice now is valid.

It may happen that a situation changes in such a way that the doing of x (for whatever reason) subsequently turns out to be an unjust action; or even that doing x was unjust from the very beginning, that is, that A had promised B to do something unjust. Is it possible that B has a claim (a right) on A's committing an unjust act? Certainly not. The promise becomes in reality vain (or reveals itself as vain or immoral from the beginning). So the promise, in reality, is not broken; by not keeping it no injustice is committed; rather the very promissory act was unjust, and it now would be according to justice that A in a way indemnifies B, who has been deceived. In order to be able to judge whether a promise keeps binding the person who made it, the consequences of doing x must be considered (an action without *any* consequence is not an action at all). But these will always be the consequences in the sphere of the question whether B continues licitly to *claim* A's keeping the promise, that is: A's doing x. The question can never arise whether such an *existing* claim may be overridden in favor of other more important or more numerous goods benefiting Q, R, S, T (even if there may be cases in which the benefits for Q, R, S, T precisely will determine whether B continues to have a claim on A's doing x). In any case, the relation between A and B established by making the promise, and the consequences relating to Q, R, S, T, are two different things; one cannot say that we are, *in principle*, responsible for all the foreseen consequences of our actions or omissions. B's being deceived by a promise which may possibly not be kept certainly cannot be regarded as simply one among many consequences of not keeping the promise. So it may be possible that not keeping a promise is unjust with regard to B even if the state of affairs resulting from not keeping it were, as such, more desirable than the one brought about by keeping the promise. In this case, not keeping it would be morally wrong because the choice of an unjust action involves the wrongness of the will.

Anyhow, this view remains far too abstract. In reality things are resolved in other ways. In reality an agent who intends justice will try, for example, to achieve a delay in repaying the debt. Or he will find (or at least try to find) a way to prevent by other means the ruin of Q, R, S, T. His refusal to commit an injustice against his creditor by breaking the promise will lead him to discover new lines of action, alternatives, and formerly unseen opportunities. To describe this, we would need to tell a story. Virtuous actions are, in this sense, rendered intelligible only in a narrative context.[25] But the right thing to do will always be the action which is consistent with the rightness of appetite, with the rightness of our will's relation to concrete persons with whom we live together in defined relationships.

Many details should be added, and there is still much to be specified. But the fundamental difference between virtue-and norm-ethics consists in the fact that for the former the morally right is always determined, *as well as* rightness of appetite, with regard to the "good-for-man" on the level of concrete actions and in relation to particular persons, persons with whom the agent encounters himself living in morally qualified relationships (be they naturally given or be they relationships established by free acts, such as promises, contracts, etc.). That is why a virtue ethic can speak about actions which are "intrinsically," "always and per se," "on account of their very object" evil (cf. *VS* 80). A norm-ethic of utilitarian character, however, that in the last analysis is an argumentatively proceeding norm-ethic, cannot do justice to such qualified relationships. Consequently, it is compelled to detach the category of the "rightness of actions" from the category of the "goodness of the will." That is why it simply will not understand that the intentional relation of the will to "justice," i.e., the "just will," is at stake in every concrete choice of a particular action.[26]

VI. The Intentional Structure of Practical Objects as "Forms Conceived by Reason"

Teleological ethics owes a large amount of its plausibility—as far as Catholic moral theology is concerned—not least to the fact that it was directed against a naturalistic (or physicalist) misunderstanding of the *"moralitas ab obiecto."*[27] Yet, despite this justified aim, adherents to these teleological approaches do not seem to have recognized the real source of this misunderstanding, which consists in overlooking the fact that practical reason is embedded in the intentional process of human acting, being a part of it. That is why, I think, these new approaches remained themselves addicted to a surprising, even extreme, naturalism. Particular actions implicitly are considered by them as analogous to events and their outcomes as state of affairs. They implicitly presuppose, on the level of particular actions, a causal-eventistic concept of action (action as causing a state of affairs). I said "implicitly," because adherents of teleological ethics do not explicitly defend such a corresponding action theory (they actually deal very little with questions of action theory).[28] That is why they are compelled to reclaim the aspect of intentionality—the aspect of willingly taking a position with regard to good and evil—on the level of fundamental options and attitudes, on the level of *Gesinnung*. So consequentialists fail to see that independently from *further* intentions required to optimize consequences or goods on the level of caused states of affairs, an action may already be qualifiable as *morally evil*. And this means: That a particular type of action, describable in behavioral terms, may be qualified as causing an *evil will* simply because it is *evil* to want (and therefore to choose) certain actions as practical objects (=as the "good to be done"). The problem is bypassed, even veiled, by describing chosen actions from the observer's viewpoint, thus leaving out of consideration precisely the act of choice. Probably the most famous example of such an argumentative reductionism is Caiaphas' advice to the Sanhedrin: "It is better for you that a single man dies for the people, than that the whole people perishes." As a judgment about a simple event or a state of affairs and its desirability, this obviously is quite true. But it is well known that Jesus did not simply die but was killed.

Precisely because objects of our actions are intentional objects, that is, objects of acts of the will, they can only be shaped by reason; for the will is the appetite which follows the judgment of reason. As Aquinas emphasizes: "Species moralium actuum constituuntur ex formis, prout sunt a ratione conceptae."[29] This "form conceived by reason" is nothing other than the object of an action in its *"genus moris."*

This again is closely connected with the fact that every human action is an *intentional* action. And this is why it is something that does not simply happen, but something *willingly pursued* and as such *formed* or shaped by reason. A concrete practical matter (*materia circa quam*)—the same applies to the matter of natural inclinations—is *as such*, considered in its pure materiality, always *less* than the content or object of an action with respect to the natural inclination of a *human person*. If in greeting somebody or giving a starting signal, I raise my arm, then raising my arm (the matter of action) is *as such* something which can neither be chosen or performed. The real content of an act of choice and of the describable behavior is exclusively the intentional, i.e., human, action "greeting somebody" *or* "giving a starting signal." In this, however, the practical reason which judges the action as a practical good (something good to do here and now) is already involved. To know what a person is doing by raising his arm, one must know why (in the sense of "what for") he raises his arm. The "why" here is the formal aspect, the *forma rationis* which only renders understandable the event of the raising of an arm as a human action. This "why" (or "what for") confers on the action its *intentional identity*, which is able to inform and shape the agent's will.[30]

In his "Philosophical Investigations," Ludwig Wittgenstein asks "what is left over if I subtract the fact that my arm goes up from the fact that I raise my arm ?"[31] We might answer: What is left over is precisely the *purpose* or *intention* to greet somebody or to give a starting signal. That means that what remains is *"to want* to raise the arm *under the aspect of a specific description,"* which is a description of the intentionality involved in the performance. To choose an action under a description again involves practical reason which judges greeting somebody or giving a starting signal as something which is good to do here and now. One might object: But you could just simply raise your arm. Well, I would answer, just try to do it!

It is true that it might just happen (involuntarily, as a reflex, while sleeping); but this is not a human act. If, however, somebody wanted simply to raise his arm, he again would do more than simply raise his arm. If we subtracted from his doing this action the fact that his arm goes up, we would have left over, e.g., Wanting to show the author of this paper that he is wrong. What would be left over is a "why," the intentional content or the form of this act of raising one's arm.

Therefore, "to greet somebody by raising one's arm" is properly the object of an action, which *in itself* possesses already an intentional structure. In precisely this structure, respectively the whole (the matter of the action + its "why or "what for") is a *forma a ratione concepta*. Things like greeting or affability or gratefulness or justice, that is, corresponding actions to these, do not exist in nature. There do not exist corresponding natural forms. These acts are intentionalities *formed* by practical reason. That is why the *objective* content of human actions can be expressed each time only in an intentional description of the corresponding action. "What" we do is always a "why" we do something *on purpose*. It is a "material doing" (*materia circa quam*) chosen *under a description*, while it is the description which actually contains the intentional content of the action. That is why it seems to me correct when Elizabeth writes: "We must always remember that an object is not what what is aimed at *is*; the description under which it is aimed at is that *under which* it is *called* the object."[32]

It is often overlooked (as, for example, by L. Janssens) that an object of the will necessarily is an action-matter *apprehensum et ordinatum a ratione*. For this reason, it possesses by itself a moral specificity; it never can be wanted or chosen as a non-moral good or end.[33] Equally one overlooks that the end (*finis*) is not only an object of *further* intentions, but also that the particular choice of an action has its proper end: the action as an object.

That is why, each time Aquinas speaks about *finis*" an author like L. Janssens reads *finis operantis*, overlooking thereby that the object of the exterior act of the will is in itself an end, but not this *further* end for the sake of which the action itself is chosen; instead it is the sort of end which Aquinas sometimes (very few times) calls the *finis operis*.[34] This *finis operis*, however, is the *basic* intentional content of a concrete action (without which it would not be a human action at all), and therefore something like the formal object of an action.[35] Such basic contents are not events like "the raising of an arm," but rather "greeting somebody" or "giving a starting signal." They are neither "things" nor "qualified things" as, for example, a *res aliena*; but actions "under a description" as "misappropriate a *res aliena*," that is "stealing." The arm itself is not able to greet or to give a starting signal; and an action in which a *"res aliena"* is involved is not necessarily a theft (it may also be the action of seizing something stolen carried out by the police). Equally the so-called *"finis operis* is an *agent's* goal; but it is the goal he pursues independently of the *further* goals he may pursue by choosing this concrete action. It is the goal which specifies the performed action as a determinate *type* of intentional action, the one which Aquinas usually calls the *finis proximus* of a human act, i.e., its object.

The "species" of an action is precisely the species *"ab obiecto relato ad principium actuum humanorum, quod est ratio."*[36] The *finis operis* is nothing other than the object of *choice* (the choice of the action), which by itself is an act of the will informed by reason.

The so-called "absolute prohibitions," that is, normative propositions which indicate that certain, describable actions may *never* be licitly chosen and willingly performed, therefore relate to actions described *intentionally*. It is impossible to do this independently from the content of the acts of choice which relate to such actions. So, for example (although this is not the case with such prohibited actions), a "norm" cannot refer simply to "raising one's arm" but to "greeting somebody by raising one's arm" or "giving a starting signal by a movement of one's arm." Only to actions described in such a way can a moral norm reasonably relate. The norm "never kill" receives, in this way, a clear structure.[37]

VII. Natural Law: The Fundamental Rule for the Goodness of Will

As Aquinas says in one of his most concise phrasings, "natural law is nothing other than the light of the intellect given us by God by which we recognize what is to be done and what is to be avoided, a light and law which God has bestowed to man in creation."[38] Natural law is not simply an object of human reason. But like all kinds of law, it consists precisely in judgments of practical reason itself, it is a specific set of *"propositiones universales rationis practicae ordinatae ad actiones,"* a set of "universal propositions of practical reason directed to actions."[39]

As I have shown elsewhere, there exists a parallelism between the constitution of objects of actions as moral objects on the one hand and the constitution of the precepts of natural law on the other.[40] Both objects of human actions and precepts of natural law refer to an *"appetibile apprehensum et ordinatum per rationem."* Both the *praeceptum* of the natural law and the object of a concrete action (which is the object of choice, in itself prescriptive) are *"aliquid a ratione constitutum"*[41] and spring from an *"ordinatio rationis."*[42] By natural law, this *objective*—that is, rationally ordered—meaning of natural inclinations is expressed *in universali*. And therefore natural law is properly the law by which particular judgments of practical reason are rectified.[43] So in two senses natural law is a " law of reason": it is a law *constituted by* reason (on the universal level), and a law *referred to* and *regulating* reason (on the level of particular judgments).

In this way the precepts of the natural law are recognizable as properly *practical principles* of the practical intellect determining concrete actions. This intellect possesses its perfection in prudence (practical wisdom). The questions dealt with here were not questions of "normative ethics"; I did not claim to ground specific moral norms. It concerned a question which first had to be clarified before one could even speak about the grounding of moral norms and normative ethics. I wanted to clarify *how*, from a properly *moral* perspective, we have to speak about moral norms and normative ethics and what the term moral norms refers to. Briefly we now can say: Moral norms are, in ethics and in the moral life, a quite specific way of *speaking* about intentional human actions and their practical principles. More precisely, norms are *normative propositions* (propositions in the mode of "ought," "may," "must not," etc.) about intentional actions *based on* practical principles."[44]

Theories like teleological ethics (consequentialism and proportionalism) sometimes present themselves as natural-law theories. They on principle rightly do so, because every natural-law theory consists of a theory about practical reason and the structure of moral judgment performed by human reason. And teleological ethical theories, defending the cognitive moral autonomy of man, in fact *are* theories about what is meant by "to act according to reason".[45] However, we may now be able to give a critical evaluation of these theories. First, they do not properly have a conception about *principles* of practical reason. This can also be regarded as a consequence of their lack of action-analysis. Teleological ethics essentially and exclusively is a decision-making theory: it tries to explain how we work out decisions about what to do here and now. If adherents of this theory speak of *principles*, they do so only to establish some more-general rules for the orientation of decision-making. These rules or principles, however, do not have, according to this theory, a *proper* origin, that is, an origin different from the very logic of a particular decision-making process. So consequentialism and proportionalism do not really provide a natural-law theory. They provide a theory about reasonable action, which basically fails to acknowledge what is most essential for natural law: The existence of real practical *principles* that are not derived from determinate forms of decision-making procedures but are the real *moral measure* for the decision-making process.

Secondly, by measuring the moral rightness of single types of action exclusively on the basis of their foreseeable consequences related to non-moral goods and bads, this theory presupposes a concept of action which simply leaves out of consideration a basic aspect of human actions: The fact that the acting subject, that is, its *will*, takes a position with regard to good and evil already by *choosing* concrete actions which bring about such consequences. This taking a position relates to the agent's own person and to other persons (including God). So it seems that the theory does not acknowledge what actually follows from a more adequate analysis of human action: That *in the will* of the agent the properly moral qualities of good and evil may also appear *independently* from the whole of foreseeable consequences. Adherents of teleological ethics consequently omit in principle an *intentional* description of those particular types of action which afterwards they qualify, on the basis of their decision-making procedure, as right or wrong. To defend their theory, they are *compelled* to describe these actions as mere events. Then at the same time they indicate the difficulties and aporias which logically derive from such a non-intentional concept of action, difficulties and aporias regarding the concept and the respective determination of the object of an action, so that, finally, they are able to offer their theory as the only reasonable solution for these problems, problems, however, created by their very approach rather than by the subject matter of ethics itself.[46] The solution offered by adherents of teleological ethics maintains that action-events brought about by acting subjects may be qualified as right or wrong according to whether they bring about the best overall consequences for all the concerned, an optimum of goods or a minimum of bads.

I have argued, however, that even if the non-moral consequences of an action are optimal and mostly desirable, the action by which they have been brought about may nevertheless be an *evil* action. I would insist that everybody knows that this is possible. Whoever brings about the best of all worlds (the world with an optimum of non-moral goods or a minimum of non-moral bads) can, at the same time, be a murderer or a villain, and this not simply because he acted, say, to assure his own glory and therefore with a fundamentally evil intentionality, but precisely because we would judge as wicked the *actions* he performed. This obviously shows already that such a world would not be the best of all. The problem with consequentialist ethics is not that it does not share this conviction or that its adherents are inclined to plead for amorality, but that consequentialism is not able to *explain* what all of us know. The secret of consequentialism does not consist in denying this truth, just as it does not deny the truth of the proposition that a good intention cannot "sanctify" evil means. Instead the secret of these methodologies consists in making the *acting* subject disappear which, in its concrete choices of particular actions, takes a position with his will with regard to good and evil. As a result, the verdict about the good intentions which cannot "sanctify" evil means is simply rendered *irrelevant* and *pointless*. For if the means (that is: the concrete actions we choose and willingly perform) only can be right or wrong, and this depending on their foreseeably resulting consequences in the field of non-moral goods and bads, then *by definition* there cannot exist such a thing as an evil means. Instead there can be, at most, "wrong" means, that is, means chosen on the basis of an error about which means would be the right one in order to achieve a determinate goal. To justify the concept of "intrinsically evil action," an intentional concept of action is required, and a corresponding concept of the intentional basic contents of concrete types of actions. This "intentional basic content" of an action is what we usually call its moral object."[47]

We all understand a "good person" to be a person whose *will* is a good one, even if to be good, such a will must often pay a high price: The price of accepting mostly undesirable consequences of its being a good will. But it is better to suffer injustice than to commit it.[48] This proposition precisely means quite specifically that it is *morally better* to abstain from an action the performance of which would be unjust, even if as a consequence of refraining from it, a much greater injustice committed by others would foreseeably result, an injustice that, however, I will suffer. If we set aside the acting subject, the injustice *committed* by me and the injustice *suffered* by me (and committed by another person) appear just as two different states of affairs. The point (long ago expressed by Democritus) is that one cannot and *may* not compare these two consequences, nor may one weigh the action to be avoided against the undesirable consequences of refraining from this action. And this simply for the reason *that the action as such, considered in itself, is an unjust action.* This is precisely what a consequentialist (teleological) ethic is unable to justify.

It can be seen that the natural law manifests itself as the totality of principles of practical reasonableness, which not only moves us to act and to do the truly good but also compels us to refrain from committing injustice. Natural law is the proper law of a good will. It orients human persons, as *striving* subjects, to the good-for-man, on the level of himself and of his fellowmen. It equally makes him refrain from evil, from poisoning his soul. A life that maintains this orientation to the good-for-man in each and every single act of choice may rightly be called a successful life. A person who lives such a life therefore deserves praise, and we consider him or her as a person who is on the way to sharing in true happiness, of participating in what the Greek philosophers called *eudaimonia*.

It will always remain difficult to disprove convincingly teleological ethical theories (consequentialism, proportionalism) as long as one tries to do so in the logic proper to norm or rule ethics. The Church's teaching about "law"—"eternal," "natural," or "positive," "divine," or "human," "old" and "new"—was, in the past centuries, profoundly and not very happily influenced by the logic of norm and rule ethics. For different reasons, moral theologians emphasized the "observers' viewpoint." Unlike the classical and medieval tradition of moral theory, the modern tradition was not interested in exposing a comprehensive conception of the good life as part of the intellectual enterprise involved in coming to an understanding of man and of the sense of his existence. From the sixteenth century onward, moral theology, intensively permeated with casuistry, was rather concerned with judgments about whether particular acts were compatible, or not, with a conception of the good life already established by revealed positive law and the corresponding moral norms.

This concern, however, falls short of the genuine way we arrive at a proper understanding of the real requisites of morality. For this, also in a Christian context, a virtue-centered moral theory is needed, be it on the level of philosophical ethics or on that of moral theology.[49] Teleological ethics has not yet escaped from the logic of a legalistic approach; it only now tries to "save freedom from a supposed menace by law. By asserting in n. 78 that "to be able to grasp the object of an act which specifies that act morally, it is therefore necessary to place oneself *in the perspective of the acting person,*" the encyclical *Veritatis splendor* opens a new way directed to rediscovering the perspective proper to virtue ethics, which is the genuine perspective of morals.

Endnotes

1. I thank Prof. John M. Haas of Philadelphia for having carefully reviewed my English version of this paper, originally written in German (and not yet published).
2. The term "teleological" as a characterization of ethical theories became successful through C. D. Broad's essay, "Some of the Main Problems of Ethics," *Philosophy* 21 (1946), reprinted in C. D. Broad, *Broad's Critical Essays in Moral Philosophy*, ed. D. R. Cheney (London: Allen & Unwin; New York: Humanities Press, 1971), 223–46. Broad simply identified any "teleological" argumentation with a consequentialist one. So he says (p. 230 of the reprinted essays): "One characteristic which tends to make an act right is that it will produce at least as good consequences as an alternative open to the agent in the circumstances (. . .) We can sum this up by saying that the property of being *optimistic* is a very important right-tending characteristic. I call it *teleological* because it refers to the goodness of the ends or consequences which the act brings about." Broad, then, goes on to say that a "non-teleological" characteristic of an action would be, for example, the obligation, independent from considering consequences, to perform what one has promised. But already in 1930 Broad had distinguished "teleological" from "deontological" ethical theories; see C. D. Broad, *Five Types of Ethical Theory* (London: Routledge & Kegan Paul, 1930), 206 ff. Many, today, call non-teleological ethics (in Broad's sense) "deontological"; cf. William K. Frankena, *Ethics* (Englewood Cliffs, N.J.: Prentice Hall, 1963). The term "teleological ethics" was thus "imported" by German moral theologians, mainly by Bruno Schüller; see his *Die Begründung sittlicher Urteile: Typen ethischer Argumentation in der Moraitheologie*, 2nd ed. (Düsseldorf: Patmos, 1980), 282–98 (first published in 1973). According to Schüller, a normative ethic would be "teleological" if it affirms that "the moral character of *all* the actions and the omissions of man is *exclusively* determined by its consequences" (282). So he uses "teleological ethics" as synonymous with "consequentialism" (a term in fact created by G. E. M. Anscombe) and even with "utilitarianism." Its counterpart would be "deontological ethics," which holds that there are *some* actions the moral rightness of which should *not* be judged exclusively on the basis of their consequences; see also Bruno Schüller, "Various Types of Grounding for Ethical Norms," in *Readings in Moral Theology No.1: Moral Norms and Catholic Tradition*, ed. Charles E. Curran and Richard A. McCormick, S.J. (New York: Paulist Press, 1979), 184–98. However, as it seems to me, these distinctions are not very clarifying; they rather seem to confuse judgments of prudence ("such and such is the right thing to do") with judgments of conscience ("I must do what I know to be the right thing, whatever the consequences"). Everyone must be a "deontologist" on *this* (second) level if he does not want to deny that one must follow one's conscience (see for this some of my publications to which I refer further on). For supplementary terminological clarifications, see J. M. Finnis, *Fundamentals of Ethics* (Washington, D.C.: Georgetown University Press; Oxford: Clarendon Press, 1983), 81–86.
3. Compare this also with n. 1761 of the *Catechism of the Catholic Church*, quoted in *VS* 78: ". . . there are certain specific kinds of behavior that are always wrong to choose, because choosing them involves a disorder of the will, that is, a moral evil."
4. See a more detailed account in my following books and articles: *Natur als Grundlage der Moral* (Innsbruck-Wien: Tyrolia Verlag, 1987); *La prospettiva della morale: Fondamenti dell'etica filosofica* (Rome: Armando Editore, 1994); "Menschliches Handeln und seine Moralitat: Zur Begrundung sittlicher Normen," in Martin Rhonheimer, Andreas Laun, Tatjana Goritschewa, Walter Mixa, *Ethos und Menschenbild* (St. Ottilien: EOSVerlag, 1989), 45–114; "Zur Begründung sittlicher Normen aus der Natur," and "Ethik-Handeln-Sittlichkeit," *Der Mensch als Mitte* und *Massstab der Medizin*, ed. Johannes Bonelli (Wien-New York: Springer Verlag, 1992), 49–94 and 137–74; finally, my investigations into Aquinas's interpretation and completion of Aristotle's action

theory are expected to be published under the title *Praktische Vernunft und Vernünftigkeit der Praxis* (Berlin: Akademie Verlag, 1994).*

5. *STh* I–II, q. 20, a. 1 ad 1. In *STh* I–II, q. 18, a. 10, Aquinas affirms that the object which specifies an action morally is a "forma a ratione concepta."

6. "... ab obiecto relato ad principium actuum humanorum, quod est ratio" (*STh* I–II, q. 18, a. 8). The "bonum virtutis" consists "ex quadam commensuratione actus ad circumstantias et finem, *quam ratio facit*" (*In II Sent.*, d. 39, q. 2, a. 1).

7. Germain Grisez, "A New Formulation of a Natural-Law Argument against Contraception." *The Thomist* 30:4 (1966): 343.

8. The distinction between (*"actus"* or *"finis"*) *proprium* on the one side, and *debitum* on the other, goes back to *STh* I–II, q. 91, a. 2. See for this my *Natur als Grundlage der Moral*, 72 ff.

9. Cf. *STh* I–II, q. 18, a. 8: Aquinas arrives at identifying an act as indifferent *"in specie"* by the assertion that the *act as such* has no proportion to the *"ordo rationis"*; considered in itself the choice of such an act is not yet meaningful for practical reason, "sicut levare festucam de terra, ire ad campum et huiusmodi." It is something quite different to consider an act, which by itself *does* possess such a "proportio ad rationem," *independently* from this relation to reason, that is, on its merely natural level (e.g., an act of eating or nutrition, an act of sexual copulation). In this case, this will be a biological, physiological or psychological viewpoint which in no way allows a moral judgment. The qualification of an act as "indifferent," however, *is* precisely such a moral judgment.

10. Aquinas also sometimes uses the expression "consideratio *absoluta*," that is, a consideration of acts detaching them from the wider context in which a moral qualification would be possible. Cf. *In IV Sent.*, d. 16, q. 3, a. 1, q. 1, a. 2, ad 2: "aliqui actus ex suo genere sunt mali vel boni (. . .). Hoc autem ex quo actus reperitur in tali genere, quamvis sit de substantia eius inquantum est ex genere moris, tamen est extra substantiam ipsius secundum quod consideratur ipsa substantia actus absolute: unde aliqui actus sunt idem in specie naturae qui differunt in specie moris; sicut fornicatio et actus matrimonialis." Both fornication and a matrimonial act are, as sexual acts considered in their *"genus naturae"* and in their corresponding physiological, biological, and in a sense also in their affective aspects, strictly identical acts. Nevertheless the human sexual act is not *an "actus indifferens"* if considered in its *"genus moris."*

11. This is not an argument against teleology in nature; just the opposite is the case: this teleology exists because we affirm both (1) that birds do not *intend* the goal of building a nest and (2) that they indeed do what they do *for the sake* of building a nest; so the "intention" is inherent in nature.

12. Compare again *VS* 78 (the emphasis is mine) : "The object of the act of willing is in fact a freely chosen kind of behavior. To the extent that it is in conformity with the order of reason, *it is the cause of the goodness of the will; it perfects us morally.*"

13. This reproach, which I have invoked against adherents of so-called "teleological ethics," is not, it seems to me, sufficiently refuted by W. Wolbert in his critique of my position; cf. Werner Wolbert, "Naturalismus in der Ethik: Zum Vorwurf des naturalistischen Fehlschlusses," *Theologie und Glaube* 79 (1989): 234–67, especially 259ff.

14. Bruno Schüller, *Die Begründung sittlicher Urteile*; Werner Wolbert, *Ethische Argumentation und Paränese in 1 Kor 7* (Düsseldorf: Patmos, 1981).

15. About the importance of the perspective of the "first person" see J. M. Finnis, *Fundamentals of Ethics*, 114ff.; Giuseppe Abbà, *Felicità, vita buona e virtù* (Rome: LAS, 1989); Angel Rodriguez Luño, *Etica* (Florence: Le Monnier, 1992) and finally my own *La prospettiva della morale*.

16. This, it seems to me, is an often overlooked differentiation. An example is provided by Louis Janssens, "Ontic Evil and Moral Evil," *Louvain Studies* 4 (1972): 121 (note 34) and 135ff. The bodily dimension of man is here conceived simply as "material part of the material world"; it is named "human" only insofar as this "material part of the

material world" participates at the same time in the subjectivity of single human individuals. Therefore, Janssens considers the body, in a consequent way, as a "means to action," as an instrument of man's subjectivity for his being able to act in the sphere of the external world. With this, the properly "human" is restricted to a spiritually understood subjectivity (without taking into account that also the body originally forms part of man's subjectivity). This, however, is not a personalist view of man, but a view which we could call a "personalistic spiritualism." The consequences of this view are, in the case of Janssens, absolutely clear, e.g. when he says that the exterior act ("*actus exterior*") is an "exterior *event*" (120) which, in itself, does not possess a moral meaning because it does not yet participate in the subjectivity of man, i.e., before it is assumed by the spiritual "ego" as a "means to action." So bodily acts are, according to this view, a sort of "raw material," determined in their moral meaning exclusively by the spirit. This is obviously true as far as bodily acts need to be "operationally" integrated into the whole of the person. It is not true, however, as an anthropological thesis which reduces "moral meaning" to what proceeds from the spiritual part of the soul or even as a thesis which reduces "human person" to "spirit." See also Martin Rhonheimer, "Contraception, Sexual Behavior, and Natural Law," *The Linacre Quarterly* 56:2 (1989): 20–57. Also published in *"Humanae vitae": 20 anni dopo. Atti del II Congresso Internazionale di Teologia Morale, Roma 9–12 novembre 1988* (Milano: Edizioni Ares, 1989), 73–113.

17. The distinction between the goodness and the rightness of an action was introduced by W. D. Ross, *The Right and the Good* (Oxford: Clarendon Press, 1930). The terms right-making and good-making characteristics (wrong-making and bad-making characteristics) of an action was first used in 1946 by C. D. Broad, in his famous, above-quoted essay "Some of the Main Problems of Ethics."

18. See for this also Rüdiger Bubner, *Handlung, Sprache und Vernunft*, 2nd ed. (Frankfurt/M: Suhrkamp, 1982), 74–90.

19. Of course it may be considered as good (desirable) that P finally dies (and we may even pray for it); in this sense we also say: "It was precisely the right thing for him (and probably also for his relatives) that he finally died." With this, however, we do not qualify an action or the choice of an action, but a state of affairs and its desirability. The goodness, rightness or desirability of such a state of affairs, however, cannot serve as a criterion for qualifying a possible *action* of mercy killing. Because in such an action a will set against P's life is involved, with the *further* intention of bringing about a desirable state of affairs.

20. This affirmation, as is obvious, presupposes that killing as the execution of capital punishment (pronounced by the competent judicial authority) and taking into account the fact that the punished is really *guilty* according to the standards of penal law, cannot be described as a *choice* of the death of a person. Intentionally this action is (as *any* type of punishment is) "restoration of the order of justice," violated by the criminal and in danger of being disrupted without imposition of punishment. However, it is precisely not the choice of the death of a person as resulting from weighing the good of a person's life against other goods which by this person's death would be brought about (whether capital punishment can be considered as an *adequate, proportionate*, and in this sense just kind of punishment *at all* is another question, which still may be answered negatively; but in an objective-intentional sense it is "punishment" and therefore an act intentionally and objectively belonging to the virtue of justice, and not the choice that a person not be, whether as a means or as an end). Cf. the excellent treatment of this question in John Finnis, *Fundamentals of Ethics*, 127ff.; and my own remarks in *Natur als Grundlage der Moral*, 371–74 and in *La prospettiva della morale* V, 3, d. Secondly, the above affirmation also implies the concept of non-intentional side-effects, e.g., in the case of self-defense which (physically) causes the aggressor's death. This means quite precisely that the aggressor's death was not *chosen for the sake* of defending one's life; cf. *STh* II–II, q. 64, a. 7: "illicitum est quod homo intendat occidere hominem ut seipsum defendat." Here, "intendere" means the elec-

tive will referring to the concrete action ("occidere hominem"), while the defense of one's life is the *further* intention *with which* the concrete action is chosen.

21. Compare Peter Geach, "Good and Evil," *Analysis* 17 (1956): 33–42; republished in *Theories of Ethics*, ed. Philippa Foot (Oxford: Oxford University Press, 1967), 64–73; see esp. 72.

22. This is why *VS* 77 rejects in a very specific and restricted way the method of balancing goods and evils: "The weighing of the goods and evils foreseeable as the consequence of an action is not an adequate method for determining whether the choice of that concrete kind of behavior is 'according to its species,' or 'in itself,' morally good or bad, licit or illicit."

23. Cf. Bruno Schüller, "Die Quellen der Moralität: Zur systematischen Ortung eines alten Lehrstückes der Moraltheologie," *Theologie und Philosophie* 59 (1984): 535–59.

24. This category of "moral relationship" and its importance for explaining responsibility in moral decision-making was very well emphasized by Robert Spaemann, "Wer hat wofür Verantwortung? Zum Streit um deontologische oder teleologische Ethik," *Herder Korrespondenz* 36 (1982): 345–50 & 403–8. The subsequent criticisms by A. Elsässer, F. Furger, and P. Müller-Goldkuhle (ibid. 509ff.; 603ff.; 606ff.) unfortunately do not enter into the fundamental question posed by Spaemann; Spaemann himself remarks upon this in his concluding reply (*Herder Korrespondenz* 37 [198]: 79–84).

25. This is one of the very valuable insights of Alasdair MacIntyre's *After Virtue*, 2nd ed. (Notre Dame: University of Notre Dame Press, 1984).

26. This, it seems to me, explains why virtue ethics do not require a "personalistic complement." Recent personalism often seems to be an attempt to overcome the one-sided views of modern rule-ethics. Ethics based on the concept of moral virtue are intrinsically "personalistic," but are also probably more open to rational discourse than many forms of actual personalism.

27. See, e.g., Franz Scholz, *Wege, Umwege und Auswege der Moraltheologie: Ein Plädoyer für begründete Ausnahmen* (München: Bonifatius, 1976), 16f.; Joseph Fuchs, "'Intrinsece malum': Überlegungen zu einem umstrittenen Begriff," in *Sittliche Normen: Zum Problem ihrer allgemeinen und unwandelbaren Geltung*, ed. Walter Kerber (Düsseldorf: Patmos, 1982), 76f.; Peter Knauer, S.J., "The Hermeneutic Function of the Principle of Double Effect," in *Readings in Moral Theology* n. 1, 1–39.

28. A more recent attempt to do so by referring to Kant is not very satisfying, and it remains unclear to what extent the author may be called a representative of teleological ethics. Cf. Gerhard Höver, *Sittlich handeln im Medium der Zeit: Ansätze zur handlungstheoretischen Neuorientierung der Moraltheologie* (Würzburg: Echter Verlag, 1988). However, this book contains some valuable criticisms of positions defended by adherents of "teleological ethics."

29. *STh* I–II, q. 18, a. 10.

30. Cf. for this G. E. M. Anscombe, *Intention*. Professor Anscombe conceives, in the course of her analysis, the question "Why?" in a larger sense (any sort of motives, or also involuntary causes of actions); it includes the "what for?," without being reduced to it. But insofar as we are concerned with properly human, voluntary actions, the "why?" precisely is the "what for?" It properly concerns "intentions."

31. Ludwig Wittgenstein, *Philosophical Investigations*, n. 621, translated by G. E. M. Anscombe, ed. G. E. M. Anscombe, R. Rhees (Oxford: Basil Blackwell, 1958), 161e. Wittgenstein thinks that nothing is left over ("Are the kinaesthetic sensations my willing?"). Wittgenstein refuses (see the next number) to differentiate conceptually, besides the physical fact, an act of willing. Anyhow, Wittgenstein here clearly mixes up the observer's viewpoint ("the fact that my arm goes up") and the acting person's perspective ("I raise my arm"). Nobody ever can really observe "I raise my arm"; only "the fact that my arm goes up" is observable. "I raise my arm" can properly be described only as a choice by a willing subject. Everybody has personal interior experience of such choices as something different from "kinaesthetic sensations."

32. Anscombe, Intention, 35, 66.
33. Here we may find probably the most decisive misjudgment of Janssens; for he assumed that the Will is able to relate to "ontic" goods as ontic; so he asserts that it is possible to want *"per se"* an ontic evil on the level of its being only an ontic state of affairs, and that, as such, it can be the object of a choice which, then, would not be subject to moral qualification as a "good" or an "evil" choice. Only if the ontic evil is the end of the further intention with which a choice is performed, if it, therefore, were the proper reason of bringing such an evil about, could a corresponding will be called an evil will. Such an objectifying of ontic goods by the elective will, however, is simply impossible; it contradicts the very nature of the will which is *"appetitus in ratione"* or "intellectual appetite"; the will receives its object *through reason.* Janssens' argument is simply naturalistic.
34. Cf. e.g. *In IV Sent.*, d. 16, q. 3, a. l, q.l, a. 2, ad 3.
35. About formal and material objects of actions cf. Anthony Kenny, *Action, Emotion and Will*, 5th ed. (London: Routledge & Kegan, 1976), 187ff.
36. *STh* I–II, q. 18, a. 6.
37. Equally does the norm of never lying; see my *Natur als Grundlage der Moral*, 346ff.; 367ff. About both, killing and lying, see also *La prospettiva della morale*, chapter V, section 3 d. About contraception, see my paper *Contraception, Sexual Behavior, and Natural Law.*
38. Thomas Aquinas, *In duo praecepta caritatis et in decem praecepta, prologus:* "lex naturae. . . nihil aliud est nisi lumen intellectus insitum nobis a Deo, per quod cognoscimus quid agendum et quid vitandum. Hoc lumen et hanc legem dedit Deus homini in creatione." And further on: ". . . lumen scilicet intellectus, per quod nota sunt nobis agenda."
39. *STh* I–II, q. 90, a. 1, ad 2.
40. See *Natur als Grundlage der Moral*, mainly part 2.
41. *STh* I–II, q. 94, a. 1.
42. *STh* I–II, q. 90, a. 4.
43. "Lex naturalis est secundum quam ratio recta est" (*In II Sent.*, d. 42, q. 2, a. 5). This would be the appropriate place to speak about the constitution of "prudentia" (practical wisdom or "prudence") by the "fines virtutum," and about the twofold (intentional and elective) aspect of moral virtue; finally one must say something about the relation between "synderesis" and prudence. See for this *STh* II–II, q. 47, a. 6.
44. About the relation of moral absolutes to intentional actions, see also the excellent Marquette Lecture by William E. May, *Moral Absolutes: Catholic Tradition, Current Trends, and the Truth*, The Père Marquette Lecture in Theology 1989 (Milwaukee: Marquette University Press, 1989), esp.40ff.
45. See Bruno Schüller, "Eine autonome Moral, was ist das?" *Theologische Revue* 78 (1982): 103–6. See for this my above-quoted article, "Zur Begründung sittlicher Normen aus der Natur," esp. 67ff.
46. This approach, however, is not so different from traditional approaches that can be found in some classical manuals of moral theology. Some of them used to look at actions as physical processes or events, relating them afterward to the "norma moralitatis," an extrinsic rule determining whether it is licit or illicit to perform such and such an "action." What most classical manuals failed to do was precisely to render intelligible what a human action is and that its moral identity is *included* in it because it is included in the *intentional* structure of an action.
47. For a full account of the concept of "intentional basic content" and "intentional basic action," see my *La prospettiva della morale.*
48. For the following I am indebted to A. W. Müller, "Radical Subjectivity: Morality versus Utilitarianism," *Ratio* 19 (1977): 115–32.
49. See an example of the latter in Romanus Cessario, O.P., *The Moral Virtues and Theological Ethics* (Notre Dame and London: University of Notre Dame Press, 1991).

Moral Absolutes in the Civilization of Love[1]

Romanus Cessario, O.P.

As an authentic expression of magisterial teaching, the encyclical *Veritatis splendor* enunciates Christian truth for God's people who live within the economy of faith.[2] Still, as many commentators have observed, this encyclical also represents a new initiative in the history of magisterial teaching. The magisterium of course has addressed "the sphere of morals" and has even taught "specific particular precepts" throughout the course of the Church's history.[3] But because *Veritatis splendor* undertakes to expound "fundamental questions of the Church's moral teaching," it provides authoritative norms for establishing the morality of all kinds of human actions.[4] In other words, the encyclical takes up the challenge of helping each believer to answer what the Holy Father calls, "the primordial question: *What is good and evil? What must be done to have eternal life?*" (*VS* 111.2).

An episode in the life of St. Thomas's commentator Cajetan illustrates both the nature and the difficulty of the challenge that Pope John Paul II engaged in writing this encyclical. In the sixteenth century, Cajetan advanced the view that the personal condition of an agent should figure in the moral evaluation of his or her actions. But because Cajetan's effort to discuss morality from "the perspective of the acting person" was premature, it earned him a reputation, even among some of his fellow Dominicans, for promoting moral laxism—a high misdemeanor during this period of nascent casuistry. Why this reaction? Cajetan's opponents reasoned in this way: to hold that an adequate moral evaluation of an action must take account of its "object" as "*rationally chosen by the deliberate will*"—to borrow an important phrase from the encyclical (see *VS* 78.1)—means considering the psychological condition of the person who makes a moral choice. This in turn leads to making subjective excuses for violations of the moral law. Cajetan of course was neither a laxist nor a revisionist *ante nomen*. He was simply applying what Aquinas had developed theologically from Aristotle's *Nicomachean Ethics*. Aquinas speaks about the nature of moral science, namely, that it concerns practical knowledge. Unlike theoretical knowledge, which informs the mind with specific truths, practical knowledge is ordered ultimately to what a person either makes or does. For this reason, practical knowledge depends on the character of the one who possesses it in a way that speculative knowledge does not. To give a concrete example, a person can engage in bad actions and still function as a good mathematician. However, no one should expect to receive good advice about sobriety from a person who habitually drinks too much.[5]

In continuity with the teaching of the Apostles, *Veritatis splendor* talks about practical knowledge; specifically, it concerns *"the right conduct of Christians"* (*VS* 26.1). As an exercise in practical knowledge, Christian moral theology includes accounts of the "good," the Commandments, the virtues, the gifts of the Holy Spirit, and the Beatitudes as well as of moral judgments, for example, "It is good to help others in distress," at whatever level of generality such judgments are expressed. But unlike geometry, which can draw a true conclusion from its own theoretical principles, moral science ensures completely practical knowledge, the knowledge incarnate in action, only up to a certain point.[6] Why? Completely practical knowledge requires moral agency, and choice always implies the exercise of human freedom. On the basis of this analysis, we might speculate that Cajetan's opponents regarded moral teaching to be more like geometry than in fact is the case: the important thing is to get the [moral] theorem right. Cajetan, on the other hand, understood that it is one thing to affirm the orthodox doctrine on the Trinity, and another to affirm the moral truth that "it is good to help others in distress." When the Christian believes the orthodox doctrine of the Trinity, he or she can be said to possess the truth in faith, whereas when the believer learns that "it is good to help others in distress," he or she still needs to move to the moment of completely practical knowledge, to render the knowledge incarnate in action. In other words, the believer must choose the good and, shaped by the virtue of prudence, command the good action.

To recognize the way that moral truth informs prudence is not to deny the value of moral science, together with its postulates and arguments, for the Christian life. Moral norms are important, and the Church must proclaim them as constitutive elements of Christ's call to conversion. A lesson from history illustrates the importance of sound teaching. In her study of women, the family, and Nazi politics entitled *Mothers in the Fatherland*, Claudia Koonz relates that during the period of the National Socialist Party in Germany women reacted no differently than men when it came to opposing unjust laws.[7] The only exception Koonz discovered were Roman Catholic nurses, who, because they had been taught that sterilization was wrong, objected to its inclusion in the health care directives of the Third Reich. Normative instruction, then, is important. Even so, *Veritatis splendor* invites us to look at the moral life from the point of view of the acting person. In this paper I would like to argue that a specific strength of the encyclical lies in its presentation of the moral life as situated within the larger context of the theological life. While the Holy Father touches many aspects of the Christian moral life, I develop three of these: the connaturality of virtue, especially prudence; freedom in Christ; and the happy life, what the classical authors call beatitude.

* * *

Today Cajetan is not much remembered as a moralist. While his commentaries on the *Summa theologiae* inspired a great deal of philosophy and dogmatic theology during the period of the twentieth-century Leonine revival, his teaching on morals, even his important commentaries on prudence, remained relatively unknown.[8] Instead, the sixteenth century witnessed the development of legalistic casuistry, which eclipsed the classical moral teaching on the virtues. By developing treatises on the virtues, the ancient Christian authors concretized the graced connaturality between man and the true good.[9] The casuist systems controlled the moral context of the Church for roughly four centuries, from the mid-sixteenth century through the first half of the twentieth century.[10] In my view, many of the difficulties that moral theology has suffered over the past thirty years, and which *Veritatis splendor* addresses, derive in large measure from the fact that one of the least publicized events that took place at the Second Vatican Council was the bringing of a four-hundred-year-old casuist tradition to closure.

Veritatis splendor indeed introduces a new era in the history of moral theology. Certain of my fellow Catholic moral theologians interpret the significance of the encyclical differently. Some claim that the text should be read as mere exhortation, a "papal *cri de coeur*,"[11] whereas others predict that its influence will be short-lived.[12] I am not persuaded by these dismissive arguments. As Alasdair MacIntyre's analysis of the encyclical points out, *Veritatis splendor* presents us "with what is in effect a theology of moral philosophy embedded in a theology of the moral life."[13] Except for a truncated account of the four last things (death, judgment, heaven, and hell), the casuist theologians offered the Church no theology of the moral life.

Again, *Veritatis splendor* signals a new beginning for moral theology. In an unambiguously clear way, the encyclical sets forth the need for exceptionless moral norms (*VS* 82.1), but without recapitulating the rigid legalism and confusion of the old casuistry. In other words, we should not expect that post-*Veritatis splendor* moral theology will produce a new collection of moral manuals, complete with detailed lists of moral precepts and instructions for resolving "cases of conscience" in a way that mimics legal jurisprudence. Rather, the moral theology of the new evangelization aims to develop first a communion of persons (*communio personarum*) in which individuals are shaped by the truth of the divine and evangelical law. Among other benefits of the new personalism, educated believers can speak confidently even about the *"universality and immutability"* of the natural law because they know, with St. Augustine, that these norms reflect divine truth.[14] The Holy Father makes an especially bold claim: *"This universality does not ignore the individuality of human beings,* nor is it opposed to the absolute uniqueness of each person. On the contrary, it embraces at its root each of the person's free acts, which are meant to bear witness to the universality of the true good" (*VS* 51.3). This means that *Veritatis splendor* requires us to think now in terms of a virtue-centered approach to moral theology, one that relies on the cardinal virtue of prudence, as much as on the canons of moral jurisprudence. The better that moral theologians work out the principles set down in the encyclical, the more easily the Church will be able to show that "man's *genuine moral autonomy* in no way means the rejection but rather the acceptance of the moral law, of God's command . . ." (*VS* 41.1). Consequently, the prudent man or woman is able to embrace the complete truth-value of Catholic moral teaching, and at the same time exercise a full measure of personal freedom. In the technical language of the encyclical, this state is described as one of "theonomy" or of "participated theonomy."[15] In short, Pope John Paul calls us to a vertical transcendence, which is at the source of every love, and which alone can perfect the spiritual nature of the human person.[16] Aquinas captures the same truth when he says, "God alone satisfies."[17]

It is not surprising, then, that the Holy Father makes a central point of Thomist moral theology his own: "It is the 'heart' converted to the Lord and to the love of what is good which is really the source of *true* judgments of conscience. Indeed, in order to 'prove what is the will of God, what is good and acceptable and perfect' (Rom 12:2), knowledge of God's law in general is certainly necessary, but it is not sufficient: what is essential is a sort of *'connaturality' between man and the true good*."[18] As the Swiss philosopher Martin Rhonheimer points out, only this kind of virtuous connaturality enables a person to develop "the genuine perspective of morals," which, Rhonheimer argues, is one of the truly innovative parts of the encyclical's teaching about moral objects.[19] The moral condition of the person affects the judgment of prudence. Upright living supports prudence, whereas vicious habits impair, and can even destroy, a person's capacity to realize completely practical knowledge in accord with moral truth. The Holy Father reserves the term *freedom* to characterize the person who not only knows what the moral law teaches, but who also is able to render moral truth incarnate in his or her actions.

*   *   *

So we come to another feature of the theology of the moral life found in *Veritatis splendor*, the notion of freedom. Pope John Paul II has accomplished what Cardinal Cajetan had been unable to achieve. The pope has elaborated a moral theology that places the individual person and personal freedom at the center of moral analysis. He expresses his understanding of the relation between freedom, truth, and the human person, but he does so without endorsing the moral subjectivism that Cajetan's "conservative" adversaries feared in the sixteenth century. Of course, neither does he countenance the moral waffling that many neo-casuists in the twentieth century consider inescapable. The success of Pope John Paul in setting forth a teaching that both upholds moral truth and takes full account of human freedom is due, at least in part, to his acquaintance with modern philosophy, especially modern theories of ethics and anthropology.

In *The Acting Person*, Karol Wojtyla took the characteristically modern notions of self-possession, self-determination, and self-governance and placed them within the biblical context of conditional stewardship and respect for the divine sovereignty. As Kenneth Schmitz has explained in his illuminating work, *At the Center of the Human Drama*, Karol Wojtyla was uniquely prepared to talk from the Chair of Peter about the absolute character of moral truth, while at the same time affirming that human freedom forms part of "the ontological structure of man."[20] "It seems to me," writes Schmitz, "that to John Paul II's mind the modern practical tendency to obscure or forget the conditional nature of our stewardship is the direct outcome of the modern theoretical tendency to treat human consciousness as an absolute."[21] The ethics of health care, for example, requires a renewed commitment to conditional stewardship, including the stewardship of one's own physical life. Moral absolutes represent one way of concretizing the requirements of this conditional stewardship, so that the enthusiasm generated by technological developments, which has shaped the modern mind since the seventeenth century, will not frustrate the development of the civilization of love.

It would be misleading, however, to suggest that the pope's acquaintance with modern philosophical categories alone enables him to supply a moral teaching that takes account of human freedom and at the same time reaffirms the universal validity of the negative precepts of the natural law, which "oblige each and every individual, always and in every circumstance" (*VS* 52.1). For the Church could not adequately account for the place that human freedom holds in the Christian life unless she had also determined the nature of Christ's human freedom. Recall that the encyclical gives us a "theology of the moral life." This theology owes much to the sixth ecumenical council, III Constantinople (681), which rejected the Monothelitist heresy (DS 556). It is illustrative to reflect on the fact that the "monophysitic mentality" about Christ endured for more than two centuries after the Council of Chalcedon (451). In this view of the Incarnation lurks the conviction that human freedom disappears in the presence of divine grace. In other words, no human action or genuine human autonomy remains once a divine action has begun to work in a person. As pious as this explanation may appear, it in fact destroys the Christian view of man and empties the expression "participated theonomy" of any meaning. Rather, the biblical doctrine on creation obliges us to accept that human actions have a value in their own right: God created man a unity of body and soul—*corpore et anima unus*.[22] More to the point, the first person to demonstrate that human actions can possess divine value is Christ himself. So the pope can affirm that "human freedom and God's Law are not in opposition; on the contrary, they appeal one to the other" (*VS* 17.2). In the person of Jesus Christ, the Church beholds the "concrete norm"—to borrow a phrase from Hans Urs von Balthasar—of human freedom and divine law appealing one to the other. This "concrete norm," moreover, is not a luxury for the human race, as if believers enjoy a slightly better position than non-believers do when it comes to distinguishing right from wrong. For as the "concrete norm" of the moral life, Christ himself alone makes it possible for the human person to achieve his or her most high calling through the exercise of both the theological virtues and the infused moral virtues.[23]

"Christ the new Adam, in the very revelation of the mystery of the Father and of his love, fully reveals man to himself and brings to light his most high calling."[24] This cardinal principle of post-conciliar theology is put to new use in the encyclical: The pope reminds us that only the Lord bestows on us the full enabling condition of freedom. The Scholastic discussions about the relative sufficiency of the acquired virtues addressed this same issue in premodern categories. Let us return to Cajetan for a moment. As a Christian humanist, Cajetan was willing to grant that since the acquired virtues are true virtues, they could establish a relative perfection (what he termed the "essence of virtue"). But he also held that the acquired virtues by themselves could not produce what he called the state of virtue, the full "*status virtutis*." For only charity orders the virtues to the Ultimate End in an unqualified fashion. If we follow Cajetan's view on the relative sufficiency of the human virtues, then we must conclude that before the salvific life and death of the God-man, human autonomy could not even achieve the ultimate good of the very nature that it served. For only the charity of Christ makes the virtues of human life exist in full existential possession of their efficacy. This is the first principle of the theology of the moral life that provides the matrix for the encyclical's specific moral teaching. Just as Christ, because he remains the Eternal Word of Truth, exercises his authentic human freedom in a way that always embodies the greatest charity or love, so the one who remains united to Christ enjoys the assurance that his or her actions embody the full measure of moral truth.

In Chapter 3 of *Veritatis splendor*, entitled "Lest the Cross of Christ Be Emptied of Its Power" (1 Cor 1:17), the pope urges the Church, and especially her priests, to undertake "an intense pastoral effort" so that the "essential bond between truth, the good and freedom" will be better known in the world (*VS* 84.3). If the Church is to avoid endorsing the measures of expediency that are so seductive to the modern spirit, each member of the Church must be completely persuaded of this fundamental Christian truth, namely, "when all is said and done, the law of God is always the one true good of man" (ibid.).[25] To avoid raising expediency to the level of a moral principle, however, we cannot remain only at the side of Christ the Divine Teacher. We must also be ready to stand by the Cross of the Crucified Christ; in other words, we must become disciples of the Cross. It is incumbent on the Pastors of the Church, but also on every Christian believer, to show that this vocation does not go against the good of reason. We need to affirm unequivocally that the wisdom of the Cross creates neither foolishness nor a stumbling block (see 1 Cor 1:23). Rather, to circumvent the wisdom of the Cross means inviting death-dealing disobedience. St. Irenaeus writes: "The Lord, coming into his own creation in visible form, was sustained by his own creation which he himself sustains in being. His obedience on the tree of the cross reversed the disobedience at the tree in Eden."[26] Aquinas teaches the same truth when he explains the true purpose of the Incarnation. While the end, or objective, of the Incarnation entails the perfection of our godly image, the motive for the Incarnation remains the fact that a disobedient people required a Savior to reverse their lot. An essential feature of the ministry of the moral theologian is to help people acknowledge their sins, so that Christian believers can move beyond the stage of image-restoration, which entails sorrow and conversion, to that of image-perfection, which is the state of genuine freedom. In fact, the pope states that *"The crucified Christ reveals the authentic meaning of freedom; he lives it fully in the total gift of himself* and calls his disciples to share in his freedom" (*VS* 85).

Veritatis splendor is really a soteriological document, for it urges us to confront the false voices of freedom that cry out in "many different 'areopagi.'"[27] Given the secularization of the West, these voices are numerous, heard especially in the areopagus of social welfare agencies as well as that of health-care professionals. For this reason, special discernment is required in these fields in order to distinguish the "authentic meaning of freedom," a freedom that always leads to excellence, from freedom that is false because it is "not in harmony with the true good of the person" (*VS* 72.2). The true good of the person can never be compromised for reasons of expediency. For even one bad choice, so the Holy Father affirms, puts "us in conflict with our ultimate end, the supreme good, God himself" (ibid.).

* * *

If freedom is the distinctive feature of ethical action, practical action reaches completion only in the good. When discussing the nature of human action, the *Catechism of the Catholic Church* (part 3, section 1) generally follows the outline of Aquinas's *prima secundae*. The *Catechism* treats first our vocation to beatitude (1716–24), next human freedom (1730–42), and then the virtues and gifts of the Holy Spirit (1803–32), which account for our personal transformation as well as our free participation in beatitude. (It is significant that Aquinas retained the patristic view that the virtues and the gifts remain with the saints in heaven, even though they no longer face moral choices.) In order to stress the order of development in the human person, I have reversed the order of presentation in this essay, namely, virtue, freedom, beatitude. This also allows me, while discussing Christian happiness, to refer more explicitly to the important question of the gospel of life. On 25 March, 1995, the feast of the Annunciation of the Lord, the Holy Father signed the encyclical *Evangelium vitae*. The title reveals that this encyclical treats specific moral questions relating to safeguarding human life. The 1995 encyclical should be read as a companion to the 1993

Veritatis splendor. Today health-care ethics raises some of the most serious challenges to the observance of moral absolutes. And we know that the Holy Father repeatedly warns us about the "culture of death." In *Evangelium vitae* he issues an urgent appeal to modern society to recognize that "life is always a good" (No. 31). Even at its highest level of perfection, the human good must include provision for sustaining the physiological and biological level of the human person. As Pope John Paul has had occasion to teach repeatedly, the failure to respect human life from the moment of conception to natural death devastates the civilization of love.

Let me introduce the general issue of respect for human life in light of the three points that I am making in this paper. *Veritatis splendor* affirms the significance of the "objective moral order" for bringing about true Christian personalism.[28] Many of our contemporaries are persuaded that individual conditions, especially those which surround difficult health-care situations, make it nearly impossible to apply general moral principles or "to establish any particular norm the content of which would be binding without exception" (*VS* 82.2). I have argued, however, that the variables associated, for example, with caring for the sick and dying should urge Christian believers to rely on the virtue of prudence. This means that having been shown "the inviting splendor of that truth which is Jesus Christ himself" (*VS* 83.2), their minds will be conformed to the full moral truth about human life. While it is true that only the prudent person acts virtuously in a particular circumstance, the Church—as *Donum vitae* reminds us—must proclaim to the world that human life is sacred and that God alone is the master of life (see No. 5). So both the 1980 "Declaration on Euthanasia" and the 1974 "Declaration on Procured Abortion" assert, as the latter puts it, that "the first right of the human person is the right to life" (No. 11). Now in *Evangelium vitae*, this fundamental principle of the natural law receives a fresh and developed expression, confirmed by the authority of the Church's magisterium. Earlier, *Veritatis splendor* set the stage for this pronouncement of the Holy Father when it taught that abstaining from the intentional killing of innocent human life remains, no matter what the circumstances or further intentions, *semper et pro semper* an indispensable condition for attaining Christian happiness. No prudent person can choose to act against this norm: it grounds the drive to happiness.

The encyclical cites St. Augustine's *Commentary on John*: "The beginning of freedom is to be free from crimes. . . such as murder, adultery, fornication, theft, fraud, sacrilege and so forth. Once one is without these crimes (and every Christian should be without them), one begins to lift up one's head towards freedom" (*VS* 13.4). Thus Catholic moral teaching on respect for human life aims to ennoble Christian believers, to make them perfectly free, to bring them toward a perfection that is due each human person. The *Catechism of the Catholic Church* recalls that Jesus repeats the Commandment "Thou shalt not kill," during his Sermon on the Mount (see Mt 5:21).[29] This biblical text invites us to consider the context of moral absolutes. The norms enshrined in documents such as the *1994 The Ethical and Religious Directives for Catholic Health Care Services* should not be treated as burdensome obligations that Catholics have to endure, but rather accepted as reliable guides to beatitude.[30] A text from St. Augustine, which is not found in the encyclical, helps us understand the importance of making the proper decision in matters of health care: "For in the way you decide to follow Christ, this you have intended, this you have chosen, this is your judgment."[31] Even in seemingly difficult cases, such as assisted suicide, direct sterilization, human embryo research, and the treatment of rape victims, the reason for determining a wise and truthful course of action is to ensure that the Christian believer as well as those who care for him or her attain the positive goal of Christian happiness. As the Christian believer acts under the influence of infused prudence and with the aid of the gift of the Holy Spirit, he or she already possesses the Good. "Genuine freedom is an outstanding manifestation of the divine image in man. For God willed to leave man 'in the power of his own counsel' (see Sir 15:14) so that he would seek his Creator of his own accord and would freely arrive at full and blessed perfection by cleaving to God" (*VS* 34.1).[32]

Although some are not optimistic about the future of Catholic hospitals, it is my firm opinion that the Church should do everything to maintain Catholic health-care services.[33] The sick and dying should enjoy the same opportunity to continue in the path of blessedness that Catholic moral teaching marks out for them as do those members of the Church who enjoy good health and the prospect of many years. As a Catholic has lived a virtuous life, so he or she has a right to proper health care and, when the Lord comes, to die virtuously, to die choosing Christ. We still refer to this as the grace of a happy death. To die well belongs to the happy life.[34]

In conclusion: *Veritatis splendor* makes three important contributions to an authentic expression of Christian ethics. First, it affirms that since natural law properly "understood does not allow for any division between freedom and nature" (*VS* 50.2), we must develop, by nature and in grace, the connaturality of virtue. Second, it explains that since true freedom flows from "communion of life with Christ" (*VS* 16.3), it poses no hardship for the believer to accept that "there are certain specific kinds of behavior that are always wrong to choose, because choosing them involves a disorder of the will, that is, a moral evil" (*VS* 78.1).[35] Third, in this life, the pursuit of beatitude entails suffering. "Christ's witness is the source, model and means for the witness of his disciples, who are called to walk on the same road: 'If any man would come after me, let him deny himself and take up his cross daily and follow me' (Lk 9:23)" (*VS* 89.2). In my view, these three principles form the heart of the encyclical's teaching and establish the ground for all specific moral claims, such as respect for human life.

But we must remember that the New Testament puts us under the sign of the diminutive. The Kingdom grows like the mustard seed; only ideologies look for sudden success. Yet ideologies are destined to fail, whether they appear incarnated in the omnicompetent state or are promulgated in the form of prevailing cultural wisdom. To preach the efficacy of universal and unchanging norms is an invitation to follow the littleness of the Beatitudes it is not a plan for world conquest. And always, the first soul to be converted to this new way of life is our own. The new evangelization begins, then, with each one of us, as we renew our own love of the truth. And this is a grace, one that comes from Christ, reminding us that the Church lives with the sure hope that "all that Christ is we shall become."

Endnotes

1. A version of this essay appeared in *Crisis* 13 (1995), 18–23.
2. "The service to Christian truth which the magisterium renders is thus for the benefit of the whole People of God called to enter the liberty of the truth revealed by God in Christ" (*Instruction on the Ecclesial Vocation of the Theologian* [1990], n. 14).
3. See *VS* 110 for the encyclical's explanation as to how the magisterium properly intervenes in moral theology, which it defines as "a scientific reflection on the *Gospel*

as the gift and commandment of new life, a reflection on the life which 'professes the truth in love' (cf. Eph 4:15)." In *VS* 114, the Holy Father further explains that this task belongs to the threefold *munus, propheticum, sacerdotale, and regale* of the priestly office, as set down in the conciliar documents on the Church (*Lumen gentium*) and on bishops (*Christus Dominus*).

4. The Holy Father himself makes this point: "This is the first time, in fact, that the magisterium of the Church has set forth in detail the fundamental elements of this [Christian moral] teaching, and presented the principles for the pastoral discernment necessary in practical and cultural situations which are complex and even crucial" (*VS* 115.1).

5. Jacques Maritain reflected extensively on the way in which a person's moral character affects his or her moral science. For a discussion of the nuance with which Maritain treats practical knowledge, see Ralph McInerny, *Art and Prudence* (Notre Dame: University of Notre Dame Press, 1988), especially chapter 5, "The Degrees of Practical Knowledge," 63–136.

6. See Ralph McInerny, *Ethica Thomistica* (Washington, D.C.: The Catholic University of America Press, 1982), 38–40.

7. Claudia Koonz. *Mothers in the Fatherland: Women, the Family and Nazi Politics* (New York: St. Martin's, 1987). See also Claudia Koonz. "Eugenics, Gender, and Ethics in Nazi Germany: The Debate about Involuntary Sterilization, 1933–1936" in Thomas Childers and Jane Caplan, eds., *Reevaluating the Third Reich* (New York: Holmes and Meier, 1993), 66–85.

8. For a treatment of Cajetan's views on moral theology, see Joseph Mayer, "Cajetan comme moraliste," *Revue Thomiste* 39 (1934–35): 343–57.

9. For a thorough study of this theme in the history of moral theology, see Servais Pinckaers, O.P., *The Sources of Christian Ethics,* trans. Sr Mary Thomas Noble, O.P. (Washington, D.C.: The Catholic University of America Press, 1995).

10. Casuist moral theology divided human actions into two categories: on the one hand, those actions controlled by law, either as enjoined or as forbidden, and, secondly, those actions for which no rule was applicable. These latter, the so-called "free" actions, occurred only because no existing law applied to them. Thus, casuistry placed "free" actions in a secondary place within the moral life. And, in fact, they occurred principally in the areas of piety and devotion.

11. See the report of the remarks made by John Boyle and Anne Patrick at the Moral Theology Group of the Catholic Theological Society of America's 1994 meeting in Baltimore in the *Proceedings of the Catholic Theological Society of America* 49 (1994), 200–201.

12. See Richard McCormick's essay in *America* 30 October 1993: "*Veritatis splendor* at key points attributes to theologians positions that they do not hold. It will, I predict, eventually enjoy a historical status similar to that of *Humani generis*" (11).

13. See MacIntyre's essay, above, p. 75.

14. See *De Trinitate* 14.15, 21 (*Corpus christianorum. Series latina* vol. 50/A, p. 451) as quoted in *VS* 51.

15. See *VS* 41. For background on this notion, see Joseph de Finance, "Autonomie et Théonomie," in *L'agire morale,* ed. M. Zalba (Naples: Edizioni Domenicane Italiane, 1974), 239–60.

16. See Kenneth L. Schmitz, *At the Center of the Human Drama: The Philosophical Anthropology of Karol Wojtyla/Pope John Paul II* (Washington, D.C.: The Catholic University of America Press, 1993), 86ff. The author explains how this theme appears even in Wojtyla's early dramas *Radiation of Fatherhood* and *The Jeweler's Shop.*

17. *Expositio in symbolum apostolicum,* 1.

18. *VS* 64, citing *STh* II–II, q. 45, a. 2. Pope Pius XII made a similar point in *Humani generis* when he affirmed that "never has Christian philosophy denied the usefulness and efficacy of good dispositions of soul for perceiving and embracing moral and religious truths" (n. 34).

19. See Rhonheimer's essay "'Intrinsically Evil Acts' and the Moral Viewpoint: Clarifying a Central Teaching of *Veritatis splendor,*" above, pp. 171ff. Rhonheimer goes on

to point out that a genuine perspective of morals reveals an intimate relation between the "object" and the "will" or "choice," so that the object becomes understood as "the proximate end of a deliberate decision which determines the act of willing" (*VS* 78).

20. See Schmitz, *At the Center*, 104.
21. Ibid., 97.
22. The *Catechism* cites an important text from *Gaudium et spes* n. 14.1:
    > Man, though made of body and soul, is a unity. Through his very bodily condition he sums up in himself the elements of the material world. Through him they are thus brought to the highest perfection and can raise their voice in praise freely given to the Creator. For this reason man may not despise his bodily life. Rather he is obliged to regard his body as good and to hold it in honor since God has created it and will raise it up on the last day.

    The encyclical turns to this text in order to support its refutation of the charge that the traditional concept of natural law entails a physicalism or biologism.
23. See *Gaudium et spes*, n. 22. See the *Catechism of the Catholic Church*, nn. 1812–13 for the theological virtues, and nn. 2803 & 2607 for the use of the term *theological* to describe the life lived according to the theological virtues.
24. Vatican Council II, Pastoral Constitution on the Church in the Modern World (*Gaudium et spes*), n. 22.
25. This remark is taken from an address to those taking part in the International Congress of Moral Theology (10 April 1986), 2: *Insegnamenti* IX, 1 (1986), 970–71.
26. *Adversus haereses* 5.19.1 (*Sources chrétiennes* vol. 153, pp. 248–50).
27. "*The more the West is becoming estranged from its Christian roots, the more it is becoming missionary territory*, taking the form of many different 'areopagi'" (*Tertio millennio adveniente*, n. 57).
28. Citing *Dignitatis humanae*, n. 7 at *VS* 82.
29. CCC 2262
30. For the full text of these guidelines issued by the Bishops of the United States, see *Origins* 24, n. 27 (15 December 1994).
31. *Ennarationes* 36.1.7 (*Corpus christianorum. Series latina*, vol. 38, p. 342).
32. The text cites *Gaudium et spes* n. 17.
33. See Richard McCormick, S.J., "The Catholic Hospital Today: Mission Impossible?," *Origins* 24 (1995): 648–53.
34. In *Evangelium vitae*, the Holy Father traces this loss of appreciation for dying well to the alienation of man from God endemic in modern society:
    > [Man] no longer considers life as a splendid gift of God, something "sacred" entrusted to his responsibility and thus also to his loving care and "veneration". . .He is concerned only with "doing," and, using all kinds of technology, he busies himself with programming, controlling and dominating birth and death. Birth and death, instead of being primary experiences demanding to be "lived," become things to be merely "possessed" or "rejected" (*EV* 22).
35. CCC 1761

III. Reception

John Paul II, Moral Theology, and Moral Theologians[1]

William E. May

Within weeks of the promulgation of Pope John Paul II's encyclical *Veritatis splendor*, a number of theologians known as proportionalists, pre-eminently Richard A. McCormick, S.J., claimed that the Holy Father had seriously misrepresented their position. According to McCormick "the vast majority of theologians known as proportionalists will *rightly* say that they do not hold or teach what the encyclical attributes to them."[2] If McCormick is correct, then John Paul II's repudiation of proportionalism in his encyclical simply erects a chimera or a caricature of what he calls "trends of theological thinking . . . incompatible with revealed truth" (*VS* 29.4). It also follows that it would be a terrible injustice to attribute the views he repudiates to "the vast majority of theologians known as proportionalists."

It is thus a matter of grave justice, both to the Holy Father and to theologians known as proportionalists, to determine whether or not these theologians indeed hold the views alleged to be "proportionalist" in *Veritatis splendor*. To achieve this goal I will proceed as follows:

- First, I will summarize relevant material from *Veritatis splendor*;.
- Second, I will examine the pre-*Veritatis splendor* writings of major theologians commonly recognized as proportionalists to see whether the claims they make are recognizably those identified as "proportionalistic" by John Paul II;.
- Third and finally, I will examine some post-*Veritatis splendor* writings of these theologians to see what light they shed on the subject of the accuracy of the pope's presentation of their views.

I. Relevant Teaching of *Veritatis splendor*

Toward the end of the third chapter of his encyclical, in reminding bishops of his and their responsibilities as pastors, John Paul II identifies the "teaching which represents the central theme of this Encyclical," the teaching "being restated with the authority of the Successor of Peter." This is the teaching reaffirming *"the universality and immutability of the moral commandments,* particularly those which prohibit always and without exception *intrinsically evil acts"* (*VS* 115.3). The pope, in other words, reaffirms as Catholic teaching that there are *moral absolutes* or *exceptionless moral norms* valid always and everywhere (*semper et pro* or *ad semper*) and that, corresponding to these absolute norms, there are *intrinsically evil acts.*

John Paul II's reaffirmation of this teaching in *Veritatis splendor* did not come as a surprise. He had previously reaffirmed it in strong terms. For example, in his Apostolic Exhortation *Reconciliatio et poenitentia* he declared that there is a "doctrine, based on the Decalogue and on the preaching of the Old Testament, and assimilated into the kerygma of the Apostles and belonging to the earliest teaching of the Church, and constantly reaffirmed by her to this day." What doctrine? The doctrine that "there exist acts which, *per se* and in themselves, independently of circumstances, are always seriously wrong by reason of their object" (n. 17.12). Correspondingly, as he elsewhere said, "there are moral norms that have a precise content which is immutable and unconditioned . . . for example, the norm . . . which forbids the direct killing of an innocent person."[3]

Note that in *Reconciliatio et poenitentia* John Paul II asserted that the doctrine regarding intrinsically evil acts is "based on the Decalogue." He returns to this theme in the first chapter of *Veritatis splendor*, where he is at pains to show the essential link between obedience to the Commandments of the Decalogue and eternal life. There he observes, in reflecting on the dialogue between Jesus and rich young man of Matthew's Gospel (19:16–21), that the first three Commandments of the Decalogue call "us to acknowledge God as the one Lord of all and to worship him alone for his infinite holiness" (*VS* 11.1; cf. Ex 20:2–11). But the young man, responding to Jesus' declaration that he must keep the Commandments if he wishes to enter eternal life, demands to know "which ones" (Mt

19:18). As John Paul II notes, "he asks what he must do in life in order to show that he acknowledges God's holiness" (*VS* 13.1). Replying to this question, Jesus reminds the young man of the Decalogue's precepts concerning our neighbor. These precepts, John Paul II affirms, are rooted in the commandment that we are to love our neighbor as ourselves, a commandment expressing "*the singular dignity of the human person*, the 'only creature that God has wanted for its own sake'" (*VS* 13.2).[4]

At this point in the encyclical John Paul II develops a matter of crucial importance to the meaning of our lives as moral beings, namely, that we can love our neighbor and respect his dignity as a person only by cherishing the real goods perfective of him and by refusing to damage, destroy, or impede these goods. Appealing to the words of Jesus, he emphasizes the truth that

> the different commandments of the Decalogue are really only so many reflections of the one commandment about the good of the person, at the level of the many different goods which characterize his identity as a spiritual and bodily being in relationship with God, with his neighbor, and with the material world. . . . The commandments of which Jesus reminds the young man are meant to safeguard *the good* of the person, the image of God, by protecting his *goods* (*VS* 13.2–13.3).

He continues by saying that the negative precepts of the Decalogue—"You shall not murder; You shall not commit adultery; You shall not steal; You shall not bear false witness"—"express with particular force the ever urgent need to protect human life, the communion of persons in marriage," and so on (*VS* 13.3). These negative norms of the Decalogue are moral absolutes, prohibiting without exception the sorts or kinds of human acts identified by them. One willing to engage in such deeds cannot love his neighbor, nor can he love God.

Recall now that in *Reconciliatio et poenitentia* John Paul II had affirmed that "there exist acts which, *per se* and in themselves, independently of circumstances, are always seriously wrong *by reason of their object*" (n. 17.12; emphasis added). In the second chapter of *Veritatis splendor*, in the part devoted to an analysis of "The Moral Act" (*VS* 71–83), he makes crystal-clear what is meant by the "object" of an act. He does so because, as he says, "*the morality of the human act depends primarily and fundamentally on the 'object' ra-*

tionally chosen by the deliberate will" (VS 78.1). In a critically important passage he then shows what is meant by the "object" rationally chosen by the deliberate will. He writes: "In order to be able to grasp the object of an act which specifies that act morally, it is therefore necessary to place oneself *in the perspective of the acting person.* The object of the act of willing is in fact a freely chosen kind of behavior. To the extent that it is in conformity with the order of reason, it is the cause of the goodness of the will; it perfects us morally. . . . By the object of a given moral act, then, one cannot mean a process or an event of the merely physical order, to be assessed on the basis of its ability to bring about a given state of affairs in the outside world. Rather, that object is the proximate end of a deliberate decision which determines the act of willing on the part of the acting person" (*VS* 78.1). In short, the "object" that is the primary source of the morality of a human act is precisely *what one freely chooses to do,* and, in so choosing, ratifies in his heart and endorses. It is, one could say, the intelligible proposal that one adopts by choice and then executes externally. For example, "adultery" is a human act specified by the choice—and in this sense, the intention—to have genital sex with someone other than one's spouse.

Here it must be noted that acts so specified by their objects are not specified already as *morally wicked.* One could ask, without making a fool of himself, "why ought one not," given certain conditions, have intercourse with someone other than one's spouse. It is not self-evident that a willingness to do a deed of this kind is morally wicked. The acts in question are simply identified accurately by describing "what" they are in light of the object freely chosen and willed by the acting person. It is obviously necessary to know precisely "what" one is freely choosing to do in order to determine whether or not this is in conformity with "the order of reason." Note too that John Paul II explicitly rejects the view that the "object" specifying an act morally is a mere process or event in the physical world, described independently of any will act of the acting person. Rather, the object is specified precisely by what the acting person freely chooses to do. The pope clearly acknowledges that a human act, a moral act, cannot be evaluated without relating it to an act of the agent's will, in particular, the will act of choosing, the *voluntas eligens.* A human or moral act is not something given in nature.

With this understanding of the "object" of the human act in mind, one can then readily grasp John Paul II's further argument, which he summarizes by saying, "reason attests that there are objects of the human act which are by their nature 'incapable of being ordered' to God *because they radically contradict the good of the person made in his image*. These are the acts which, in the Church's moral tradition, have been termed 'intrinsically evil' [*intrinsece malum*]: they are such *always and per se*, in other words, on account of their very object, and quite apart from the *ulterior* intentions of the one acting and the circumstances" (n. 80; emphasis added).

Recall now that in the first chapter of *Veritatis splendor* John Paul II had been at pains to show that the negative precepts of the Decalogue, concerned with our neighbor, protect the inviolable dignity of the human person made in the image of God precisely by protecting his good, i.e., by protecting the real goods of human existence perfective of him as a human person, goods such as life itself, the marital communion, and the like. Thus if the precise object of one's will act, one's choice, is intentionally to deprive one's neighbor of goods of this kind, one simply cannot be making a choice and executing an act in conformity with reason or with love of one's neighbor. John Paul II's teaching here is utterly reasonable as well and in complete fidelity to the tradition of the Church and to its biblical foundations.[5]

Moreover, as John Paul II is at pains to show in the third and final chapter of *Veritatis splendor*, absolute moral norms proscribing *semper et ad semper* acts intrinsically evil by reason of their object go hand-in-hand with inviolable human rights. Such norms, he emphasizes, "in fact represent the unshakable foundation and solid guarantee of a just and peaceful human coexistence, and hence of genuine democracy, which can come into being and develop only on the basis of the equality of all its members, who possess common rights and duties. *When it is a matter of the moral norms prohibiting intrinsic evil, there are no privileges or exceptions for anyone*" (*VS* 96.2). Innocent persons, for instance, have an inviolable right to life if and only if all other persons have an absolute obligation to forbear intentionally killing them.

From this it also follows, as John Paul II insists, that "*one must therefore reject the thesis*, characteristic of teleological and proportionalist theories, *which holds that it is impossible to qualify as*

*morally evil according to its species—its 'object'—the deliberate choice
of certain kinds of behavior or specific acts, apart from a consideration
of the intention for which the choice is made or the totality of the foreseeable consequences of that act for all persons concerned"* (*VS* 79.1).

In this passage, John Paul II refers to "teleological and
proportionalist theories." While acknowledging that the "moral life
has an essential *'teleological' character,* since it consists in the deliberate ordering of human acts to God, the supreme good and ultimate end (*telos*) of man" (*VS* 73.2), he rejects theories that he terms
teleologisms. "Certain *ethical theories,*" he writes, "called *'teleological,'* claim to be concerned for the conformity of human acts with
the ends pursued by the agent and with the values intended by
him. The criteria for evaluating the moral rightness of an action are
drawn from the *weighing of the non-moral or pre-moral goods* to be
gained and the corresponding non-moral or pre-moral values to be
respected. For some, concrete behavior would be right or wrong
according to whether or not it is capable of producing a better state
of affairs for all concerned. Right conduct would be the one capable of 'maximizing' goods and 'minimizing' evils" (*VS* 74.3).

One type of "teleologism" identified by John Paul II—"consequentialism"—"claims to draw the criteria of the rightness of a
given way of acting solely from a calculation of foreseeable consequences deriving from a given choice." Another variant—"proportionalism"—"by weighing the various values and goods being
sought, focuses rather on the proportion acknowledged between
the good and bad effects of that choice, with a view to the 'greater'
good or 'lesser' evil actually possible in a given situation" (*VS*
75.1).

Teleological theories, whether consequentialist or proportionalist, the pope continues, claim that it is not possible to determine
whether an act traditionally regarded as intrinsically evil by reason of its object would really be morally evil until one has considered, in the concrete situation, the "premoral" good and evil state
of affairs it is likely to cause. They conclude that the foreseen proportions of "premoral" goods and evils in the alternatives available
can at times justify exceptions to precepts traditionally regarded as
absolute (cf. *VS* 75).

John Paul II's central teaching on "The Moral Act" can be summed up in the following theses:

1. It is possible to judge that specific sorts of human acts, identifiable by reason of the object freely chosen by the acting person, are intrinsically evil or contrary to the order of reason, i.e., because "they radically contradict the good of person made in the image of God." To judge that acts so specified are morally evil there is no need to consider the further or ulterior intentions of the acting person, the circumstances in which acts so specified are done, or the consequences that might come about were acts so specified chosen and done. The reason is simple: one cannot be ready intentionally to deprive a human person of goods perfective of him without being willing *to do evil* and to make himself *to be an evil-doer.*

2. Corresponding to acts intrinsically evil by reason of the object freely chosen are moral absolutes, i.e., specific moral norms proscribing those acts unconditionally and unequivocally, without any possible exception.

3. Those moral theories are to be repudiated which claim that it is impossible to qualify as morally evil according to its kind or species the deliberate choice of certain specific acts without taking into account the further intention for which the choice is made or the totality of the foreseeable consequences of that act.

According to John Paul II, "teleological" theories, whether consequentialist or proportionalist, deny Thesis 1 and Thesis 2 and accept the claim repudiated by Thesis 3.

Consequently, if theologians commonly recognized as proportionalists deny Thesis 1 and Thesis 2 and accept the claim repudiated by Thesis 3, it follows that they do in fact hold the positions attributed by Pope John Paul II to "consequentialism" and "proportionalism" in *Veritatis splendor.* We shall now see whether theologians commonly regarded as proportionalists in their writings both prior to and after *Veritatis splendor* deny Theses 1 and 2 and accept the claim repudiated in Thesis 3.

II. Positions Taken by Theologians Commonly Known as Proportionalists Prior to *Veritatis splendor*

A. The Seminal Significance of the Papers of the Majority Report

I will begin this survey with the papers of the so-called Majority Report of the Papal Commission for the Study of Population, the Family, and Natality. These papers, prepared in 1966 by a group of theologians including Joseph Fuchs, S.J., were made public in 1967.[6] At that time the authors of these papers accepted, as did all Catholic theologians of that day, the teaching that some sorts of acts, specified by the object freely chosen, are intrinsically evil, for they vehemently rejected as intrinsically immoral the choice to engage in such acts as anal and/or oral sex when their opponents on the Commission challenged them to show why, if contraceptive intercourse can be morally good, other masturbatory-type acts by spouses cannot be made such.[7] However, as Charles E. Curran, writing only a few years later, forthrightly acknowledged, the moral reasoning used by these theologians to justify contraceptive intercourse for married couples inevitably led to the justification of other kinds of acts previously considered to be intrinsically evil.[8] It is thus useful to note key claims made by the authors of the celebrated Majority Report in order to understand this line of moral reasoning and how it contributed to the development of proportionalism in Catholic moral thought.

In one of their documents, the authors set forth the following normative statement: "To take his or another's life is a sin not because life is under the exclusive dominion of God, but because it is contrary to right reason *unless there is question of a good of a higher order*. It is licit to sacrifice a life for the good of the community" (emphasis added).[9] According to this "principle," it is morally permissible intentionally to destroy human life (even, apparently, innocent human life or other human goods) if doing so is necessary for some alleged higher good. Today this principle is commonly referred to as the "preference principle" or the "principle of proportionate good."

In another passage claiming that married couples may rightly contracept individual acts within marriage so long as these contracepted acts are ordered to the expression of marital love, which culminates in fertility responsibly accepted, the authors have this to say:

> When man intervenes in the procreative purpose of individual acts by contracepting, he does this with the intention of regulating and not excluding fertility. Then he unites the material finality toward fecundity which exists in intercourse with the formal finality of the person and renders the entire process human. . . . Conjugal acts which by intention are infertile [obviously, the authors see no moral difference between recourse to the infertile period and the use of contraceptives] or which are rendered infertile [by the use of contraceptives] are ordered to the expression of the union of love; that love, moreover, reaches its culmination in fertility responsibly accepted. For that reason other acts of union are in a sense incomplete and receive their full moral quality with ordination toward the fertile act. . . . Infertile conjugal acts constitute a totality with fertile acts and have a single *moral specification* [namely, the fostering of love responsibly toward generous fecundity].[10]

This passage presents an understanding of the "totality" of a human act central, as shall be seen, to proportionalist thinking. According to this argument, there is an admitted "material privation" (or what later will be termed a "premoral," "nonmoral," or "ontic" evil) in contraceptive activity, because, after all, one does deprive a genital act of its openness to new life. However, the contraceptive intervention is only, so this argument goes, a partial aspect of a whole series of contracepted conjugal acts, and this entire ensemble or "totality," "receives its *moral* specification from the other finality, which is good in itself [namely, the marital union] and from the fertility of the whole conjugal life."[11] According to this argument, married couples who use contraception rightly are not choosing to exclude children selfishly from their marriage (or expressing what the authors elsewhere call pejoratively a "contraceptive mentality").[12] They are not, according to this argument, acting in a way "which is contraceptive and opposed to a prudent and generous fruitfulness"; rather, they are acting responsibly.[13] Indeed, the object morally specifying their act—what they are doing—is that of fostering love responsibly toward a generous fecundity. But this "object" can be grasped *only* by looking at the act—or rather ensemble of acts—as a totality given its unity by the end or purpose for whose sake the couple uses contraceptive in a "non-contraceptive," i.e., unselfish, way.

According to the authors of the papers in the Majority Report, the moral analysis which led to the condemnation of contraception actually misconstrued the moral meaning of human acts by equating their moral objects narrowly with "physical processes," failing to consider them in their totality.

B. Consequentialism and Proportionalism

Before describing more fully how the kind of reasoning used in the papers of the Majority Report was subsequently developed by revisionist theologians, I believe it may be useful to comment briefly on the reasons why the terms "consequentialism" and "proportionalism" were used to identify this movement in moral theology. Briefly, as I will show, these terms were used because the theologians associated with this movement themselves used these terms to describe what they were doing.

The most influential of these theologians include Louis Janssens, Joseph Fuchs, Bruno Schüller, Franz Scholz, and Richard McCormick.[14] In a very significant way McCormick became, as it were, the historian of the movement by reason of his ongoing "Notes on Moral Theology," published annually in *Theological Studies* 1965–1985 and subsequently reprinted in two substantive volumes.[15] A review of some key "Notes" for the period 1972–1975 provides us with an insight into the reasons why the terms "consequentialism" and "proportionalism" were used to identify this movement in Catholic moral theology.

In the early 1970s, the proponents of the new moral theology themselves referred to their position as "consequentialist." Thus McCormick, writing in 1972, reviews essays by Bruno Schüller, Joseph Fuchs, and several other writers (e.g., Nicholas Crotty, John Milhaven) expressing somewhat similar ideas. He heaps high praise on Schüller's contributions (the essay in question was Schüller's "Direct Killing/Indirect Killing"), notes some ambiguities in Fuchs's "The Absoluteness of Moral Norms" but nonetheless expresses substantive agreement with Fuchs's thought. He emphasizes that the thread linking all these theologians together is their common movement toward "a morality of consequences." Again and again McCormick singles out "the key part played by consequences in the development of norms."[16] With Schüller he agrees that the moral assessment of an act must be "made 'teleologically,' i.e., from consequences."[17] He explicitly states that Fuchs's essay "appears to contain a significant shift in his methodology toward a morality of consequences."[18] Indeed, McCormick concludes that Fuchs "has obviously taken a rather giant step in the direction of a consequentialist methodology. . . . [indeed] the very 'meaning' of an action can only be gathered when all aspects of the action, *especially its consequences* have been *weighed* as far as possible."[19] Moreover, McCormick makes it clear that he agrees with Fuchs on this matter. Concluding his review of the literature at this time (1972), McCormick offers the "summary statement that contemporary theological writings have moved very markedly in the direction of a consequentialist methodology."[20]

It is also important to observe that several of these theologians (e.g., Schüller and McCormick) insisted that the terms "direct" and "indirect" must be properly understood. According to them, these terms ought not to be understood in a *psychological* sense. It is not of crucial moral significance, they maintained, that one "psychologically intend" a premoral evil, e.g., the death of an innocent person. Evil (premoral) can legitimately be the object of a will act, and one can "directly intend" such evil in a psychological sense. According to these authors, "'indirect' was (or should have been) first of all a way of saying that there was at least a proportion between the value pursued and the value left undone or the disvalue caused [and 'intended' in this way]."[21]

However, by 1975 proponents of the new theology did not like being called consequentialists and rejected as unfair and heavy-handed the charge that their methodology is "consequentialist." In his 1975 "Notes on Moral Theology"[22] McCormick begins by referring once more to Fuchs's "The Ab-

soluteness of Moral Terms," and then severely criticizes a German theologian, Gustav Ermecke, who had accused Fuchs of
making the morality of human acts depend entirely upon the
agent's intention (of effecting good or bad consequences).[23]
Both Fuchs[24] and McCormick regard this criticism as unjust.
Fuchs was not, both he and McCormick insist, advocating consequentialism or intentionalism. Rather, as Fuchs now explains
matters and as McCormick sought to make clear, what Fuchs
was really doing (and what McCormick approves) was to "nuance" the traditional understanding of the three *fontes
moralitatis* (object [or, according to Fuchs, "action"], end, and
circumstances). What Fuchs has done, McCormick says—and he
is fully in agreement with him—is to deny "that the object can
be an independent source of the moral quality of the action—
independent, that is, of the intention [of the end for whose sake
the object is chosen] and circumstances. In this sense,"
McCormick continues, "he has tightened the relationship between the traditional object-end-circumstances and argued that
it is only the combination of the three that yields the total *object of choice* [in a moral sense]. The good intended in one's
choice specifies the object without smothering it out of existence, and thus in a sense becomes an integral part of the total
object."[25] McCormick contrasts this procedure with that followed by Ermecke and, he says, the "manualist" tradition,
which "attributed a moral quality to the object independently
of the circumstances, including the end." He then concludes
this section of his "Notes" by claiming, as one of the major considerations in support of Fuchs's analysis, that "if it is only object-end-circumstances together that can yield a final moral
evaluation, the implication is that it is a *proportion* within the
entire action between the values and disvalues that justifies the
causing or permitting of the disvalues . . . It is precisely this emphasis on over-all *proportion* that Fuchs's [new] study high-
lights."[26]

   Note that in this 1975 essay McCormick characterizes the
moral methodology advocated not as a type of
consequentialism (as he had in his 1972 "Notes") but as a methodology rooted in an assessment of proportionality between the
disvalues (nonmoral evils) and values (nonmoral goods) one's

action effects. McCormick sees the same methodology operative in the important essay by Louis Janssens, "Ontic Evil and Moral Evil." After reviewing Janssens' article in some detail, McCormick, summarizing the new theology being developed by Janssens, Fuchs and others, says that these theologians are arguing that

> it is impossible to pronounce a final moral judgment on an exterior action containing ontic evil (e.g., a killing...) without attending the end of the inner act of the will. For a true moral evaluation, two things must be considered: (1) the end of the agent, the moral goodness or badness of the end; and (2) the *debita proportio* of the external action to the end. Because the action in its entirety must be evaluated morally, Janssens concludes, exactly as does Fuchs, that concrete moral norms (generalizations about such actions) *valent ut in pluribus*.[27]

In this set of "Notes" McCormick also reviews and criticizes an article, "Morality of Consequences: A Critical Appraisal," by John Connery, S.J.[28] Connery had accused Fuchs (and McCormick) of being consequentialists. McCormick and Fuchs disavow this name, insisting that all aspects of the action, and not only the consequences, need to be taken into account in order to render a moral judgment. McCormick notes that Connery, in his critique of Fuchs, had claimed that Fuchs's reasoning would justify the "direct killing of an innocent person" and that Fuchs would have to "attach a rider to every rule, e.g., killing is wrong except when there is a proportionate reason."[29] To this objection McCormick responds: "'Exactly so," and then claims that this is indeed the way Catholic theology has traditionally operated.[30] The key principle is that of proportionality.

I believe it obvious, from this review of the genesis of the terms "consequentialism" and "proportionalism," that theologians commonly known today as "proportionalists" deny Theses 1 and 2 of *Veritatis splendor* and affirm the position repudiated in Thesis 3 of that encyclical. Thus the writings of these theologians suffice to show that John Paul II did not misrepresent their views in his encyclical, as McCormick and others have charged.

But it will be worthwhile to examine more closely the positions developed by Fuchs, Janssens, McCormick, and other theologians known as proportionalists in their writings. Hence I will now offer a summary of the views set forth by these authors not only in the essays summarized so neatly by McCormick in our review of the genesis of the terms "consequentialist" and "proportionalist" but in other published material as well.

C. The Developed Articulation of the Proportionalist Theory

Recall now the "principles" to which the authors of the papers of the Majority Report appealed, namely, that it is against right reason to take the life of a person (a "premoral" or "nonmoral" or "ontic" good) or to destroy other human goods "unless there is a question of a good of a higher order." As formulated in later writings of theologians commonly known as proportionalist this became known as the "preference principle" or "principle of proportionate good." The expression "preference principle" was advocated by Bruno Schüller. Thus he wrote: "Any ethical norm whatsoever regarding our dealings and omissions in relation to other men . . . can only be a particular application of that more universal norm, 'The greater good is to be preferred.'"[31] According to this principle it is morally right to intend a premoral evil, such as the death of an innocent person, *if* this is required by a "proportionately related greater good." This is Schüller's way of articulating the "principle" at the heart of the Majority Report's analysis of human action. Richard McCormick articulates the "preference principle" this way:

> Where a higher good is at stake and the only means [human act] to protect it is to choose to do a nonmoral evil, then the will remains properly disposed to the values constitutive of human good. . . . This is to say that the intentionality is good even when the person, reluctantly and regretfully to be sure, intends [in the "psychological" sense] the non-moral evil if a truly proportionate reason [i.e., good] for such a choice is present.[32]

This principle does not, proportionalist theologians claim, mean that a good end can justify *morally* evil means. But they do hold that the intention [in the sense of one's *further* intention or *ulterior end*] and realization of a "greater" nonmoral good can justify the "psychological" intending and doing of any nonmoral evil.

Some proportionalists (for instance Peter Knauer[33] and Fuchs)[34] claim that when one chooses to cause evil only as a means to a greater good, the evil or harm is *not intended*. But most proportionalist theologians clearly acknowledge that this principle justifies the deliberate [psychological] intention to do nonmoral or premoral evil. Thus McCormick explicitly proposed, in noting the "ambiguity" in the way Fuchs articulated the position, that it would be clearer and more precise to say that

> it is legitimate to intend [psychologically] premoral evil *in ordine ad finem proportionatum*. . . . The "greater good" does not mean that the premoral disvalue is not intended; it means that it is not intended *propter se*. Therefore, would it not be better to say that it is legitimate to intend a disvalue *in se sed non propter se?* When there is no proportionate reason, the disvalue caused is chosen and intended *in se et propter se*, and it is this *propter se* which makes the act immoral. I believe that this is what Fuchs means by "intending evil *as such*," but his occasional use of the simple and unqualified word "intend" leaves the matter a bit murky.[35]

It is most instructive to observe here that in the early 1970s McCormick acknowledged a significant difference between a will that "psychologically" intends evil and one that merely permits it. Thus in his 1973 Père Marquette Lecture he wrote: "The will relates differently to what it intends and what it permits. . . . the intending will (hence the person) is more closely associated with the evil than is the permitting will. This bespeaks (in some admittedly obscure way) a greater willingness that it [the evil] occur."[36] As a result, at that time McCormick claimed that a "greater" proportionate good is required if one is to intend the nonmoral evil than if one only "permits" or "indirectly intends" the nonmoral evil involved in one's action. Bruno Schüller, however, pointed out to McCormick that "the person who is prepared to realize the good even by intending evil is more willing that the evil exists, but only because he is more willing that the good exist."[37] Thus Schüller concluded: "Therefore, I am strongly inclined to believe that in point of fact *'intend as a means' and 'permit,' when referring to a non-moral evil, denote exactly the same mental attitude.*"[38] Schüller's remarks so impressed McCormick that by 1978 he had abandoned his earlier view, declaring that Schüller's objection to his original position was "fatal."[39]

The point is this: since there is no significant moral difference between deliberately intending a "nonmoral" evil and merely permitting it, the person who intends and does evil for the sake of a proportionately greater good has a greater love for the good than does one who refuses to intend and do evil yet at times does permit it. In the judgment of these proportionalist theologians this is an admirable character trait: they contend that the refusal intentionally to do evil would be a moral weakness when intending and doing such evil is demanded by the "preference principle" or "principle of proportionate good."

Obviously, one cannot judge whether intending and doing evil, i.e., having a so-called nonmoral or premoral evil as the "psychological object" but not yet "moral object" of one's choice, until one knows that "greater good" toward which this object is directed, and one can know this only teleologically, i.e., by taking into account the foreseeable consequences of one's choice (direct intention) to do evil. Obviously too, those holding this view deny Theses 1 and 2 which *Veritatis splendor* affirms and affirm the view rejected by Thesis 3 of the encyclical.

Other proportionalists, preeminently Fuchs, have developed the "totality argument" of that Majority Report according to which one cannot grasp the "object" morally specifying a human act and can hence make no judgment, either negative or positive, regarding a proposed action, without considering all the traditional *fontes moralitatis*. Only by considering all these factors simultaneously can we discern the "object" morally specifying the act.[40] Thus, to use an example of this line of reasoning provided by McCormick, if a married couple resorts to contraceptive sterilization (the "object" narrowly conceived in abstraction from the "totality" of the act) because any further pregnancy might endanger the mother's life, the choice to sterilize her, when viewed within the totality of what the couple is doing, can truthfully be described as a "marriage-stabilizing" act. The moral object, on this understanding, is not contraceptive sterilization but rather "saving or stabilizing the marriage."[41]

Recall that Fuchs, in his version of the new morality, consistently identifies the controverted moral absolutes he denies with "material" or "concrete behavioral" norms specifying "physical acts" or "material acts," including, in some cases, their "direct'" effects, described independently of *any* purpose or intention of the agent.[42] In his view and in that of other revisionist theologians the tradition affirming as moral absolutes norms such as those proscribing the "direct" killing of the innocent, sexual union with someone other than one's spouse, etc., arbitrarily abstracted some elements of an act from its total, concrete reality, falsely absolutizing "nonmoral," "premoral," "ontic" goods, goods such as human life itself. In this view norms protecting particular goods, such as human life, can never be more than generalizations about what usually serves to promote human well-being; such norms have only a prima facie validity and may rightly be set aside if one correctly assesses the whole or totality of the action in question.[43] Indeed, as Fuchs wrote, "a strict behavioral norm, stated as a universal, contains unexpressed conditions and qualifications which as such limit its universality."[44]

According to Fuchs and his followers, material, concrete behavioral norms such as those prohibiting the direct killing of the innocent, sexual union with someone who is not one's spouse, etc., are formulated on the basis of reflection on shared human experience. But this is an ongoing, open-ended process. It therefore follows, as another revisionist theologian expressed the matter, that

> we can never exclude the possibility that future experience, hitherto unimagined, might put a moral problem into a new frame of reference which would call for a revision of a norm that, when formulated, could not have taken such new experience into account.[45]

As a result, these moral norms, which include the norms the Catholic tradition and the magisterium had regarded as absolute or without exception, are "valid only for the most part," and admit of exceptions in light of the "total" or "whole" context in which they are chosen and done.[46]

From the foregoing it should be evident that Fuchs and others who claim that one can determine the "moral object" of the human act only by considering the "action" (or "object" narrowly considered), "end," and "circumstances" together deny Theses 1 and 2 of *Veritatis splendor* and accept the proposition repudiated by Thesis 3 of the encyclical.

From all this, too, it seems evident that John Paul II did not attribute to theologians commonly regarded as proportionalist positions that they do not hold and teach. Their writings prior to the encyclical provide abundant evidence that the positions attributed to the "teleologisms" repudiated by John Paul II as incompatible with Catholic faith are positions advanced and defended by them.

I wish now to look briefly at some post-*Veritatis splendor* writings of proportionalist theologians in order to see whether the positions attributed to "proportionalists" in the encyclical are still held by them.

III. Representative *Post-Veritatis splendor* Writings of Proportionalist Theologians

Here I will consider some writings of McCormick, Joseph Selling, and Louis Janssens in response to *Veritatis splendor*.

A. Richard McCormick

McCormick, as we have seen, complains that the encyclical attributes to proportionalists positions that they do not hold.[47] The encyclical, he says, "repeatedly states of proportionalism that it attempts to justify *morally wrong* actions by a good intention" and that this is a "misrepresentation."[48] This is McCormick's way of summarizing the major criticism of proportionalism made by John Paul II, and I have placed emphasis on the words "morally wrong." For McCormick's major complaint, namely, that the encyclical has attributed to proportionalists views that they do not hold, seems to have some kind of plausibility if the Holy Father's critique is summarized in this way, for, after all, no intelligent person—let alone a proportionalist theologian—would attempt the ludicrous, and the ludicrous would be the attempt to justify an action already known to be morally wrong. If the action is already known to be morally wrong, then one cannot make it morally right, and proportionalists do not try to do this.

Yet this is not the central critique by *Veritatis splendor* of their position. Rather, the issue lies in identifying the criteria to be used in determining whether an action is morally good (right) or morally wrong. *Veritatis splendor*, as we have seen, holds that a human act is specified morally primarily by the object freely chosen and that if this object is not in conformity with the order of reason because it contradicts the good of the person made in God's image, then one can judge that an act so specified is morally bad (intrinsically evil) and need not inquire further regarding its circumstances or ulterior purpose, for these could not give the act a different moral species. The encyclical, as we have also seen, rejects the claim, which it attributes to "proportionalism," that one cannot judge an act to be morally bad without taking into account, in addition to the object, the circumstances and ulterior end intended by the agent.

But it is precisely this claim, attributed to proportionalist theologians by the encyclical, that McCormick makes again in developing his complaint that John Paul II has simply failed to understand what proportionalists are trying to do. He faults the pope for "missing the point of what proportionalists are saying." They are not, McCormick assures us, saying that we can justify morally wrong actions by a good intention. "When contemporary moral theologians," McCormick writes, "say that certain disvalues [="premoral" evils] in our actions can be justified by a proportionate reason they are not saying that *morally wrong actions (ex objecto) can be justified by the end* [emphasis in the original]. They are saying that an action cannot be judged morally wrong simply by looking at *the material happening* [emphasis added] or *at its object in a very narrow and retricted sense* [emphasis added]. This is precisely what the tradition has done."[49]

This is precisely the issue, namely, properly identifying the "object" of a human act. In reviewing key elements of *Veritatis splendor*, I noted how carefully John Paul, following St. Thomas,[50] did this. Note now that McCormick, in his complaint, first says that the objection to proportionalism stems from identifying the moral object with the "material happening." But those who, in the tradition, affirmed that there are acts intrinsically evil by reason of their object did not identify object with "material happening" (or what St. Thomas called the "natural species," as opposed to the "moral species" of the act). Most important of all, however, for understanding John Paul II's teaching, is the fact that he explicitly says: "by the object of a given moral act . . . one cannot mean a *process or an event of the merely physical order*" (*VS* 78.1; emphasis added). Obviously, the Holy Father is not guilty of the rather jejune error McCormick attributes to critics of proportionalism.

McCormick, again, adds that opponents of proportionalism at times render a moral judgment by looking at the action's "object in a very narrow and restricted sense." His point is that we can grasp the "moral object" only by considering the act in its totality, i.e., by considering the "object" "narrowly conceived" together with the circumstances, including the consequences, and the further end intended by the agent. But this, as we have seen, is precisely the thesis rejected by *Veritatis splendor* and accurately attributed to proportionalists—and it is now being reasserted by McCormick.

A good way of illustrating the difference between this proportionalist way of identifying the moral object and the way taught by John Paul II (and the Catholic moral tradition) is to see how they regard the human act involved in contraception and contraceptive sterilization. As we have seen, proportionalists like McCormick claim that the moral "object" of contraceptive practices, if rightly and unselfishly chosen, is "to foster love responsibly toward a generous fecundity," obviously something very good. And contraceptive sterilization, if done because a woman has been told that any further pregnancy may threaten her life, is, McCormick avers, truthfully specified as being a "marriage-stabilizing" act.

John Paul II, however, undoubtedly agrees with Pope Paul VI in describing the moral object specifying contraception and contraceptive sterilization as the "impeding of procreation": "to be rejected is every act which, either in anticipation of the conjugal act, or in its accomplishment, or in the development of its natural consequences, *proposes, either as end or as means, to im-pede procreation*" (*Humanae vitae*, n. 14; the Latin text of the material emphasized is: "*id tamquam finem obtinendum aut viam adhibendam intendat ut procreatio impediatur*").

John Paul II and Paul VI are correct in so identifying the object freely chosen by those who contracept (and arguments can then be advanced to show that a choice so specified is contrary to the order of reason because it contradicts the good of the person made in God's image). Contraceptors freely choose to impede procreation (to effect what proportionalists call a "premoral" or "nonmoral" or "ontic" disvalue or evil) in order to achieve some good purpose—their further or ulterior end, e.g., to foster love responsibly or to stabilize a marriage. But of itself contraception does *not* "foster love responsibly toward a generous fecundity" nor does contraceptive sterilization "stabilize a marriage." What McCormick and other proportionalists are actually doing is redescribing the object chosen in terms of its hoped-for benefits, and this is precisely what John Paul II criticizes as philosophically and theologically flawed and irreconcilable with Catholic faith. In his very effort to show that John Paul II did not know what he was talking about, McCormick convincingly shows us that he surely did.[51]

B. Joseph Selling

Selling, dean of the faculty of moral theology at the University of Leuven and Janssens' successor, is co-editor, with Jan Jans, of a volume of essays entitled *The Splendor of Accuracy: An Examination of the Assertions Made by Veritatis splendor.*[52] It is not possible here to give adequate consideration to Selling's essay. By focusing attention on a few of his criticisms, however, it is possible to see how he seeks to undermine the teaching of the encyclical and how flawed his major complaints are.

He first seeks to compare *Veritatis splendor* with Pius XII's *Humani generis* in an effort to discredit the former. He flatly asserts that "nearly everything that . . . *Humani generis* stood for was reversed by the close of the Second Vatican Council," implying that the notion of theology and its work as set forth by Pius XII was repudiated by the council Fathers.[53] But he ignores the fact that in a council document explicitly concerned with the teaching of theology, not least of all moral theology, the council Fathers make the teaching of Pius XII's encyclical their own. The document in question, *Optatam totius*, emphasizes that for Catholic theology to be carried out rightly, it must be done "in the light of faith and *under the guidance of the Church's magisterium*" (n. 16; emphasis added). At precisely this point in the directives for the "renewal" of theology, the council Fathers explicitly referred to the teaching of Pius XII in *Humani generis* on the work of Catholic theology. Hence Selling's bald assertion is falsified by documents of the very council which he avers repudiated the views of Pius XII. But his strategy was to analogize John Paul II's encyclical on moral theology with Pius XII's. Just as Pius's thought, so Selling claims, is now repudiated, so too, the implication goes, will John Paul II's *Veritatis splendor* be repudiated in the future.

With respect to human acts and their moral evaluation, Selling finds "rather bizarre" the concepts of freedom and the will found in the following passage of *Veritatis splendor*: "Some authors do not take into sufficient consideration the fact that the will is dependent upon the concrete choices which it makes: these choices are a condition of its moral goodness and its being ordered to the ultimate end of the person" (*VS* 75.1, as given in the translation Selling provides).[54] Here it is important first of all to note that the Latin text, and the official English translation, is more precise than the translation Selling provides. The Latin reads as follows: "*Nonnulli non satis aspiciunt voluntatem definitis implicari delectionibus, quas ipsa operatur*" (translated, in the authorized translations, as "some authors do not take into consideration the fact that the will *is involved in* the concrete choices which it makes"). The point is that the person's moral character is dependent upon his own free choices—in and through them he determines himself. Selling claims that the idea that the action of the will is dependent upon its choices for its goodness is a "relatively new idea that has developed in the literature in order to substantiate the theory of the 'basic goods.'"[55]

I will return to the "theory of the 'basic goods'" below. But it is first necessary to note how false is Selling's claim that the position taken by John Paul II regarding human action and human freedom in *Veritatis splendor*, n. 75, is "rather bizarre" and a "relatively new idea." Earlier in the encyclical John Paul II had stressed that we determine ourselves through our freely chosen acts. He emphasized that "[freely chosen deeds] do not produce a change merely in the state of affairs outside of man but, to the extent that they are deliberate choices, they give moral definition to the very person who performs them, determining his *profound spiritual traits*" (*VS* 71.2). That this is not a "relatively new" idea should be clear from the fact that John Paul II goes on to say that the precise point he is making has been "perceptively noted by St. Gregory of Nyssa." He then cites a beautiful passage from Gregory's *De vita Moysis* (II.2–3; PG 44:327–28), to wit:

> All things subject to change and to becoming never remain constant, but continually pass from one state to another, for better or worse. . . . Now, human life is always subject to change; it needs to be born ever anew. . . . but here birth does not come about by a foreign intervention, as is the case with bodily beings. . . ; it is the result of a free choice. Thus we *are* in a certain way our own parents, creating ourselves as we will, by our decisions. (Cited in *VS* 71.2).

Now to the "theory of 'basic goods'" to which Selling referred in the passage previously cited. Selling contends that the encyclical has been profoundly influenced by the "novel" doctrine of "basic goods" developed principally by Germain Grisez and John Finnis.[56] Selling makes no effort to show the truth of his claim that the natural law thought of Grisez and his associates profoundly influenced the encyclical. Perhaps the thought of these contemporary theologians who seek to develop the natural law thought of St. Thomas did influence the encyclical; perhaps not. This is not, in my opinion, of crucial concern. But what is crucial is Selling's way of characterizing the "basic goods" theory of Grisez. According to Selling, "when we look below the surface" at the "basic goods theory" we will discover that according to this theory, it is natural to accumulate possessions beyond one's needs, to stratify society into leaders and followers, to destroy one's enemies, to accept that white European male persons are superior to non-white persons, non-Europeans, and non-males.[57] Such an erroneous characterization of this theory is an indication that Selling's critique of *Veritatis splendor*'s "inaccuracies" is perhaps not entirely reliable.

C. Louis Janssens

In his contribution to *The Splendor of Accuracy* Janssens defends the thesis repudiated by John Paul II in *Veritatis splendor*, the thesis namely *"which holds that it is impossible to qualify as morally evil according to its species—its 'object'—the deliberate choice of certain kinds of behavior or specific acts, apart from a consideration of the intention for which the choice is made or the totality of the foreseeable consequences of that act for all persons concerned"* (*VS* 79.1; cf. Thesis 3, above).

The bulk of Janssens's article is devoted to defending this thesis and to denying Thesis 1 and Thesis 2. Early on Janssens appeals[58] to the "Vatican Declaration on Euthanasia" (1981) to support his thesis that we can determine whether an action is morally good or morally bad only by evaluating it in its totality and by seeing whether or not any evil involved in the deed is "proportionate" or "disproportionate" to the good intended as the end of the deed.

While it is true that this Vatican document suggested that the terms "proportionate" and "disproportionate" might be used to designate medical treatments previously called "ordinary" and "extraordinary," its use of these terms in no way supports the "proportionalist" method of making moral judgments. For prior to considering the reasons for judging that some means of medical treatment are proportionate (ordinary, obligatory) or disproportionate (extraordinary), the "Declaration" had affirmed that euthanasia, or mercy killing, is intrinsically immoral, not because it is "disproportionate" but simply because it is the intentional killing of an innocent human person, an act specified by reason of its chosen object as intrinsically evil and incapable of being made morally right by any further intentions of the agent (e.g., to relieve suffering), its circumstances, etc.[59]

In the balance of this essay Janssens basically reiterates the thesis of his enormously influential earlier article, "Ontic Evil and Moral Evil," in which he claimed St. Thomas's support for the proportionalist method of making moral judgments—a method according to which no moral judgment can be rendered without taking into consideration not only the "object" (which Janssens identified with the "external act" considered as a material event) but also the proportionality of the object chosen to the final end intended by the agent, which serves as the "form" of the entire moral act, giving it its species. In other words, in the balance of the essay Janssens again seeks to defend Thesis 3, the thesis attributed to proportionalist theologians by John Paul II and firmly rejected by him.

Janssens offers no new arguments to support his claims (other than his appeal to the "Declaration on Euthanasia"), nor does he even attempt to respond to those who have tried to show that in "Ontic Evil and Moral Evil" he seriously misinterpreted St. Thomas.[60] The same criticism can be leveled against the present essay.

Moreover, Janssens insists that "official church documents maintain that contraception . . . and homosexual acts are intrinsically evil according to their object. *All these terms refer simply to factual events.*"[61] This is patently false, for contraception and homosexual acts are morally specified, as John Paul II insists, by the object *freely chosen by the acting person*, and not by a mere physical happening. Here Janssens attributes to the magisterium (and by implication to Pope John Paul II) a position explicitly rejected by John Paul II in *Veritatis splendor*, n. 78.

In short, in this post-*Veritatis splendor* essay Janssens clearly defends the thesis accurately attributed to proportionalists by John Paul II in his encyclical while at the same time attributing to John Paul II a position that he explicitly rejects.

IV. Conclusion

I believe that I have shown here, with abundant use of the writings of proportionalist theologians both prior to and after *Veritatis splendor*, that they indeed do teach and hold the views attributed to them by John Paul II. I think that the evidence presented here also shows that these theologians have been quite inaccurate in their portrayals of John Paul II's teaching. If any injustice has been done, it has not been done to proportionalist theologians by the Holy Father but rather to him by the proportionalist theologians.

Endnotes

1. This essay incorporates some material found in earlier articles of mine on the reaction of theologians to *Veritatis splendor*: "Theologians and Theologies in the Encyclical," *Anthropotes: Rivista di Studi sulla Persona e la Famiglia* 10 (1994): 41–59; "Moral Theologians and *Veritatis splendor*," *Homiletic and Pastoral Review* 95.3 (December 1994): 7–16; "*The Splendor of Accuracy*: How Accurate?" *The Thomist* 59 (1995): 465–83.

2. Richard A. McCormick, S.J., "*Veritatis splendor* and Moral Theology," *America* (30 October 1993): 11; the same article was published under the title "Killing the Patient" in *The Tablet* of London (30 October 1993): 1410–11. Among other proportionalists who rejected the encyclical as flawed, claiming that the pope had been poorly advised, are Joseph Fuchs, S.J., "Good Acts and Good Persons," *The Tablet* (6 November 1993): 1444–45; Lisa Sowle Cahill, "Accent on the Masculine," *The Tablet* (11 December 1993): 1618–19; Joseph Selling, "Ideological Differences: Some Background Considerations for Understanding *Veritatis splendor*," *The Month* (January 1995): 12–14.

3. John Paul II, "Address to Moral Theologians," 10 April 1986, par. 4; *Acta apostolicae sedis* 78 (1986): 1101.

4. The internal citation in *Veritatis splendor*, n. 13, is from Vatican Council II, Pastoral Constitution *Gaudium et spes*, n. 24.

5. On this see St. Thomas Aquinas, *ScG* III, c. 122: "*Non enim Deus a nobis offenditur nisi ex eo quod contra nostrum bonum agimus.*"

6. Three of the papers from the Commission were leaked to the press and published, in English, by *National Catholic Reporter* on 19 April 1967. Later, all of the papers of the Commission, along with other material, were published in *The Birth-Control Debate*, ed. Robert Hoyt (Kansas City, Mo.: National Catholic Reporter, 1969). Detailed accounts of the Commission's work, highly favorable to the "majority position" and critical of *Humanae vitae* and of the "minority report" can be found in Robert Blair Kaiser, *The Politics of Sex and Religion* (Kansas City, Mo: Leaven Press, 1985); and Robert McClory, *Turning Point: The Inside Story of the Papal Birth Control Commission and How "Humanae Vitae" Changed the Life of Patty Crowley and the Future of the Church* (New York: Crossroad, 1995).

7. On this see the "Documentum syntheticum de moralitate nativitatum" (translated as "The Question Is Not Closed") in *The Birth-Control Debate*, p. 76, where the authors declare that "the new theory" they champion "is extremely strict. . . since it does not permit them [masturbatory-type acts]. For in these acts there is preserved neither the dignity of love nor the dignity of the spouses as human persons according to the image of God." As John Finnis has observed, however, this is a "'picture-thinking' conception of dignity" and "is no explanation at all, since an act accords with human dignity in the morally relevant sense by being reasonable and right in accord with God's call to us." See John Finnis, "The Natural Law, Objective Morality, and Vatican II," in *Principles of Catholic Moral Life*, ed. William E. May (Chicago: Franciscan Herald Press, 1981), 120.

8. See Charles E. Curran, "Divorce from the Perspective of a Revised Moral Theology," in *Proceedings of the Canon Law Society of America 1974* (Washington, D.C.: Canon Law Society of America, 1974), 6. This essay is reprinted in Curran's *Ongoing Revision: Studies in Moral Theology* (Notre Dame, Ind.: Fides, 1975), 78. Curran accepts the reasoning of the authors of the so-called Majority Report and the subsequent revising of other moral norms in light of the reasoning found in it.

9. "Documentum syntheticum de moralitate nativitatum" ("The Question Is Not Closed"), in *The Birth-Control Debate*, 69.

10. Ibid., 72; emphasis added.

11. Ibid., 75; emphasis added.

12. On this see another document from the Majority, "Schema documenti de responsabili paternitate" (translated as "On Responsible Parenthood"), in ibid., 88–90.

13. See this remarkable passage in ibid., 89–90:
    The true opposition is not to be sought between some material conformity to the physiological processes of nature and some artificial intervention. For it is natural to man to use his skill in order to put under human control what is given by physical nature. The opposition is to be sought really between one way of acting *which is contraceptive* and opposed to a prudent and generous fruitfulness, and another way *which is in an ordered relationship to responsible fruitfulness and which has a concern for education and all the essential human and Christian values.* (Emphasis added)

    This passage is instructive because it sharply distinguishes between "a way of acting which is contraceptive," that is, selfish, and using contraceptives in order to be responsible in one's fruitfulness. Note, moreover, the dualism implicit in this passage. Our power to generate life is merely some "physiological process of nature;" it belongs to "what is given by physical nature" to be put under human control. I will return to this issue below, in considering the way John Paul II responds to the charge of "physicalism" leveled against magisterial teaching on issues in sexual morality by proportionalist theologians.

14. A handy collection of representative essays in which these authors set forth their position is found in *Readings in Moral Theology No. 1: Moral Norms and Catholic Tradition,* ed. Charles E. Curran and Richard A. McCormick, S.J. (New York: Paulist Press, 1979). This volume includes the following: Peter Knauer, "The Hermeneutic Function of the Principle of Double Effect" (originally published in *Natural Law Forum* 12 [1967]); Louis Janssens, "Ontic Evil and Moral Evil" (originally published in *Louvain Studies* 4 [1972]; Joseph Fuchs, "The Absoluteness of Moral Terms" (originally published in *Gregorianum* 52 [1971] and reprinted as "The Absoluteness of Behavioral Moral Norms" in Fuchs's *Personal Responsibility and Christian Morality* (Washington, D.C.: Georgetown University Press, 1983); Bruno Schüller, "Direct Killing/Indirect Killing" (originally published as "Direkte Tötung/Indirekte Tötung," in *Theologie und Philosophie* 47 [1972]; Bruno Schüller, "Various Types of Grounding for Ethical Norms" (originally published as "Typen der Begrundung sittlicher Normen" in *Concilium* 120 [1776]; and Franz Scholz, "Problems on Norms Raised by Ethical Borderline Situations: Beginnings of a Solution in Thomas Aquinas and Bonaventure" (originally published as "Durch ethische Grenzsituationen aufgeworfene Normenprobleme" in *Theologische-Praktische Quartalschrift* 123 [1275].

    Other important sources for this movement in contemporary moral theology are: Richard A. McCormick, S.J. *Ambiguity in Moral Choice,* Père Marquette Lecture in Theology 1973 (Milwaukee: Marquette University Press, 1973), reprinted along with McCormick's later "nuancing" of his view, "Commentary on the Commentaries," in *Doing Evil to Achieve Good,* ed. R. A. McCormick, S.J., and Paul Ramsey (Chicago: Loyola University Press, 1978); McCormick, *Notes on Moral Theology: 1965–1980* (Washington, D.C.: University Press of America, 1981), especially 349–67, 521–43, 576–91, 684–722; Louis Janssens, "Norms and Priorities in a Love Ethic," *Louvain Studies* 6 (1977): 207–38. The position has been developed at length in several textbooks designed for seminary use, in particular Timothy E. O'Connell, *Principles for a Catholic Morality* (New York: Seabury, 1978) and Richard Gula, S.S., *Reason Informed by Faith* (New York: Paulist Press, 1989). In a revised version of his text, published in 1991 by Harper, O'Connell says that he rejects the proportionalism he advocated in the 1978 edition; however, a careful reading of the volume shows that he does not, but rather introduces proportionalistic reasoning into his methodology without seeming to realize that this is what he is doing.

15. McCormick, *Notes on Moral Theology 1965–1980*; and idem, *Notes on Moral Theology 1981–1985* (Washington: University Press of America, 1985).
16. McCormick, *Notes on Moral Theology 1965–1980,* 349–67, passim.
17. Ibid., 352.
18. Ibid., 359.

19. Ibid.; emphasis added.
20. Ibid., 371.
21. Ibid., 352.
22. Reprinted in McCormick, *Notes on Moral Theology 1965–1980*, 521–74 (esp. 529–44)
23. Ermecke's essay, in which he had severely criticized Fuchs, was: "Das Problem der Universalität oder Allgemeingültigkeit sittlicher Normen innerweltlicher Lebensgestaltung," *Münchener theologische Zeitschrift* 24 (1973): 1–24.
24. Joseph Fuchs, "Sittliche Normen—Universalien und Generalisierungen," *Münchener theologische Zeitschrift* 25 (1974): 18–33.
25. McCormick, *Notes on Moral Theology 1965–1980*, 532.
26. Ibid., 533; emphasis added. The "Fuchs's study" to which reference is made is "Sittliche Normen—Universalien und Generalisierungen."
27. Ibid., 535.
28. Connery's essay had appeared in *Theological Studies* 34 (1973): 396–414. It is reprinted in *Readings in Moral Theology No. 1. Moral Norms and Catholic Tradition*, 244–66.
29. John Connery, S.J., "Morality of Consequences: A Critical Appraisal," in *Readings in Moral Theology No. 1*, 255.
30. McCormick, *Notes on Moral Theology 1965–1980*, 542.
31. B. Schüller, "What Ethical Principles Are Universally Valid?," *Theology Digest* 19 (1971): 24; translation of "Zur Problematik allgemeinen ethischer Grundsatze," which appeared originally in *Theologie und Philosophie* 45 (1970): 4.
32. McCormick, "Ambiguity in Moral Choice," as reprinted in *Doing Evil to Achieve Good*, 39.
33. See Peter Knauer, "The Hermeneutic Function of the Principle of Double Effect," in *Readings in Moral Theology No. 1*, 10–11.
34. See his *Personal Responsibility and Christian Morality*, 136.
35. McCormick, *Notes on Moral Theology 1965–1980*, 355–56.
36. McCormick, "Ambiguity in Moral Choice," reprinted in *Doing Evil to Achieve Good*, 30–31; cf. 35–36.
37. Bruno Schüller, "The Double Effect in Catholic Thought: A Revolution," in *Doing Evil to Achieve Good*, 191. See McCormick, "A Commentary on the Commentaries," in ibid., 241.
38. Schüller, "Double Effect," 191; emphasis in the original.
39. McCormick, "A Commentary on the Commentaries," 241.
40. See Joseph Fuchs, "The Absoluteness of Behavioral Moral Norms," in his *Personal Responsibility and Christian Morality*, 138ff.
41. McCormick, "A Commentary on the Commentaries," 241.
42. See note 35 above. Other proportionalists who speak this way are Jansens, Franz Bockle, and Peter Knauer.
43. On this see Joseph Fuchs, *Christian Ethics in a Secular Arena*, 82; Fuchs, *Personal Responsibility and Christian Morality*, 142, 212; Janssens, "Ontic Evil and Moral Evil," 144; Janssens, "Norms and Priorities in a Love Ethic," 231.
44. Fuchs, "The Absoluteness of Behavioral Moral Norms," in *Personal Responsibility and Christian Morality*, 124.
45. Francis Sullivan, S.J., *Magisterium: Teaching Authority in the Catholic Church* (New York: Paulist Press, 1983), 151–52; see Fuchs, "The Absoluteness of Behavioral Moral Norms," 140. Sullivan, who professionally is an ecclesiologist and not a moral theologian, acknowledges that here he is relying on the thought of what he terms "mainstream" Roman Catholic moral theology today, including Charles Curran, Franz Böckle, Joseph Fuchs, Bruno Schüller, and Bernard Häring.
46. Fuchs, "The Absoluteness of Behavioral Moral Norms," 142.
47. See endnote 2 above and also McCormick's "Some Early Reactions to *Veritatis splendor*," *Theological Studies* 55 (1994): 481–506.
48. McCormick, "*Veritatis splendor* and Moral Theology," 10; emphasis added.
49. Ibid.

50. In the official notes included in the encyclical, John Paul II explicitly referred to the teaching of St. Thomas in *STh* I–II, q. 18, a. 6 in note 126 appended to n. 78 of the encyclical, immediately after John Paul II's careful description of the meaning of moral object.

51. For a brilliant and extended critique of McCormick's criticism of *Veritatis splendor* see Martin Rhonheimer's essay in this book, "Intentional Actions and the Meaning of Object: A Reply to Richard McCormick," pp. 255ff.

52. Kampen: Kok Pharos Publishing House; Grand Rapids, Mich.: Eerdmans, 1994. In addition to the introduction by Selling and his co-editor, Jan Jans, the volume includes the following articles: Joseph Selling, "The Context and Argument of *Veritatis splendor*"; Gareth Moore, "Some Remarks on the Use of Scripture in *Veritatis splendor*"; Louis Janssens, "Teleology and Proportionality: Thoughts about the encyclical *Veritatis splendor*"; Brian V. Johnstone, "Erroneous Conscience in *Veritatis splendor* and the Theological Tradition"; Bernard Hoose, "Circumstances, Intentions and Intrinsically Evil Acts"; and Jan Jans, "Participation-Subordination (The Image of) God in *Veritatis splendor*." The volume also includes an "Index of Persons, Documents and Scriptural References in *Veritatis splendor*" prepared by Leon Derckx.

   With the exception of Johnstone's essay (a reflection on the teaching of St. Alphonsus Ligouri on the question of an erroneous conscience) and Derckx's Index, the essays in the volume constitute a massive critique of the encyclical, in many places gravely misrepresenting the teaching found in it. Here I will comment on the contributions by Selling and Janssens. For a fuller discussion of the volume see my article referred to in endnote 1.

53. Selling, "The Context and Arguments of *Veritatis splendor*," in *The Splendor of Accuracy*, 19.

54. Ibid., 47.

55. Ibid.

56. Cf. ibid., 67, note 52.

57. Ibid., 68.

58. Janssens, "Teleology and Proportionality: Thoughts about the encyclical *Veritatis splendor*," 100–102.

59. For a more detailed critique of Janssens' use of the "Declaration on Euthanasia" see my "*The Splendor of Accuracy*: How Accurate," *The Thomist* 59 (1995): 477–80.

60. On this see my "Aquinas and Janssens on the Moral Meaning of Human Acts," *The Thomist* 48 (1984): 566–606.

61. Janssens, "Teleology and Proportionality," 110; emphasis added.

Intentional Actions and the Meaning of Object:
A Reply to Richard McCormick

Martin Rhonheimer

In his article "Some Early Reactions to *Veritatis splendor*,"[1] Richard McCormick discusses my article on *Veritatis splendor* and its teaching about intrinsically evil acts.[2] He challenges my defense of the encyclical's views and poses some concrete questions for me. At the same time, McCormick complains once more about what he calls the encyclical's misrepresentation of the proportionalists' views, as well as about a general misunderstanding on the part of critics of what proportionalism, consequentialism, and their teleological approach are really about.

To begin with, I find it somewhat surprising that McCormick presents intentional understanding of human acts and their objects as something discovered by proportionalists. By this he obscures the fact that most critics of proportionalism, consequentialism, and so-called teleological ethics (I will not further distinguish these different labels) work with what is precisely an intentional conception of moral objects.[3] For example, my own position, situated in the context of virtue ethics,[4] is one in which an intentional conception action plays a crucial role. McCormick seems to evade this level of argument, however, and in this way appears to beg the question about one of the central issues in the debate.

At the same, it is not entirely surprising that McCormick had some difficulty in dealing with the central point of my argument (and of similar arguments[5]), because his methodology is so entangled in the categories of the strongly legalistic and casuistic manual tradition.[6] In my article, I explicitly dealt with the difficulty of understanding a virtue and first-person-centered view from the perspective of the manual tradition:

> It will, however, never be possible to render intelligible this
> moral methodology on the grounds of an ethic which from
> the beginning is concerned with justifying "moral norms."
> This is so because in such an approach the *distinction* be-
> tween "object" and *further* intentions necessarily drops out
> of view. The only thing which a norm ethic can produce in
> the way of an action theory are the particular "occurrences"
> ("actions") on the one hand, and the consequences brought
> about by them, on the other. If an agent *intends* the best con-
> sequences, then it is these which come to be designated the
> "object" of his "act." (21–22)

McCormick's article thus confirms this assertion, since the author finally arrives at the conclusion that talking about "objects"
and wrongness *ex obiecto* is not a helpful terminology and should
be abandoned.[7] I shall return to this point.

The questions put to me by McCormick, and which I shall try
to answer, deal with the following issues: 1) The meaning of "object" (which is, as he rightly states, the central point); 2) the closely
related "question of intentionality"; and 3) what is according to
McCormick "a key question" for my position: "Why in choosing to
kill a person or deceive a person, does one necessarily 'take a position with his will with regard to "good" and "evil"'?"[8] Finally, I
shall also have to say something about what McCormick falsely
calls the encyclical's misrepresentation of proportionalism, because
this is intimately connected with all the rest.

I. "Object" in *Veritatis splendor*: Not Just a "Kind of Behavior"

Let me start by specifying some points about *Veritatis splendor*'s
teaching. In his presentation of the encyclical's understanding of
the "object," McCormick says that according to the encyclical (and
presumably also to me) an object simply is "a freely chosen kind
of behavior." But it seems that he fails to grasp what the
encyclical's text wants to stress in this passage. Its intention is not
to tell the reader that objects are "kinds of behavior," but that objects are to be understood as something related to the acting
person's *choices*. Therefore the point made by the encyclical is about
intention involved in choice of kinds of behavior and not about
"kinds of behavior" as such.

The entire text (which I quoted at the very beginning of my article) runs as follows:

> In order to be able to grasp the object of an act which specifies that act morally, it is therefore necessary to place oneself *in the perspective of the acting person.* (*VS* 78.1)

What *Veritatis splendor* is saying is this: Do not look at human acts "from outside"; do not focus only on what happens, what is the case, and on the state of affairs brought about by a behavioral performance; but rather put yourself in the perspective of the acting subject, for whom "actions" or "behaviors" are objects of choice, informed by reason, as immediate goals of the will. Thus the encyclical continues:

> *The object of the act of willing is in fact a freely chosen kind of behavior.* . . . By the object of a given moral act, then, one cannot mean a process or an event of the merely physical order, to be assessed on the basis of its ability to bring about a given state of affairs in the outside world. Rather, *that object is the proximate end of a deliberate decision which determines the act of willing on the part of the acting person.* (*VS* 78.1, emphasis added)

In his reading of this passage, McCormick's attention seems to be entirely conditioned by *his own* methodology—which adopts the standpoint of the observer, as is typical for norm-ethics and casuistry—and by the argumentative problems that logically arise in *this* perspective. Therefore he does not enter at all into the rather sophisticated argument set forth by the encyclical.

It is significant that immediately after this statement, *Veritatis splendor* quotes n. 1761 of the *Catechism of the Catholic Church* (which also focuses on choice): "There are certain specific kinds of behavior that are always wrong to choose, because choosing them involves a disorder of the will, that is, a moral evil." In n. 1755, the *Catechism* gives an example, fornication, to illustrate its teaching. Clearly, "fornication" is not simply a material behavioral pattern (this would be "sexual intercourse between male and female"). The encyclical's verdict about moral evil is not about *this* pattern, but about the *choice* of it, that is, *about a specific case of this choice,* called "fornication," that is describable in universal terms (as a "species" of human act), a description that applies to a multiplicity of particular acts independently from further circumstances or consequences. Notice that the description of an (observable) behavioral pattern as such and the description of the *choice* of this behavior may be two quite different things.[9]

Let me spell this out in more detail. When Jim chooses to have sexual intercourse with Jane, Jim actually not only chooses a behavioral pattern (to have intercourse with a female, or with Jane), because Jane either is or is not his wife. This is a circumstance relevant for practical reason that judges about the corresponding behavior as a practical good to be either pursued or avoided. It is a circumstance that, in this specific situation, is given and is thus prior to choice. It is not, however, inherent in the behavioral pattern as such; it is recognizable only for reason and it confers on the chosen behavior an inherent, though not simply naturally given, "form." The behavior could not be chosen at all *apart from this "form."*[10] Therefore, provided Jim and Jane are not married, Jim necessarily chooses, not just "intercourse with a female," but "fornication."[11]

Accordingly, the concrete behavior considered as an object of choice is much more than merely a material behavioral pattern. In choosing a concrete behavioral pattern, one necessarily chooses it "under a description," which is precisely the description of an intent formed by reason. Sexual intercourse, as a chosen kind of behavior, is the object of a judgment of reason of the following sort: "Having sexual intercourse with Jane, who is *not* my wife (or even is another's wife, etc.), is a good here and now to be pursued." This precisely indicates an intention that *defines* the act in question. If there were no intention—which is impossible—there would be no reason, nor would there be a perceived good to be pursued. There would exist nothing but an observable behavioral pattern, not a human act. Thus the chosen act is precisely what *Veritatis splendor* calls the "proximate end of the [choosing] will." As such, the *very act includes an intention, formed by reason, without which it could not be described as a human act.* This intention (choice) of Jim to have intercourse with somebody who is not his spouse is perfectly describable and morally qualifiable *independently* from further intentions (e.g., the intention of doing it for the sake of obtaining some information necessary to save the lives of others).

The encyclical's understanding of the object of a human act explains the formulation in n. 79, which I quoted in the opening section of my article. This sentence, which contains the key formulation, is, however, mostly ignored by revisionists. The verdict here concerns "*choice* of certain kinds of behavior." In *Veritatis splendor,* n. 80, "intrinsically evil" is referred to the object, and this again means: to kinds of behavior, insofar they are objects of choice. What is called "intrinsically evil," therefore, is concrete choice, describable in behavioral terms, that cannot be reduced to simple "behavior," however, because every choice includes an intention of the will and a corresponding judgment of reason. That is also the reason why the encyclical speaks here about *ulterior* intentions, and not about intention as such: because "object" and intention are not mutually exclusive terms. There is some intentionality required so that an object of a human act can be constituted.[12]

McCormick affirmed in his article that proportionalism makes precisely this point, imputing to *Veritatis splendor,* and to critics of proportionalism generally, a different view, one rather easy for him to criticize. In this way he avoids the real issue and conceals the weakness of proportionalism and consequentialism. This weakness, however, is that a consequentialist refuses to speak about "actions" or about intention involved in the choice of concrete actions; he or she talks only about intentions as related to foreseeable consequences, thereby describing, and continuously redescribing, "actions" from the standpoint of a value-balancing observer; in this way he arrives at what he calls the "expanded notion of object." When McCormick says, "Intention tells us what is going on," he is perfectly right. But he neglects to ask: How are intentions shaped? Upon what do they depend? and, finally, What is, not intention and intentionality, but intentional *action*?

II. Intentionality and "Intentional Actions": The Implicit Physicalism of Proportionalism

Perhaps the reader of my article on *Veritatis splendor* will remember the example of "arm raising," "greeting," and so on. It was a simple example—inspired by Wittgenstein and Anscombe—of showing how intentional actions are structured. I asserted:

> The so-called "absolute prohibitions," that is, normative propositions which indicate that certain, describable actions may *never* be licitly chosen and willingly performed, therefore relate to actions described *intentionally*. It is impossible to do this independently from the content of the acts of choice which relate to such actions. (32)

I have always conceded that proportionalism and consequentialism in Catholic moral theology have aspired to overcome the limitations and flaws of a traditional physicalist understanding of the
"moral object."[13] At the same time, however, I have contended that
they have not succeeded because they have overlooked, and thus con-
served, the basic error inherent in this tradition: to fail to understand
human acts as embedded in an intentional process, that is, to fail to
understand them from the perspective of the acting person.

This can be seen very well in the case of Josef Fuchs (one of
McCormick's chief witnesses for the proportionalists' innocence).
According to my judgment, Fuchs speaks about "intentions," but
he does not seem to have a notion of what an intentional *action* is.
He speaks only of (premoral) "physical acts" or behavioral patterns
(realized, performed, etc.) to which he *adds* intentions (as a
"premoral" element!). What Fuchs calls the "act" in itself or the
"act as such" has no moral identity. Only the combination of the
three premoral elements "act," "circumstances," and "intentions"
becomes for him a moral whole.

The problem is that "physical act" plus "intention" (defined by
some "reason") will never result in an "intentional action." "Intentional action" is a concept belonging to action theory, not to moral casuistry. It is not part of a theory about how to combine "reasons" and
"intentions" in order to justify an action normatively (that is, to know
whether it is "allowed" and right or "illicit" and wrong). The concept
of "intentional action" expresses the very nature of human acting. So
one has to talk about the acting person and about what is going on
in his or her will when he or she acts. The discourse will be about
choice and about intention *involved* in human acts, that is, in chosen
acts (or behaviors, to use the encyclical's term).

Let us have a look at Fuchs's well-known article, "The Absoluteness of Moral Terms."[14] In this article, Fuchs argues that "human acts" are composed of three elements: the (physical) act; special circumstances; and the intention. He first points out correctly
that: "Morality, in the true (not transferred or analogous) sense is
expressible only by a human action, by an action which originates
in the deliberate and free decision of a human person."[15] So a human action, Fuchs continues, must be performed "with the intention of the agent." He then adds the following example:

> One may not say, therefore, that killing as a realization of a
> human evil may be morally good or morally bad; for killing
> as such, since it implies nothing about the intention of the
> agent, cannot, purely as such, constitute a human act.[16]

The problem here is that "killing as such" is not an act, not even
an "act as such," because "as such" it is not described as a *chosen*
act, that is, as an act that is the object of choice. Of course, "killing" as behavioral pattern (putting another person to death) could
also be the performance of a robot. Considered on this level, "killing" is nothing but a behavioral pattern defined by a specific outcome. But, we should ask, what is going on when John chooses to
kill Harry (for whatever reason: either because John simply wants
Harry to be dead; or because John wants his uncle Harry to be dead
for the sake of getting an inheritance or for the sake of revenge or
for the sake of marrying Harry's wife)?

The point is that "killing as such" is not conceivable as a describable action, as if this could be understood apart from intention. If John kills Harry, he already has, in *choosing* the killing, an
intention: he wants Harry to be dead (this independently of
whether he chooses "killing Harry" for its own sake or as a means
to a further end). Fuchs, however, falling into the trap of dealing
with acts as if they were pure events ("realizations of goods and
evils"), continues:

> The conclusion in definitive terms is:
>
> 1. An action cannot be judged morally in its materiality
>   (killing, wounding, going to the moon) without refer-
>   ence to the intention of the agent; without this, we are
>   not dealing with a human action, and only with
>   respect to a human action may one say in a true sense
>   whether it is morally good or bad.[17]

From this it obviously follows that, *prima facie*, any "act" (in his
sense of performing a behavioral pattern) can be justified, even if
it brings about a (premoral) evil (e.g., "death"). This brings us to
Fuchs's second criterion:

> 2. The evil (in a premoral sense) effected by a human
>   agent, must not be intended as such, and must be jus-
>   tified in terms of the totality of the action by appro-
>   priate reasons.[18]

Therefore, if I do not kill just for killing—without further reason besides the victim's death itself—then *any* killing *could* be, on principle, morally justified, provided there are "appropriate reasons." Or do I somehow grossly misunderstand Fuchs?

In this way, we are presented with an action analysis in which "acts" are simply physical events ("realizations of goods and evils" or of "lesser evils") to be given a moral character by intentions that justify these performances on the ground of "appropriate" (commensurate) reason. The acting subject focuses exclusively on the overall outcome of his or her doings, not on what he or she concretely does. The acting subject disappears as a subject that *chooses* and thus willingly performs concrete acts, acts that are not simply events causing consequences, but proximate ends of a choosing will.[19]

Fuchs sums up his argument by asserting:

> A moral judgment is legitimately formed only under a *simultaneous* consideration of the three elements (action, circumstance, purpose), premoral in themselves; for the actualization of the three elements (taking money from another, who is very poor, to be able to give pleasure to a friend) is not a combination of three human actions that are morally judged on an individual basis, but a single human action.[20]

The example given by Fuchs, of course, is revealing and confirms what I reproach. The problem is that "taking money from another" is not a good description of a "chosen kind of behavior." A better description would be: "Appropriating money, taking it from its legitimate owner, against his will." This is an intentional description of an action called "theft." It has its moral form independently from whether the acting person has this or another "purpose" (intention), and from whether the outraged person is poor or not. Provided he or she in fact is poor, then the theft may be more condemnable and called "mean." If the purpose is frivolous ("to give pleasure to a friend"), then the whole theft will be a frivolous action in addition. Such a theft, however, will not only be a frivolous one, but also, *by its very object*, an unjust one! If the purpose ("further intention") is laudable, the intention remains laudable, but not the action as such, which remains unjust, though it probably will be, despite of its wrongness, more understandable. In any case, on the whole it will be an evil action, *malum ex quocumque defectu*. On the grounds of Fuchs's and McCormick's methodology, however, these kinds of differentiations are completely ruled out in favor of a uniform overall judgment about "rightness" or "wrongness" of the act.

To sum up, this methodology has three main characteristics. First, it confounds the intentionality involved in actions with the reasons one might have to judge certain outcomes as desirable. Proportionalism, of course, does not forget intention or intentionality, but it reduces "acting" to "intending" and to "having appropriate reasons." What is lacking is an intentional concept of *action itself*. For proportionalists, action remains a purely physical event that realizes the state of affairs one has a "reason" to bring about. Splitting up human acts into "acts as such," on one side, and "reasons" and "intentions related to foreseeable consequences," on the other, proportionalists seem to assert that choice proceeds on a double track: One first chooses, on the grounds of appropriate reasons, the state of affairs to be brought about, and afterwards the physical "act as such" that will cause it (e.g., "killing as such") is chosen. The second choice—according to the theory—receives its moral species exclusively from the first ("as such," it has none); it has a purely instrumental relation to the first. That is precisely what I would call an "eventistic" and thus non-intentional notion of action.

The second characteristic derives from this: The "basic action," the concrete act or behavior immediately chosen and then referred to whatever end, is not conceived as an intentional action. This is a very important point, because I take the "object" of a moral act to be precisely the content of what I have called an "intentional basic action,"[21] which itself can be distinguished from *further* intentions. This inability to isolate the *basic intentional content* of actions in relation to further intentions leads to the third feature of proportionalism, what McCormick calls the "expanded notion of object," an "object" that is to be understood as being already the *result* of a process of weighing and "commensurating" all foreseeable consequences. The "expanded object" thus contains the intentions that define what in a morally significant sense the acting person is doing (and so, *prima facie* everything becomes morally possible, provided there is an appropriate reason). The expanded notion of object, however, in reality is equivalent to the abolition of the notion of object altogether, for the very notion of "object" necessarily implies a distinction between the *basic* intention that characterizes the object and *further* intentions.

III. McCormick's "Expanded Notion of Object"

The problem of the proportionalist "expanded notion of object" can be well illustrated with the case of Paul Touvier, a French Nazi collaborator in the Vichy regime, recently condemned, who was ordered to shoot seven Jews on June 28, 1944. On trial fifty years later, Touvier argued that both he and the chief commander of the militia of Lyon knew that Gestapo chief Werner Knab was planning to execute a hundred Jews in reprisal for the Resistance's killing of Philippe Henriot, the head of Vichy's propaganda organization. By convincing Knab to execute only thirty, and then in fact executing seven Jews, Touvier argued that they had in fact prevented the execution of one hundred desired by the Gestapo commander. The key point here is their argument that *what they did in reality (the morally relevant "object" of their doing) was not kill seven Jews, but save the lives of ninety-three of them.*

That is an argument based on an "expanded notion of object."[22] The corresponding reasoning that would, in proportionalist terms, justify such an action, begins by affirming that "killing as such"— that is "without reference to the intention of the agent"—is neither good nor evil, but only the "realization of a (premoral) human evil" that can be justified, provided one does not directly intend this evil as the goal of the action, and that there be a "commensurate reason." Taking into account "the whole of the action," circumstances and foreseeable consequences, Touvier came to the conclusion: If I do not kill the seven, then one hundred (these seven probably included) will be killed. Therefore, in killing the seven (which *as such* is beyond good and evil), I can save ninety-three Jews. Thus Touvier reasoned: The morally relevant "object" of my action—that is, *what I am really doing*—has to be called meritorious or at least responsible and justified as life-saving.

Although a proportionalist can produce reasons why Touvier should have refrained from killing the seven Jews, this will be a consequentialist argument and will be accomplished by an even greater expansion of the object. For example, one could argue: "Acting in that manner could have foreseeably weakened consciousness of the criminal character of the Nazi regime, which would have cost the lives of even more Jews in the long run."

The problem here is not the *result* of the proportionalist reasoning, but rather its very structure. It is precisely the methodology of weighing the consequences, taking into account premoral "values"—in this case, lives of innocent human beings—so as to determine whether or not there is a "commensurate" reason for "realizing the premoral evil" of killing them. Why not simply admit that the intentional killing of innocent persons is immoral, unjust, criminal, that one is never allowed to do such a thing?

According to proportionalism, however, what one chooses are mainly the consequences of one's actions (actions therefore conceived as simple behavioral performances), but not the actions themselves. As Fuchs put it:

> The object of the ethical decision for an action is, therefore, not the basic (e.g. physical) act as such (in its ethical relevance, such as killing, speaking falsehood, taking property, sexual stimulation), but the entirety of the basic act, special circumstances, and the chosen or (more or less) foreseeable consequences.[23]

A problem here is that everything depends on your preferences—including the determination as to which reasons are commensurate and which are not. Yet is preference ever sufficient as a basis for moral judgment? Who would not prefer the killing of only seven, instead of a hundred innocent people? Who would not, to use McCormick's famous wording, prefer "to choose the lesser evil"?[24]

Of course, I prefer the lesser evil, too. I am happy when I learn that not one hundred but only seven innocents were killed, as I am happy to know that only seven instead of one hundred persons were killed in an air crash or by an earthquake. But I will not *choose* and willingly perform an evil action because I think it to be less evil then another and because otherwise foreseeably somebody else would commit the greater evil (I shall try to prevent that, of course). The proportionalist will rebut: "Sorry, you did not understand me. I meant that choosing the lesser evil signifies that this action was precisely the good one." I then would reply: "So you really think that when choosing and freely performing an action, nothing else happens than what happens in an air crash or an earthquake? Are the evil results of certain actions somehow simply given, beyond both my power to change and my responsibility? Or are they rather intrinsically bound up with the action that I perform?"

On the grounds of this and similar examples, we can better understand why *Veritatis splendor*, n. 77 pronounces a very important warning, a warning overlooked, it seems, by most proportionalists:

> The weighing of the goods and evils foreseeable as the consequence of an action is not an adequate method for determining whether the choice of that concrete kind of behavior is "according to its species," or "in itself," morally good or bad, licit or illicit.

Of course, in the light of the preceding example this statement is perfectly intelligible. The proportionalist "expanded notion of object," however, renders it meaningless because in proportionalist terms there simply *is no possible choice of a concrete kind of behavior* that could be called morally bad "by its species" or "in itself" *before* the foreseeable consequences having been weighed—consequences that change from case to case—and *before* a judgment about commensurate reasons has been reached. The problem here is with what are called intrinsically *wrong* or *evil* actions; in such cases already the very object should serve as an indication that one should not persist along this line of action. McCormick avoids facing this problem directly by employing examples like "one takes a vacation trip in order to commit adultery" to maintain that only in such cases can one discern "an intention in addition to the object," because "there are two distinguishable actions here, each with its own object."[25] This is then a simple means-end relation. In the example, the basic action is perfectly indifferent or even good, but not the end. Yet is not the situation radically different in the case, for example, of one who commits adultery in order to rescue an innocent person and save his life or one who kills seven Jews in order to save the lives of ninety-three? Are there not also "two distinguishable actions here, each with its own object"? McCormick's choice of examples serves to avoid the real issue.

Proportionalists thus describe and redescribe concrete chosen basic actions, without looking at what the acting person chooses on the level of action (or "means"); rather, they concentrate on what he or she chooses in the order of consequences and on the corresponding commensurate reasons, all of which finally constitute the "expanded object." As we have seen, however, the expanded notion of object is in reality not a notion of "object" at all, but precisely its abolition, because "object" means the basic intentional content of a human act, distinguishable from *further* intentions.[26]

To borrow an example from William May, it would be more truthful to say that Macbeth *killed* Duncan instead of saying that Macbeth *stabbed* Duncan and as a result Duncan died. Stabbing Duncan "as such" is not a sufficient description of a chosen kind of behavior or of an action. A description of the object must include, in Aquinas's terminology, both the *materia circa quam*,[27] "matter about which," and the "form" of the action: Macbeth stabbed Duncan for the sake of causing his death, or, because he wanted him dead (that was precisely his *reason* and his intention or purpose). We rightly call this kind of act an act of "killing." That is what he chose and what he did; that is the object of his action. In order to express our moral disapproval, we also call it "murder." It would not make any sense to say: Macbeth chose stabbing Duncan with the *further* intention of causing his death, of killing him. You cannot describe "stabbing Duncan" as a reasonable, freely chosen action without indicating an intention.

This way of describing an act by the intention involved in it is not always truthful. Thus it is not truthful to say that Touvier "saved ninety-three Jews" instead of saying that "Touvier killed seven innocent Jews, and as a result ninety-three were saved." We cannot call this action an act of "life saving" merely because the foreseeable result (the sparing of the ninety-three) was a "commensurate reason" for shooting the seven, and thus "life itself" was "better served." We are not calculating with quantities of the "good of life," but relating to concrete *living persons*. To speak truthfully, Touvier killed seven innocent people (he shot at them with the intent of ending their life)—which is murder—with the *further* intention of preventing the killing of a hundred.

Thus it is not truthful to say that abortion, given that it means killing an innocent human being, is either an act of life saving when done for the sake of saving the mother's life or an act of saving family stability in certain difficult family situations. Nor can the manipulation and sacrifice of human embryos for the sake of health research (considered as a commensurate reason) be taken as simply an act of health care by virtue of its (expanded) object. The notion of expanded object does not work; or, better, it works for

anything whatsoever. Again, everything depends on the preferences one has.[28]

McCormick conceals the problem by adopting examples that, in
themselves, are precisely *not* examples of "expanded objects" (and
that I would call intentional basic actions). Let us take the example
of masturbation.[29] Of course, stimulation of the genital organs "as
such" is not a kind of behavior that can be chosen or willingly performed by a human person; a basic reason, intent, or purpose is
needed.[30] That is why the *Catechism of the Catholic Church* very correctly writes in n. 2352: "By *masturbation* is to be understood the
deliberate stimulation of the genital organs in order to derive
sexual pleasure." That seems very clear. If one chooses the same
behavioral pattern (stimulating genital organs) in order to get se-
men for fertility analysis, then one simply chooses an action that
is different by its object.

What happens, however, if one chooses to masturbate for the
sake of psychological release? Is the action properly described by
calling it "deliberate stimulation of the genital organs in order to
have psychological release?" I think not. Rather, what one deliberately chooses is "the stimulation of the genital organs in order
to derive sexual pleasure" (=object), and this with the *further* intention of getting psychological release. The key here is that the release obviously does not derive from stimulating genital organs "as
such," but from the corresponding sexual pleasure. Thus what the
intentional basic action (or its object) turns out to be is not simply
a question of preference.

At the same time the behavioral pattern alone does not decide
everything and is sometimes ambiguous. Consider the following
situations. John, a college student, for the sake of forgetting his
girlfriend troubles drinks lots of whisky in order to induce a tem-
porary loss of consciousness; in other words, he gets drunk. This
is an act of intemperance, drunkenness. On the other hand, Fred,
a soldier, for the sake of avoiding the pain of an emergency operation, drinks the same amount of whisky in order to induce a tem-
porary loss of consciousness; in other words, he undergoes anesthesia. The behavioral pattern may be exactly identical,[31] but without indicating an intention (a "Why?"), it is impossible to describe
properly *what* John and Fred are doing, i.e., what, in a basic sense,
they choose.[32] If you remove *any* intention or purpose whatsoever,

there is no action. Thus in every case you arrive at a basic level, which is the level of intentional basic actions.[33]

There are also adherents of a non-intentional concept of object who fear that this consideration of intention opens the way to subjectivism[34]: Any behavioral pattern, they object, could serve for any object whatsoever: "by shifting intention to and fro, the agent constitutes out of whole cloth the moral properties of his act."[35] Moreover, their concern is "whether the *norm* of acts exists prior to human choice, or whether it comes only into being with our consideration of proportions, circumstances, and consequences."[36] And finally: Is it possible to say that intention is so important; should we not hold "that the concrete nature of acts tells us whether an intention is morally good or bad"?[37]

These formulations are, however, somewhat misleading. First, the "nature of an act" necessarily *includes* an intention, because there is no human act without an intention formed by reason. And that is precisely why Aquinas calls the species of an act, which is determined by its object, a *forma a ratione concepta*, a "form conceived by reason";[38] likewise, he defines the good that is by nature specific to each virtue as a good formed *"ex quadam commensuratione actus ad circumstantias et finem, quam ratio facit,* "from a certain commensuration of the act to circumstances and to the end, a commensuration produced by reason."[39] Such formulations seem to justify the position of Fuchs and McCormick, but only seemingly, however, because the underlying understanding of human action is different. What Aquinas and the tradition say is: One cannot simply "choose" a (physical) act and additionally *order* it to *any* intention formed by commensurate reasons that would justify the act. To deny this does not mean, however, that a human act could be described *without* referring to intention altogether.

Secondly, we have quite an extended power to organize our actions intentionally, and thus, in a sense, to constitute the moral properties of our acts. But there are what I would call *naturally given limits* to this. Therefore, (provided sound perception) I cannot shoot at a person's heart and truthfully say, "I love you," meaning that I am doing this with the intent of doing good to this person. What is crucial to recognize is that not every behavioral pattern fits for *any* intention. For example, I cannot shoot at a person and, e.g., have the intention of healing his wound.

To have a human act, one needs to have a basic intention; on this much we agree. But can one, as Hittinger fears, simply "shift intention to and fro"? Given a determined situation (which is precisely given and does not depend on the subject's will or preferences), it is not simply up to me to decide whether my shooting at a person's heart is or is not an action of punishment. And John who drinks to forget his girlfriend troubles simply *cannot* reasonably intend his act to be an act of anesthesia. Fred, on the other hand, who "does the same thing" *cannot* intend that what he does be an act of drunkenness. There are given contexts (shaped by circumstances and recognizable, as a morally significant contextual unity, only by practical reason) that, *in a basic sense*, decide what kind of intentions we reasonably *can* have if we choose a determined "kind of behavior," *independently* from *further* intentions.

From this it follows that even if there is no act (and no object) possible without an involved intention, *what* the intention reasonably can be does not depend on pure preferences, or decisions, or any other power of the subject. This is (in many cases, but not always) simply *given*.[40]

Thus Paul Touvier had no power to decide what would be his basic intention in killing seven innocent people. To describe his action properly, one must include the purpose or the intention, "wanting them to be dead" (even if he would *regret* it; that is only a motivational side feature, but not the very intention of his acting). Touvier clearly *wanted* the seven to be killed; he chose their deaths for the sake of some greater benefit.[41]

If someone should wonder why "intention" should be included in the "object" or in the "intrinsical nature of an act," he also should wonder why generally things like "will," "intellect," "reason," etc., should be included in human nature. It seems rather obvious that the very "nature" of the acts of a spiritual being—moral acts—includes spiritual elements as "purposes," or "intentions" of the will, shaped by reason, and not only observable behavioral patterns. Is this not precisely the constant teaching of Aquinas?[42] Why should "realizing the evil of death" as such be taken as the adequate description of the object of a human act or express its "intrinsical nature," when exactly the same thing could be brought about by an earthquake or by a robot? Why should simple "solitary stimulation of genital organs as such" be the definition of the object and the intrinsical nature of a human act, when this contains absolutely no indication as to why one would do such a thing?

One can therefore describe concrete choices of kinds of behavior as wrong or evil independently from further intentions. Such descriptions, however, always *include* a basic intention, an intention that itself presupposes a given ethically relevant context without which no intention, formed by reason, could come into being. This has nothing to do with the "expanded notion of object." But it includes a certain complexity that is due to the plurality and multiplicity of virtues that in turn reflect human life and its richness in relations between persons, including the differences of ethically relevant practical contexts.

IV. The Shaping of Intentional Basic Actions and the Virtues: Some "Manual Cases"

To explain accurately what I have just said at the end of the preceding section, I should explain how practical principles are generated in a moral theory based on the "ends of virtues."[43] While my approach grows out of a tradition rooted in classical virtue ethics, proportionalism is entirely situated in the context of the manualistic tradition.[44] In opposition to this classical tradition, proportionalism provides, on the basis of modern consequentialism, a relatively uniform theory of decision making, one that can be summed up in some very simple key principles: "What one does, considered *as such*, is not yet morally decisive; whatever one does, however, one ought never directly to intend premoral evil; rather, one should always act with a commensurate reason, so as to maximize benefit and/or to minimize harm or evil."

In order to justify his position, McCormick adduces a whole range of classical examples, self-defense, masturbation, lying, contraception, sterilization, theft.[45] Insofar as he deals with these problems as a proportionalist, however, he simply begs the question. By affirming that to describe a moral human action an intentional element is required, McCormick asserts what nearly all hold. There is more, however, to the proportionalist position. McCormick affirms that proportionalists "are saying that an action cannot be judged morally wrong simply by looking at the material happening, or at its object in a very narrow and restricted sense."[46] Yet by identifying the "ob-

ject in a very narrow and restricted sense" with the "material happening," he has already accepted the physicalist fallacy.[47] So he is necessarily unable to understand how an intentional basic content can be
formed. Like Fuchs, Knauer, et al., he will look only at material hap-
penings (the act "as such") and then at *all* the intentions (among which
those that will be morally decisive will be those for which one is able
to adduce commensurate reasons).[48]

What I maintain is that it is possible both not to be a
proportionalist and simultaneously to assert that there is a difference in basic intentional content, i.e., the object, in the case of the
following actions:

- Simple killing for any end whatsoever (an action against justice), even if the ulterior end is saving one's life (this is illicit murder).
- (Legitimate) killing in self-defense (killing *praeter
  intentionem*).
- (Carrying out of) capital punishment (an act of punishment,
  which *may* be regarded as unjust, but which is by its object different from simple killing for any further end whatsoever).
- Killing of combatants in war, on the battlefield.

These are not actions to be defined differently only because of
different "reasons" one might have for realizing them. Not only
their intentional *content* but also their very intentional *structure* is
very different in each case. Since they represent different intentional basic actions, they also are different by their object. Take for
example the difference between "self-defense" and "the choice of
killing in order to save one's life." On the level of "reasons" regarding the *further* end, both cases are identical: the reason for acting
is to save one's life. But if you look at the action not from outside,
but from the acting person's perspective, you will notice that there
is a different choice (and so there is a different object, too): In legitimate self-defense, what engenders my action is not a will or a
choice for the aggressor's death. A sign of this is that I use only
violence proportionate to stop his aggression. This may lead me to
kill him (*praeter intentionem*), but the reason for my action is not
wanting him do be dead (for the sake of saving my life); rather it
is wanting to stop his aggression. Thus there is a difference of intention on the level of concrete chosen behavior, and that means,
on the level of the object.[49]

Or, take "killing on a battlefield": Am I a murderer or simply a soldier who is fighting against an aggressor? Provided the war is what one calls a just war (*ultima ratio*—defense against an aggression), it entirely depends on what is going on in my heart, i.e., whether I want the enemy soldier to be dead, or simply to stop his aggression and to win the battle. Therefore if as a soldier, you do not want to be a murderer, you must care for wounded enemy soldiers. This shows that the object of your acting—the intention involved in your action—obviously was not wanting them to be dead, not even in the moment of battle, even if killing them in the moment was the foreseeable and necessary physical outcome of violence proportionate to stop their aggression.

With theft it is slightly different. Theft refers to property. Property is not a natural or physical entity, but a moral and legal one. Property is not simply "what I have in my hands," but "that to which I am entitled" or "that to which I have a right." Such entitlement and rights, in a given situation, do or do not exist (and this precisely does not depend on consequentialist reasoning). But situations may change; they are contingent. Unlike a person's life, property is not an unchangeable matter. It is a contingent matter, relativized by higher principles of justice. So there are situations of extreme necessity in which no one is reasonably entitled to say to the starving: "This is my property, you have no right to it." If the starving one takes what he needs to survive, it will simply not be the action we call "theft," meaning an action that is contrary to justice.

Therefore one has to analyze intentional contents as belonging to the structure of virtues. Admittedly, the traditional manuals were not very careful in this. Their methodology was rather legalistic, focusing on the external features of actions, referring them to positive law, and only secondarily applying some corrections to recover important intentional aspects.[50]

In any event, it seems clear that justice related to property and related to life are two quite different matters. Notice that my arguments adopted so far have nothing in common with a proportionalist reasoning. The question was not whether there was a commensurate reason to realize the premoral evil of appropriating another's property, so that the act would not be "theft" anymore. Rather, the question was whether or not in a given practical context there existed a title of property (this certainly is not a question of commensurate reason or of utility). Once the question of rights is settled, however, these rights may not be overruled by consequentialist reasoning.[51]

If one applies the proportionalist methodology of decision making to these questions, one will never discern the differences, even though in certain more simply structured cases one will probably arrive at the same result. As a consequentialist, one arrives at this result by speaking only in terms of physical acts, foreseen consequences, and commensurate reasons, a level of discourse that will prove profoundly misleading in more serious questions, as illustrated by the Touvier case. Moreover, that is not how upright people really act and live. We act in given circumstances and personal relationships that form basic intentional contexts and corresponding intentional basic actions. Some of them are simply evil by their basic content. They divert the acting person from human good, and make the will and the heart evil.

V. The "Key Question" and the Encyclical's Alleged "Misrepresentation" of Proportionalism

At this point we finally arrive at what McCormick calls the "key question." Why, he asks me, in choosing to kill a person or deceive a person, does one necessarily "take a position with one's will with regard to 'good' and 'evil'"? While some elements of my answer are contained already in what I have explained in the foregoing sections, to answer the question systematically I would have to repeat all that I have said about the misleading distinction, fundamental for proportionalists, between "rightness" and "wrongness" of actions, on the one hand, and the "goodness" and "wickedness" of persons and their actions, on the other. I invite the reader to have a second glance at the original article. Let me add, however, the following.

Proportionalists say that an action is *right* if what one does is justified by commensurate reason. In this view, a person is a *good* person if he or she does not directly intend to realize a premoral evil, but intends to act so as to maximize goods or to minimize evils ("in the long run," Knauer would add), meaning to act responsibly by commensurate reasons.

I consider this to be simply erroneous. In my article I wrote:

> It is one of the most important assertions of classical virtue ethics that there exist conditions for the fundamental rightness of actions which depend on basic structures of the "rightness of desire" and that it is therefore possible to describe particular types of actions, the *choice* of which always involves wrong desire. (20)

With regard to proportionalist decision-making theories (and their characteristic as "rule ethics") I then added that these theories

> *may not*, on the level of the concrete performance of actions, include in their reflection the acting subject and his willingly "taking a position" with regard to "good" and "evil" *in* choosing this or that particular action.

So, if I choose to kill P, I simply set my will against a fundamental right of P, which is moral evil; if I choose to have intercourse with Q, with whom I am not married, I act against the truth of sexuality, harming my own integrity (in the case of simple fornication), or, in the case of adultery, I moreover violate faithfulness due to the person to whom I am married. This implies disorder of my free will, and exactly this we commonly call an *evil will*. If I choose to utter falsehood to a person, given a practical context in which speech acts are meant to be acts of communicative justice (which is not the case in war situations, aggression, etc.), then I am lying to my fellow man. This means setting my will against social ties due to this person, and this is disorder in my will, moral evil. The same, obviously, applies to theft. At the same time, the one who carries out a capital punishment does not do what he does because he wants the executed to be dead (this could be a further motive, but a condemnable one); he may even do it after having done everything to liberate him. This is an act of punishment, that is, of retributive justice.[52]

Following proportionalist methodology, one will not see, or not concede, the point because one omits focusing on what is going on in the acting and choosing person, precisely where moral evil comes about. Proportionalists are concerned with the reasons one might have to bring about certain state of affairs as the consequences of one's doings; and only this allows a judgment about "right" and "wrong." That is why consequentialists discuss for example the question of whether it could be right to execute the innocent, instead of simply asserting: to execute an innocent person for whatever reason is *evil by its object*. Thus precisely what proportionalists do not want to acknowledge is that, according to the encyclical's quotation of n. 1761 of the *Catechism of the Catholic Church*

> there are concrete acts that are always wrong to choose, *because their choice entails a disorder of the will, i.e., moral evil,*

and that, according to *Veritatis splendor*'s key sentence in n. 79,

> one must therefore reject the thesis, *characteristic of teleological and proportionalist theories, which holds that it is impossible to qualify as morally evil according to its species—its "object"—the deliberate choice of certain kinds of behavior or specific acts, apart from a consideration of the intention for which the choice is made or the totality of the foreseeable consequences of that act for all persons concerned.*

Obviously, the encyclical goes right to the point, and McCormick's reaction, along with similar reactions, confirms that the pope was right. This relates to that for which McCormick most reproaches *Veritatis splendor*, its "misrepresentation" of proportionalism,[53] namely, the encyclical's assertion in n. 76: "Such theories however are not faithful to the Church's teaching, when they believe they can justify, as morally good, deliberate choices of kinds of behavior contrary to the commandments of the divine and the natural law." McCormick repeatedly says that with this the encyclical gravely misrepresents the proportionalists' views, reproaching them falsely "that [the proportionalist position] attempts to justify *morally wrong actions* by a good intention."

This is simply not true. McCormick's complaint would be justified if the ope held the same understanding of the nature of natural and divine law that is proper to revisionist moral theology. Unlike proportionalists, however, the encyclical holds that in natural and divine law there are included certain negative precepts that precisely refer *universally* to certain kinds of behavior that one never may choose. The encyclical does not reproach proportionalist theologians for wanting to justify by good intentions what is already determined to be morally wrong. The reproach is that proportionalism is a theory by which, in concrete cases, you can justify as morally right what the Church teaches to be universally, *semper et pro semper*, wrong. The pope therefore reproaches proportionalism for denying that there are certain negative precepts that refer *universally* to certain kinds of behavior that one may never choose (killing the innocent, adultery, fornication, theft, contraception, abortion, lying, etc.).

In fact, what the encyclical rejects is the proportionalist notion of expanded object that allows one *in every concrete case* to "redescribe" concrete actions, reducing the commandments of law simply to forbid certain immoral *attitudes*, but not choices of determined and intentionally describable *behaviors* or *acts*.

Therefore *Veritatis splendor* does not here affirm something about the *formal* structure of proportionalist moral judgment (imputing to proportionalists a theory that seeks to justify the principle "One may do good evil that good come about"); the reproach is a *material* one, that is, that proportionalism is a theory according to which such universal negative norms *cannot* exist, so that, according to this theory, one comes to declare to be morally right what natural and divine law, according to the Church's teaching, declare to be morally wrong and evil. Thus *Veritatis splendor*'s assertion in n. 76 does not characterize proportionalism as a theory, but it characterizes the *result* of this theory, its *material* implications, as leading to moral judgments explicitly contrary to what the Church teaches as morally wrong and evil.

As evidence for this judgment, I refer again to the example of Fuchs, who wrote in 1971: "What value do our norms have with respect to the morality of the action as such, prior, that is, to the consideration of the circumstances and intention? We answer: They cannot be moral norms, unless circumstances and intention are taken into account."[54] Some pages later, referring to norms related to actions that "could never be objectively justified," he concludes:

> Viewed theoretically, there seems to be no possibility of norms of this kind for human action in the inner-worldly realm. The reason is that an action cannot be judged morally at all, considered purely in itself, but only together with all the "circumstances" and the "intention." Consequently, a behavioral norm, universally valid in the full sense, would presuppose that those who arrive at it could know or foresee *all the possible combinations* of the action concerned with circumstances and intentions, with (pre-moral) values and non-values (bona and mala 'physica').[55]

Of course, Fuchs—like others—neglects to distinguish here between negative (prohibitive) and affirmative norms, which would
make all the difference. And so, in a recent paper, he even specu-
lates that in a future, yet unknown time, the command "you shall
not commit adultery" could change and no longer be valid without exceptions; there could be imaginable "rare exceptions, on the
grounds of highly important reasons and with mutual consent."[56]
     Similarly, it is not surprising that with regard to "murder, adul-
tery, stealing, genocide, torture, prostitution, slavery, etc."
McCormick cites with approval the argument of Lisa Sowle Cahill:
"These phrases, Cahill correctly notes, do not define acts in the
abstract, 'but acts (like intercourse or homicide) *together with the
conditions or circumstances* in which they become immoral.'"[57] In
their view, precisely because these "conditions or circumstances"
can be discerned only in each particular case, the general norm indicating a *species* or *kind* of behavior tells us nothing definitive
about whether the act is right or wrong, but merely provides us
with a *name* for something of which we disapprove. Yet McCormick
misses the point when he complains that Robert P. George "misrepresents proportionalists as maintaining that rape, murder, and
adultery could be justified by a proportionate reason,"[58] for what
the critics of proportionalism are arguing is that the acts that
proportionalists would not designate as "adultery" or "murder" because of the "conditions or circumstances" are in fact precisely acts
of "adultery" or "murder," regardless of the new names given to
such acts by the proportionalists. McCormick's complaint simply
begs the question.
     The notion of "expanded object" requires that any universally
formulated norm be open to exception because of a "commensurate reason" that redescribes the act in question. Proportionalism
thus teaches that *precisely on the grounds of intention*, determined
behaviors that are held by the Church's teaching to be *semper et pro
semper* immoral, evil, and wrong according to divine and natural
law may be become "right," *here and now*—when the "expanded
object" is taken into consideration.[59] The trick is precisely to affirm
this by a theory that is immune against the reproach, "you are trying to justify evil means by good intentions," since the very theory
eliminates even the *possibility* of doing such a thing, for it argues
that only evil intentions render an act evil and that a well-inten-

tioned act is necessarily good. And that is why this theory is not only erroneous, but moreover dangerously confusing moral reasoning. Proportionalism is a methodology by which one in fact always can *with good conscience* act according to the principle "let us do evil so that good come about," because the methodology gives one the conviction that, provided good comes foreseeably about, what you did was not evil at all, but just the morally right thing, so that the ominous principle does not apply in your case. Whoever nevertheless reproaches you for trying to justify, on the grounds of "good reasons," what in reality is morally evil, will be "misrepresenting" your position.

McCormick said that the reason for what he sees as my error was probably that I had "taken one general description of consequentialism and applied it indiscriminately to all recent revisionist analyses." I do not think this is the case. But even if it were true, McCormick's position is still included in what I criticized in my article. And I also think that his position is one of those reasonably rejected by *Veritatis splendor*.

Endnotes

1. *Theological Studies* 55 (1994): 481–506; see 500–502; 504.
2. Martin Rhonheimer, "'Intrinsically Evil Acts' and the Moral Viewpoint: Clarifying a Central Teaching of *Veritatis splendor*," *The Thomist* 58 (1994): 1–39; reprinted in this volume, pp. 171ff.
3. There may be some exceptions, for example, Russell Hittinger; see his article, "The Pope and the Theorists," *Crisis* 11 (December 1993): 31–36. G. E. M. Anscombe, one of the first and most incisive critics of consequentialism, attacked it on the grounds of an intentional concept of action, developed in her famous study *Intention* (Oxford: Basil Blackwell, 1957; 2nd ed. 1963). Cf. Anscombe, *Contraception and Chastity* (London: Catholic Truth Society, 1975).
4. See Martin Rhonheimer, "'Ethics of Norms' and the Lost Virtues. Searching the Roots of the Crisis of Ethical Reasoning," *Anthropotes* 9, 2 (1993): 231–43; *La prospettiva della morale: Fondamenti dell'etica philosophica*, (Rome: Armando, 1994); *Praktische Vernunft und Vernünftigkeit der Praxis: Handlungstheorie bei Thomas von Aquin in ihrer Entstehung aus dem Problemkontext der aristotelischen Ethik* (Berlin: Akademie Verlag, 1994). Contrary to the impression which McCormick gives in his article, I do not share the Grisez-Finnis theory about basic goods and practical reason, nor do I argue on its grounds, in spite of many important common views.
5. See William E. May, *Moral Absolutes: Catholic Tradition, Current Trends, and the Truth* (Milwaukee: Marquette University Press, 1989); John Finnis, *Moral Absolutes: Tradition, Revision, and Truth* (Washington, D.C.: The Catholic University of America Press, 1991); Alasdair MacIntyre, "How Can We Learn What *Veritatis splendor* Has to Teach?" reprinted in this volume, pp. 71ff. See also Robert P. George's and Hadley Arkes' contributions to "The Splendor of Truth: A Symposium," published in *First Things* (January 1994) and rather unfairly criticized in McCormick's article.

6. This is also the case with Bruno Schüller and his disciples; see the recent paper by Werner Wolbert, "Die 'in sich schlechten' Handlungen und der Konsequentialismus," *Moraltheologie im Abseits? Antwort auf die Enzyklika Veritatis splendor*, ed. Dietmar Mieth (Freiburg: Herder, 1994), 88–109.

7. He had already drawn the same conclusion in his article, "Document Begs Many Legitimate Moral Questions," *National Catholic Reporter* (15 October 1993): 17.

8. McCormick, "Some Early Reactions to *Veritatis splendor*," 501.

9. The problem is that in common speech the choice and the corresponding act tend to be lumped together under a common designation derived from some characteristic behavioral aspects of the act. In reality, however, the two can never be equated one with the other. Here, as John Finnis has pointed out, "common speech . . . is not a safe guide" (*Moral Absolutes*, 72).

10. That is why (as I pointed out in sections four and six of my article) Aquinas calls objects "forms conceived by reason."

11. If Jim or Jane is (or both are) married, but not with each other, Jim and Jane choose what one calls "adultery." That is the classic example mentioned by Aquinas (*STh*, I–II, q. 18, a. 5, ad 3); it illustrates well the difference between *genus naturae* and *genus moris*.

12. If it is said that the "object" is a *chosen* act, describable only by referring to an intention, one might wonder how one can then simultaneously affirm—as does *Veritatis splendor*, along with traditional moral theology—that the goodness of the (choosing) will *depends* on the object. Someone might claim that we should be able to describe the object as something "given" and without *immediate* reference to an intention. The solution of this apparent puzzle, however, is easy: The object, its intentional element included, is *first* an object of reason, and in this sense it is prior to choice, insofar as choice is an act of the will shaped by reason. That is the point of Aquinas's teaching. See the following statements from the *Prima secundae* : *bonum per rationem repraesentatur voluntati ut obiectum; et inquantum cadit sub ordine rationis, pertinet ad genus moris, et causat bonitatem moralem in actu voluntatis* (q. 19, a. 1, ad 3); *bonitas voluntatis dependet a ratione, eo modo quo dependet ab obiecto* (q. 19, a. 3); *actus exterior est obiectum voluntatis, inquantum proponitur voluntati a ratione ut quoddam bonum apprehensum et ordinatum per rationem* (q. 20, a. 1, ad 1). Again, the object, like the "species," is a *forma a ratione concepta* which includes the cognitive or rational element of intention, purpose. For more details, see Rhonheimer, *Natur als Grundlage der Moral: Eine Auseinandersetzung mit autonomer Moral und teleologischer Ethik* (Innsbruck-Wien: Tyrolia, 1987), 317 ff., and also *Praktische Vernunft und Vernünftigkeit der Praxis*.

13. See Rhonheimer, "'Intrinsically Evil Acts' and the Moral Viewpoint," reprinted in this volume, pp. 171 ff. and the introduction to *Natur als Grundlage der Moral*.

14. *Gregorianum* 52 (1971); reprinted in *Readings in Moral Theology No.1: Moral Norms and Catholic Tradition*, ed. Charles E. Curran and Richard McCormick (New York: Paulist Press, 1979), 94–137.

15. Fuchs, "The Absoluteness of Moral Terms," in *Readings in Moral Theology No.1*, 119.

16. Ibid.

17. Ibid., 120.

18. Ibid.

19. Of course, I have never said that proportionalists *explicitly hold* such a causal-eventistic concept of action (since it is obviously absurd). Rather, my criticism was based on showing that they hold such a concept *implicitly*—because otherwise their position would not be coherent—and that this demonstrates that their position is erroneous. Consequently I argued that they should pay more attention to action theory. See Rhonheimer, "'Intrinsically Evil Acts' and the Moral Viewpoint," reprinted in this volume, pp. 171 ff.

20. Fuchs, "The Absoluteness of Moral Terms," 121.

21. See Rhonheimer, *La prospettiva della morale*, 39, 85ff., 239ff. The term "basic action" was first introduced by A. C. Danto ("Basic Actions," *American Philosophical Quarterly* 2 [1965]: 141–48), but in quite another sense, i.e. not referring to *intentional* action.

22. Or was it, mistakenly, not expanded enough?

23. Josef Fuchs, "Das Problem Todsünde," *Stimmen der Zeit* 212 (February 1994): 83 (the English translation is that offered by McCormick in "Some Early Reaction to *Veritatis splendor*," 500). In this 1994 article about *Veritatis splendor*, Fuchs restates the same basic position he had presented in his article written more than twenty years earlier.

24. Cf. John Finnis, *Fundamentals of Ethics* (Washington, D.C.: Georgetown University Press, 1983), 93ff. For McCormick, choosing the lesser evil is simply a self-evident principle, "beyond debate; for the only alternative is that in conflict situations we should choose the greater evil, which is patently absurd" (*Doing Evil to Achieve Good*, ed. Richard McCormick and Paul Ramsey, [Chicago: Loyola, 1978], 38). This of course also means that we choose and therefore are responsible for the foreseen consequences of our omissions.

25. McCormick, "Some Early Reactions to *Veritatis splendor*," 498.

26. These, of course, are also "objects" of the will. See John Finnis, "Object and Intention in Moral Judgements According to Aquinas," *The Thomist* 55 (1991): 1–27.

27. *STh* I–II, q. 18, a. 2, ad 2.

28. In the proportionalist schema, one simply calls "object" what one concludes to be morally relevant, "what one wanted to condemn as wrong *ex obiecto*" (McCormick, "Some Early Reactions to *Veritatis splendor*," 504). In this way, one can simply keep expanding the object of one's action so as to justify one's preferences and reach the result corresponding to one's personal intuitions about what is morally relevant.

29. Cf. his example of organ transplantation, as distinguished from "killing for world peace" ("Some Early Reactions to *Veritatis splendor*," 504).

30. Likewise, one simply *cannot* choose to "remove a kidney from a living donor" purely "as such," without *any* reason that constitutes it as a human act.

31. For an intentional notion of contraception, see Rhonheimer, "Contraception, Sexual Behavior, and Natural Law. Philosophical Foundation of the Norm of *Humanae vitae*," *The Linacre Quarterly* 56, 2 (1989): 20–57.

32. Cf. Anscombe, *Intention*, 22.

33. The opposite is also possible, i.e., different or even contrary behavioral patterns, but the same intentional action, e.g., "the action of killing" and "the omission of a possible action of life saving." The objects of both choices are identical.

34. E.g., Russell Hittinger; see his article, "The Pope and the Theorists," *Crisis* (December 1993): 31–36.

35. Ibid., 34.

36. Ibid., 33–34.

37. Ibid., 34.

38. *STh* I–II, q. 18, a. 10.

39. *II Sent.*, d. 39, q. 2, a. 1. "Act" here means the physical or "material" part.

40. It belongs to the virtue of prudence to *understand* the contexts in which we act; see my *Natur als Grundlage der Moral*, 346ff., and *La prospettiva della morale*, 288ff.

41. This is precisely what does not occur in the case of capital punishment (the argument applies also if one is for other reasons opposed to capital punishment), nor in that of legitimate self-defense, nor in that of killing in a just war (which must always have a defensive, anti-aggressive character).

42. See *STh* I–II, q. 1, a. 3, ad 3: fines morales accidunt rei naturali; et e converso ratio naturalis finis accidit morali.

43. See *La prospettiva della morale*, chapter 5.

44. In order to understand correctly the Catholic tradition of moral teaching, however, one must recover the classical standpoint of virtue ethics. From this standpoint, actions are not considered from the outside—as processes that cause, by combining (premoral) goods and evils, foreseeable states of affairs—but rather in terms of "my" intentional relating to good and evil in different ethical contexts (relations between persons, to community and communities, to myself and my body, to God etc.), so that

in choosing certain concrete acts or behaviors my will becomes an evil will, whatever the consequences. Only in this perspective can one understand the shaping of "intentional basic actions" (which correspond to different "moral species" of acts and "moral objects").

45. See also his article, "Killing the patient," *The Tablet* (30 October 1993): 1410–11.
46. Ibid., 1411.
47. McCormick commits the same error, even more explicitly, in his article, "Geburtenregelung als Testfall der Enzyklika," where he asserts that the "object in a narrower sense" is identical with the Thomistic *materia circa quam* (*Moraltheologie im Abseits?* 271–84). This is clearly false and shows a physicalist reading of the tradition.
48. We have already seen in the Touvier case that this methodology does not work. Nor did it work in the case of masturbation or drunkenness. The problem with killing is that there are some apparent "exceptions," like capital punishment, killing in war, and killing the aggressor in self-defense.
49. This corresponds to the traditional distinction between "direct" and "indirect" killing, a distinction that reflects the easily misleading ambiguity of the word "killing." This is precisely what Aquinas very explicitly explains in the famous article 7 of *STh* II–II, q. 64. What proportionalists never understand in their reading of this article is that Aquinas here not only maintains that actions are morally shaped by *id quod intenditur*, but also that the shaping of intentions depends *on what you are doing*, in this case—on the amount of violence you use to stop the aggression. But in any case, he says: *illicitum est quod homo intendat occidere hominem ut seipsum defendat.* It is not a question of "proportionate reason," but of intention involved in action.
50. Thus St. Alphonsus de Liguori treated natural law as if it were a positive legal codex, teaching that *epieikeia* could be applied to it; this meant, however, not negative precepts but those positive precepts that Aquinas describes as valid only *ut in pluribus* (as *deposita sunt reddenda*). Alphonsus's spirit is absolutely correct, but his methodology is of course misleading (he tries to argue within a legalistic framework). St. Alphonsus is today abused by authors who are nevertheless interested in maintaining the "legalistic" approach, so as to apply *epieikeia* even to *negative* precepts, without however noting the enormous difference. See Günter Virt, "Epikie und sittliche Selbstbestimmung," *Moraltheologie im Abseits?* 203–20.
51. See MacIntyre, "How Can We Learn What *Veritatis splendor* Has to Teach?" reprinted in this volume, pp. 75ff.
52. See Rhonheimer, *La prospettiva della morale*, 283; also, the helpful analysis by Agnes Heller, *Beyond Justice* (Oxford: Basil Blackwell, 1987), 156ff. I want to repeat that my argument does not yet settle the question whether capital punishment is a good or proportionate, and in this sense, just punishment; it only settles the *basic* objective meaning of the corresponding acts as actions of *punishment* or retributive justice.
53. McCormick, "Some Early Reactions to *Veritatis splendor*," 490ff., 497; "Killing the Patient," 1411.
54. Fuchs, "The Absoluteness of Moral Terms," 121.
55. Ibid., 124.
56. Fuchs, "Die sittliche Handlung: das instrinsece malum," *Moraltheologie im Abseits?* 183. Of course, for Fuchs this should not be called "adultery" anymore; one would have to devise another name for it.
57. McCormick, "Some Early Reactions to *Veritatis splendor*," 492; the quotation is from Cahill's article, "Accent on the Masculine," *The Tablet* 247 (11 December 1993): 1618–19.
58. McCormick, "Some Early Reactions to *Veritatis splendor*," 487.
59. This is clearly seen in *Veritatis splendor*, n. 56, where the encyclical points out that according to the methodology that it rejects "a certain more concrete existential consideration . . . could legitimately be the basis of certain *exceptions to the general rule* and thus permit one to do in practice and in good conscience what is qualified as intrinsically evil by the moral law."

IV. Epilogue

The Impact of *Veritatis splendor* on Catholic Education at the University and Secondary Levels*

Pio Cardinal Laghi

The topic which has been proposed to me, "The Impact of *Veritatis splendor* on Catholic Education at the University and Secondary Levels," requires a note of clarification with regard to the word "impact." When this encyclical letter of Pope John Paul II appeared, it was received with much comment, both positive and negative, on the part of the press and the other media. This is one aspect of the topic proposed: to trace in a synthetic way a picture of the reactions which the document stirred. Such would certainly be an interesting study, but I would perhaps be led to traverse much terrain before arriving at the nucleus of what I feel is my duty to say to you. I shall limit myself, therefore, to commenting on two positive reactions appearing in Italian newspapers immediately after the publication of the encyclical.

The first was in the well-known Roman newspaper, *Il Tempo*, under the title "An Act of Consistency in an Epoch of Doubt." It states:

> If lighthouses had been moved every month, the sailors in the night would have seen the ships of history dashed against the rocks; and no voyager would have reached his homeland again if the North Star, within the Zodiac, had to obey vacillating positions of fashions and ideologies. . . .The papal document stirs discussions.
>
> . . . Nevertheless it is very much of current interest. While many ships finish on the rocks because they have sailed following fireflies instead of lighthouses and while the ruling classes have shipwrecked for having chosen compasses that lie, there is abroad a need to see the permanence of certain

---

* This paper was originally presented at the Forum on Catholic University Education at Duquesne Universtiy in Pittsburgh, Novermber 3, 1995.

values recognized in the midst of all that changes, the necessity of an ethical nucleus linked to principles of the human
person, honesty, freedom and responsibility.

This is a positive reaction, then, which welcomes the encyclical as a
text which says things that have to be said, giving basic directions for a
journey, and stating the things no one dares to speak but of which everyone knows the necessity in daily living. This is also the substance of another comment on the encyclical that I think it would be useful to cite.
Carlo Bo, a university professor and a well-known figure in Italian intellectual life, writes: "Modern culture no longer has objective criteria for distinguishing good from evil," and he adds, "John Paul II has fought against
Communism in defense of freedom; now he criticizes Western culture,
which makes of freedom an absolute value. . . . The exaltation of freedom
leads to ethical relativism, against which the pope raises his voice." Agreement and basic approval are transparent in these lines, but the title under which they appear is "A Call to Order." Immediately the image is
evoked—negative to the sensitivities of our times—of a commander intent on imposing order on his soldiers.

The heart of the problem perhaps, at least with regard to the
teaching of moral theology in the Catholic context, is in the clear
perception of the need for an unchanging point of reference, of a
lighthouse for the voyage, and at the same time the fear of speaking of this need, of making it the subject of reflection, communication, and teaching. There is a kind of widespread fear which
keeps us at a distance from the truth, from the permanent foundations of human acting, from the objective and the universal; a fear
which is perhaps the principal cause on account of which so great
a part of contemporary humanity risks dying of thirst while stand-
ing before a spring of cool water. In order not to appear authoritarian or negative, one keeps silent, does not speak, expresses oneself in a partial or even an erroneous way with regard to all that
is most necessary for life. It would be difficult not to see in this a
problem which is typically an educational one, upon which many
questions converge. Can one speak of what is objective without diminishing the subject? Of law, without killing freedom? Of truth,
without violating conscience? Of concrete actions, without frag-
menting the unified impulse which must animate the human person? Of the intrinsic evil of an act, without taking into consideration the circumstances and motives for that act? On what basis can

all this be done? When we speak of these things, do not our voices risk becoming that of a command, of an external order imposing itself without any opportunity for appeal?

And here we come to the second aspect of the word "impact" in the title of my presentation. With what tone of voice does John Paul II call attention to the unchangeable principles which are to direct our actions? What resonance or impact is his call meant to have within the context of our daily commitment to the formation of the future generations?

These are the questions to which I wish to respond, dividing my paper into three parts:

1. In the first, I should like to spend some time on a global presentation of the document, highlighting its context and its educational concern.

2. Secondly, I shall seek to bring to light some central ideas of the encyclical.

3. Finally, I shall try to show some concrete consequences for teaching and, in particular, for the teaching of moral theology at the university and secondary levels of Catholic education.

I. A Document That Raises an Educational Question

We find a key passage for understanding the fundamental aim of *Veritatis splendor* in n. 4 of the document. The pope, after having pointed out the constant tradition of magisterial expressions concerning specific moral questions, underlines the originality of the intervention he is about to make: "Today, however, it seems necessary *to reflect on the whole of the Church's moral teaching,* with the precise goal of recalling certain fundamental truths of Catholic doctrine which, in the present circumstances, risk being distorted or denied." In other words, the magisterium cannot be concerned only with covering all the areas of human life, *in extenso,* so to speak. It must also assume responsibility for the basic elements of the Christian ethical vision, without which the moral teaching of the Church in the individual sectors of life, no matter how well argued, cannot be assimilated, and thus will remain superficial and ineffective. Hence the effort at removing obstacles in an area of communication which today encounters particular difficulties: communication concerning moral choices.

An observation presents itself immediately: namely, one has the impression that the modern person finds it ever more difficult to perceive that his behavior, his decisions, can have need of instruction. At the pedagogical level there is, for example, a hesitation in the face of any kind of directivity or of setting forth proposals for what should be done or how it should be done. Frequently one is confronted with the idea that teaching should not carry with it a communication of contents, but should consist essentially in a "drawing out," an explication of what is already there. When one leaves the field of communicating technical skills and moves to the field of morality, this hesitation increases. Here the notion is widespread that one cannot or should not teach; that even less should there be the concern to make people aware of something objective, of what is received from outside oneself, what is independent of the will or understanding of the individual. But experience shows that, at every level, just as a true communication without the free involvement of two subjects cannot exist, so also human communication cannot exist unless it has a message, a content. Thus whoever holds that one must remain silent with regard to permanent foundations for giving direction for human choices leaves no room for the development of freedom and autonomy. Such a position instead lays the foundation for the development of a closed ideology, without any authentic opening, impenetrable to the reality of life. Against such a vision *Veritatis splendor* raises its voice.

In the pope's words, which take their point of departure from a look at the present situation of moral reflection in the ecclesial context,

> [Today] a new situation has come about *within the Christian community itself*, which has experienced the spread of numerous doubts and objections of a human and psychological, social and cultural, religious and even properly theological nature, with regard to the Church's moral teachings. It is no longer a matter of limited and occasional dissent, but of an overall and systematic calling into question of traditional moral doctrine, on the basis of certain anthropological and ethical presuppositions. At the root of these presuppositions is the more or less obvious influence of currents of thought which end by detaching human freedom from its essential and constitutive relationship to truth (*VS* 4.2).

The concern evidently is for the teaching of morality in the ecclesial context. Such teaching risks being weakened in two ways. On one hand, there is a decreased awareness in the field of moral theology of its being, no less so than dogmatic theology, at the service of the living Tradition of the Church. On the other, there is the danger of constructing a moral theology which has nothing to say to the contemporary world, a moral theology which dilutes the Gospel or even alters its nature. Moreover, the tragedy which the pope points to is that of moral thought which, for fear of appearing authoritarian and extrinsic to the subject, has in fact conferred an absolute character upon partial visions of the human reality. Ideas about man resulting from a study of limited aspects of human existence (psychological, intellectual, social, economic, etc.) have been transformed into ideologies claiming to account for the totality of man, if not ideologies which are in fact totalitarian. These, presenting themselves in the elegant and appealing vesture of scientific reality, have not always been recognized or uncovered by the moral theology of recent decades. It is in this way then that the necessity of discernment carried out and called for by the encyclical is to be seen: it is not a "call to order," but a penetrating look, an attention to the roots of the problems, an effort at clarity so as to prevent people from falling victim to their own illusions.

In this light one can see how the encyclical has in view, without neat distinctions between them, two circles of an intended audience for its teaching, two circles which are destined to intersect throughout the course of the document. In the first place obviously, the ecclesial community, with its preaching, catechesis, its reflection and teaching in moral theology. But, inseparable from the Church, the encyclical also has in view the whole of humanity in our troubled times, with its culture, its philosophical thought, its political, economic, and social order. There can be no separation between these two realms. Certainly the Church is concerned about maintaining the purity of its message, but for no other reason than to be able to continue to proclaim it. Certainly it thinks about the negative influences which some ideas can have on its thought, but while doing so it seeks to bring to the heart of these very ideas the liberating light of the Gospel. The central question, indeed, is that of keeping alive today the dialogue, the "educational" communication between Jesus and the human person. This is what we read in n. 25 of *Veritatis splendor*: "Jesus' conversation with the rich young man continues, in a sense, *in every period of history, including our own*. The question 'Teacher, what good must I do to have eternal life?' arises in the heart of every individual, and it is Christ alone who is capable of giving the full and definitive answer. . . . *Christ's relevance for people of all times is shown forth in his Body, which is the Church*." Seen within this perspective, it is difficult to place *Veritatis splendor* within the military imagery mentioned earlier.

Let us see now whether this approach holds up to an examination of the central message of the encyclical.

II. The Central Message

We have seen the profoundly dialogical, "educational" intention which animates the document. We must now try to show that this intention is concretized in the focal point to which the pope calls attention: those "certain fundamental questions regarding the Church's moral teaching" spoken of in n. 5.

As you know, the encyclical is composed of three chapters, each with a specific character: the first one is "biblical," centered on the dialogue of Jesus with the "rich young man" (Mt 19:16); the second is "doctrinal," in which the problem of the discernment of some tendencies of contemporary moral theology is addressed in a language which at certain points is technical; the third is "pastoral," concerned with indicating the consequences of this reflection for the concrete life of the Church and the world.

Notwithstanding this apparent diversity in literary genre, the document in its entirety has a profound interior unity. A kind of unifying element pervades the whole document and assures its solidity. It is the fundamental question of the relationship between freedom and truth, or better, in Christ's own words: "You will come to know the truth and the truth will make you free" (Jn 8:32). So much so that the title of the encyclical, instead of *Veritatis splendor*, could be *Libertatis splendor*.

Whence comes the necessity of insisting on this aspect? *Veritatis splendor* does not hesitate to respond to the question, pointing out explicitly that there is a "crisis "—a crisis which has developed, as far as regards fundamental moral theology, around two aspects of the present culture:

1. The more philosophical aspect, leading to the claim of human autonomy in the area of morality, beginning with the discussion of freedom and truth.

2. The more theological aspect, that is, the loss of awareness of the authentic relationship between faith and moral conduct.

On one side, then, there is a sort of "fusion" which has progressively led philosophical reflection to identify truth and freedom, making of this latter the only absolute—truth "dissolved" in freedom. On the other, there is the risk—for moral theology which is faced with this philosophical vision—of dissociating in the life of the believer the area of faith from that of particular moral choices. In one case, a kind of absolute affirmation of freedom, destined to lead to its own negation; in the other, a sort of "practical fideism" which robs faith of its influence and relevance for the effective determination of a way of acting.

This, we must acknowledge, is the decisive topic of our time, a topic which, with the fall of the Communist dictatorships, has become yet more urgent: How to learn to live correctly in freedom? A freedom which is conceived of in a purely individualistic way, which approaches arbitrariness, can only be destructive; it would in the end place everyone against everyone else. The danger of again determining freedom from outside the human person and substituting for truth the result of the "collective will" is evident. Think, for example, of the analysis which John Paul II made in his speech to the United Nations (October 5, 1995):

> Freedom is not simply the absence of tyranny or oppression. Nor is freedom a license to do whatever we like. Freedom has an inner 'logic' which distinguishes it and ennobles it: freedom is ordered to the truth, and is fulfilled in man's quest for truth and in man's living in the truth. Detached from the truth about the human person, freedom deteriorates into license in the lives of individuals, and, in political life, it becomes the caprice of the most powerful and the arrogance of power (n. 12).

Within this broad horizon we can see the crisis which the encyclical points out. Naturally, *Veritatis splendor* is a response of the magisterium. As such, it is important to emphasize, it is not a "theological" response in the technical sense of the term. That is, in the document there is not to be found—no matter how tempted one may be to think so—the canonization of a particular "theology," chosen from among those existing at the present time (cf. *VS* 29 and 116). (Such theologies are recognized in their specific role of providing *"a more appropriate way of communicating* doctrine to the people of their time" [*Gaudium et spes* 62, cited in *VS* 29.2].) Even though the encyclical treats, in great part, questions of the theoretical order concerning morality, the demands intrinsic to the Christian "way" (cf. Acts 22:4) remain its central point of reference. Therefore the source is Sacred Scripture, the living Tradition of the Church, and, in particular, the teaching of the Second Vatican Council (cf. *VS* 5; 27; 29).

From the "magisterial" character of the encyclical's response to this crisis flows the principal purpose which the document sets for itself. That purpose can be summed up in the world "discernment." In fact the title of the second chapter is: "The Church and the Discernment of Certain Tendencies in Present-Day Moral Theology." "Discernment," that is, "comparison" between some tendencies in moral theology and the *"sana doctrina,"* therefore, is certainly a "critical discernment . . . capable of acknowledging what is legitimate, useful and of value in them, while at the same time pointing out their ambiguities, dangers and errors" (*VS* 34.3)—a discernment, finally, that makes its own St. Paul's warning not to conform oneself to this age but to be transformed by the renewal of one's mind (cf. Rom 12:2).

Now to the object of this act of the magisterium. It is not easy to specify it in just a few words. The "discernment" of the magisterium focuses on a convergence of debated questions more vast and more complex than ever before. The problem can be set forth in terms of two sides of the question of the relationship between truth and freedom:

1. That of the law, that is, the Law of God, both in its universal formulation (*VS* 35–53, in which is treated the relationship between divine law and human freedom), and in its application to the concrete personal situation, that is, conscience (*VS* 54–64, in which is treated the relationship between conscience and truth).

2. That of the concrete putting of freedom into action, both in the free subject (that is, the person who acts freely, following a "fundamental option" expressed in "particular choices," *VS* 65–70), and in its result (the moral act, *VS* 71–83).

How can we come to grasp the deepest meaning of this intervention of the magisterium on these two aspects of our topic? It is necessary, I think, in the case of both of the perspectives mentioned, to look at what would be the final negative outcome of the tendencies criticized by the encyclical.

A. The Perspective of the Law

In this regard, the tendency to which encyclical calls attention derives from a presumed conflict. The Law of God is understood as external to the human subject, constraining him, lessening human freedom. A complete sovereignty on the part of human reason in determining the norms necessary for the ordering of life in this world is claimed as the fundamental premise for the autonomy of the human being.

It is not difficult to see how such a tendency leads inevitably to the canonization of man's solitude and, consequently, to the denial of the intimate structure of the person as open to dialogue and to communion. The presumed externality of God's law is eliminated by suppressing in man the capacity of listening. Thus the Word of God becomes "an exhortation, a generic paraenesis, which the autonomous reason alone would then have the task of completing with normative directives which are truly 'objective,' that is, adapted to the concrete historical situation" (*VS* 37.1).

It is a word then without "objective" content, without concrete incisiveness on the life of humanity, a word without "substance," deprived of that intrinsic gratuitous dynamism which leads it to become incarnate in history.

But the risk of canonizing man's solitude by means of a system of philosophy or moral theology has a still graver aspect. Not only must the Word of God conserve all of its power for an "objective" permanent and unchangeable proposition, but it must also be possible to grasp the interiority of the Word in all of its depth. The systems which are "ruinous" for freedom and which the encyclical denounces are also the ones which deny that the freedom in man carries within itself its own regulation such as can be recognized as the order of his nature. What is this principle of regulation? The first and fundamental reply of the pope is this: The principle of regulation is the truth, the truth which is found in our being human. Our "nature," which derives from the Creator, is the truth which guides and instructs us. The fact that we ourselves carry our truth within us, that our "nature" is our "truth," is also expressed with the term "natural law."

This idea, which goes back to pre-Christian philosophy, was developed further by the Fathers of the Church and by medieval philosophy and theology and had an entirely new relevance and urgency at the beginning of the modern era, in the face of the usurpations by the colonial lords. Those new peoples, even though not members of the Christian community, were not for that reason without rights, because man's "nature" confers rights on man as such. From this comes the principle that every man, insofar as he is man, by reason of his human nature, is the subject of fundamental rights that no one can take from him, because no human institution has conferred them on him.

Today the accusation is constantly heard that, with the concept of natural law, the Church makes man a slave of an outdated metaphysics or a backward biologism, attributing to biological processes the value of moral laws. The encyclical rejects such an accusation, citing St. Thomas: "The natural law is nothing other than the light of intelligence infused in us by God." The natural law is a "rational" law: it is the nature of man to be endowed with reason. When it is said that our nature is the regulation of our freedom, not only is reason not excluded, but its place is fully acknowledged. In this way also we acknowledge fully the dialogical nature of human conscience, which is the seat of the relationship between man's freedom and God's law. "Moral conscience does not close man within an insurmountable and impenetrable solitude, but opens him to the call, to the voice of God. In this, and not in anything else, lies the entire mystery and the dignity of the moral conscience: in being the place, the sacred place where God speaks to man" (*VS* 58).

B. The Perspective of Putting Freedom into Action

Following the same line of thought, that of the dignity of the human person as a being open, in his totality, to listening to the Word, and thus capable of recognizing in the Law of God the keystone of his freedom, we can easily approach the second perspective on the relationship freedom-truth of which the en-cyclical treats.

In this case as well, we can begin from what would be the negative outcome of the dominant tendencies of contemporary thought. Here attention is drawn to the wholeness of the re-sponse which the human person is called upon to give to God by means of his moral life. The risk to freedom under this as-pect is that of taking away the meaning and the seriousness of human action, seen either in its entirety or in the particularity of the individual act.

In accordance with his presumed incapacity to listen to a truth of which he himself is not the speaker, contemporary man tends to remove personal meaning from his concrete actions. In this con-ception of things, *"particular acts . . .* would constitute only partial and never definitive attempts to give. . . expression" to the so-called "fundamental option"; "they would only be its 'signs' or symptoms" (*VS* 65.2). But such a vision leads to a tearing which renders fragmentary and, in the end, meaningless man's histori-cal action; he is thereby, deprived of his capacity to express his deep adherence to the divine call. "To separate the fundamental option from concrete kinds of behavior means to contradict the substantial integrity or personal unity of the moral agent in his body and in his soul" (*VS* 67.2). *Veritatis splendor,* therefore, affirms that the human person cannot be defrauded of the possibility con-ferred on him to enter, with all that is connected to his being his-torical, into the dialogue of love which God offers him. Individual human actions must in fact remain open to being the expression of the person's adoration and his adherence to God's call as well as of the tragedy of his refusal of it. Only in his way is there ulti-mately guaranteed the fullness of meaning which human freedom can assume.

In the same context of safeguarding the integral dignity of the human moral response should be placed the rejection of teleologism (proportionalism and consequentialism). If the moral act does not contain within itself the ultimate reason for its own goodness or evil, this implies that the human person does not bear in himself his own meaning, but receives it from an abstract superstructure made up of limited motivations and goals. The human person thus finds himself slave to a utilitarian vision of reality. For this reason, there must be "intrinsically evil" acts in order not to condemn man to the exclusive pursuit of relative goods, not to close him within the circle of his finitude, to save for him the possibility of opening himself up to the infinite by means of each one of his acts. To say that every human act has an object, the goodness of which does not derive from circumstances or consequences, means saying that human acts do not remain forcibly trapped in the net of limited temporal meanings but can in themselves "be ordered to the good and to the ultimate end which is God" (*VS* 79.2). This gives an infinite character to even the smallest action, guaranteeing the possibility of a greatness in man of which he on his own cannot conceive.

The central message of the encyclical turns out then to be animated by a profound intention to keep open, in a theoretical reflection on morality, the full breadth of the vision of man of which the Church makes itself guarantor. Rather than closing the door to ethical reflection, *Veritatis splendor* asks that this reflection not "dissolve" the Christian paradox with illusory solutions. "No absolution offered by beguiling doctrines, even in the areas of philosophy and theology, can make man truly happy: only the Cross and the glory of the risen Christ can grant peace to [man's] conscience and salvation to his life" (*VS* 120.3).

It is now time to see, in this light, what are the educational and formational consequences on the secondary and university levels.

III. The Consequences for Teaching

A. Consequences for Education in General

In the first place, it seems important to note how the "educational" concern of the encyclical is in itself a reminder for all who teach. I think we can speak of a call to safeguard a certain "difference" in education.

In order to have dialogue, and above all educational dialogue, it is necessary to maintain a "difference." No fusion favors the growth of freedom. But perhaps it is precisely that which is happening in our time and which the encyclical criticizes. The conflictual situation in which humanity lives today pushes ever further toward finding individualistic solutions to various problems which present themselves. The confrontation with the "other"–whoever he is–is excluded a priori by a mentality which justifies the creation of values by the individual conscience. The teacher and the educator, in these circumstances, have a difficult task in reaching their students. From this there derives on every level a disorientation, which, far from aiding the exercise of autonomy and freedom, renders the maturation of the students difficult.

A first and essential impact of *Veritatis splendor* on the task of the teacher is, therefore, at this basic level, that of maintaining the essential "difference" of the educational dialogue, thanks to the proclaiming of a truth and of a concrete truth. In this regard it should be noted that it would be a grave error to think that in *Veritatis splendor* there are two parallel discourses: on the one hand, about an abstract truth, attainable by the light of reason beginning from created reality; on the other hand, about a personal truth who is Jesus Christ, Son of God, made flesh for our salvation. In reality, in the light of encyclical, Catholic teaching is called to an awareness that only one truth can be liberating for the human person and that it is a truth at one and the same time universal and concrete. In the final analysis, the traditional expression "natural law" means nothing other than this. It says that truth is a concrete possibility for the heart of every human creature, not a particular concept or idea, but a living Light, accessible to all in every circumstance, the "image of God" in man, the light of the Word "who illuminates every man" (Jn 1:9) and which the faith of the Church sees resplendent in the face of Jesus of Nazareth.

As John Paul II has himself observed recently in his talk to the Bishops of Brazil during their *ad limina* visit (October 18, 1995): "It will not be by weakening moral truth and neglecting true values that the Church will accomplish its mission on behalf of man. The Church, obedient to the Lord, who came not to judge but to save, must show mercy towards people without, however, giving up the principle of the truth and of a consistency according to which one cannot call good evil and evil good. It is an eminent form of charity towards souls not to reduce to nothing the redemptive doctrine of Christ" (n. 6).

B. Consequences for the Teaching of Moral Theology

In this light too should be seen the consequences specifically concerned with moral theology indicated in nn. 109–113 of the document. Outside of the perception of a concrete Truth, unique and unchangeable, there remains only the banality of utilitarian thought, which makes the human being a slave of a finite purpose and finally of an abstract system, intolerant and tyrannical, which humiliates the person and does not recognize his vocation to the infinite and the eternal. This type of thought certainly cannot find a place in moral theology if this latter intends to take its part in the Church's mission of evangelization. *Veritatis splendor* addresses this with the following points:

1. *The Ecclesial Character of Moral Theology
   and the Relationship with the Magisterium*

The encyclical's first point about the task or role of moral theology is its necessarily ecclesial character. Moral theology participates with full credentials in the description proper to all theology, which "by its very nature and procedures. . . can flourish and develop only through a committed and responsible participation in and 'belonging' to the Church as a 'community of faith' "(*VS* 109.3).

But the ecclesial character proper to moral theology has its specificity in a peculiar relationship with the magisterium of the Church, which "in proclaiming the commandments of God and the charity of Christ . . . teaches the faithful specific particular precepts" and "carries out an important work of vigilance" (*VS* 110.1) in service to the faithful. In the face of this teaching of the magisterium, the task of moral theology is, certainly, in the first place, that of having the faithful, especially future pastors, come to know the teaching of the magisterium. Even more there is a necessity of deepening this knowledge. "Working together in cooperation with the hierarchical magisterium, theologians will be deeply concerned to clarify ever more fully the biblical foundations, the ethical significance and the anthropological concerns which underlie the moral doctrine and the vision of man set forth by the Church" (*VS* 110.2).

Along these lines, it is necessary to develop a precise ecclesial consciousness, a consciousness which will welcome, not just in a negative way, the discernment which the magisterium will effect with regard to individual problems. More than closing off certain areas of theological research, interventions of the magisterium must be seen to be indicative of certain fixed points which are capable of marking the area of fruitful and productive theological reflection.

2. *Service to the Church, Society, and Culture*

In this way too one sees the contribution which moral theology offers not only to the growth of the Christian community, but also to society and culture. The scholarly reflection of moral theologians is essential for setting forth the dynamic and unifying aspect of Christian living. Because it cannot "be reduced to a body of knowledge worked out purely in the context of the so called behavioral sciences," moral theology must always keep in mind the questions which dwells in man.

"*What is good or evil? What must be done to have eternal life?*" (*VS* 111.2). These are the questions—already present in every human heart, even though often not explicitly and consciously—which make up the human person's concrete and operative point of reference for living.

3. *Discernment*

The third element which *Veritatis splendor* calls to the attention of moral theologians is that of discernment with regard to modern culture. It is a question of a focusing better on the critical function to be exercised with respect to relativism, pragmatism, and positivism, to which so often the contemporary mentality is exposed. In the face of the tendency to obtain by empirical methods even moral principles for the ordering of human action, moral theology must strengthen its role as guarantor of "*the spiritual dimension of the human heart and its vocation to divine love. . . .* It is the Gospel which reveals the full truth about man and his moral journey, and thus enlightens and admonishes sinners; it proclaims to them God's mercy, which is constantly at work to preserve them both from despair at their inability fully to know and keep God's law fully and from the presumption that they can be saved without merit" (*VS* 112.1–112.2).

4. *Ecclesial Responsibility*

Finally, the invitation of *Veritatis splendor* to moral theologians is synthesized in a call to assume responsibility. It is important that the person dedicated to teaching in Catholic institutions of learning grasp this aspect of the document well and not let himself be taken in by partial or reductive visions of his function within the Church and the world. The horizon indicated by the encyclical is vast, I dare say, planetary. It is a question ultimately of the defense of man in his wholeness. For that reason, courage is needed to enter fully into this dynamic, avoiding secondary aspects of polemics or dissent. Moral reflection is not simply the fruit of the comparison of opinions and respect for the democratic procedures of discussion. If it were thus, instead of aiding, it would obstruct the bursting forth of that Word which from deep within every human being calls upon his conscience. The educational dialogue, the possibility of teaching and of helping others to grow in freedom, would be cut at its roots. Within this framework should be placed the impact of *Veritatis splendor* on Catholic teaching which we have been seeking to describe in these remarks.

IV. Conclusion

Now, as a concluding word, I should like to recall an image which could almost be emblematic of *Veritatis splendor*, an image which John Paul II gave to the Church during the sixteenth year of his pontificate. It is the image of the pope who, looking forward to the beginning of the Third Christian Millennium, speaks to five hundred thousand young people gathered in Cherry Creek State Park in Denver, the fourteenth and fifteenth of August 1993. In the words he spoke on that occasion we grasp in synthesis the Church's passion for education and the universal horizon within which it unfolds. The Holy Father said:

> On many questions, especially those of moral theology, the doctrine of the Church is today in a cultural and social situation which makes it at one and the same time more difficult to understand and more urgent and irreplaceable for promoting the true good of men and women. In a technological culture in which people are used to dominating matter,

> discovering its laws and mechanisms in order to transform it according to their wishes, the danger arises of also wanting to manipulate conscience and its demands. In a culture which holds that no universally valid truths are possible, nothing is absolute. Therefore, in the end—they say—objective goodness and evil no longer really matter Good comes to mean what is pleasing or useful in a particular moment. Evil means what contradicts our subjective wishes. Each person can build a private system of values. . . . In the depths of his conscience man detects a law which he does not impose upon himself, but which holds him to obedience. That law is not an external human law, but the voice of God, calling us to free ourselves from the grip of evil desires and sin, and stimulating us to seek what is good and true.

It is truly to be hoped that this voice will be heard by each of us and that it will be able to inspire every Catholic teacher to do his share to make that voice audible in the hearts of all.

I end with a brief "story": a certain gentleman, at a very late hour of the night, is about to enter his house, but has lost the key that opens the door. He bends down under a street light and begins to search for it breathlessly. At this moment a passersby stops, wishing to help the man who lost his key. He too bends down and begins to search for the key. They do not find it. After a while the passersby turns to the man without his key and asks him: Are you sure you lost the key here? No, he replies, I lost it some distance from here, but where the key is, it is dark. I am looking for it here because I am underneath the light.

How many moral theologians bring people under an artificial light and ask them to find there the key to the truth, when instead it is to be found elsewhere, even if in a place where it is dark. Let us not be tricked by artificial lights; the pope has indicated to us where we must search for the key to the truth, even where it is laborious to find it, because the search requires effort and sacrifice: under "the shadow of the cross."

Index